the food of
FRANCE

the food of
FRANCE

Photography by Chris L. Jones
Recipes by Maria Villegas and
Sarah Randell

WHITECAP
BOOKS

CONTENTS

FOOD JOURNEYS IN FRANCE

the food of
FRANCE

THE FRENCH PRESIDE OVER ONE OF THE WORLD'S GREAT CULINARY HERITAGES, FROM RIPE CAMEMBERT TO BUTTERY CROISSANTS AND EXQUISITE PASTRIES TO VINTAGE CHAMPAGNE, AND NOWHERE IS IT BETTER, OR ENJOYED MORE, THAN IN FRANCE ITSELF.

France's reputation for wonderful food and cooking is often thought of as being based on technical skills and extravagant, expensive ingredients—on sauces that need to be reduced, and foie gras, truffles and other delicacies. This is *haute cuisine,* "classic cooking," which was developed by the chefs of the French aristocracy and reached its heyday in the nineteenth century under legendary French chefs like Auguste Escoffier. *Haute cuisine* is a time-consuming art form that adheres to strict rules, and this elegant form of cooking requires an understanding of its special methods and techniques, skills honed by long apprenticeships in the kitchens of great restaurants, particularly in creating the subtle sauces that are its foundation. Nowadays this style of cooking is found mostly in expensive restaurants, but it can represent the highest art of cooking, one celebrated in stars by the famous Michelin guide.

Nouvelle cuisine, "new cooking," was a reaction to the dominance of *haute cuisine* in the 1960s, when chefs, including Paul Bocuse and the Troisgros brothers, banded together to create lighter dishes with less reliance on heavy sauces and a willingness to experiment with nontraditional ingredients and cooking styles. *Nouvelle cuisine* encouraged innovation, and though some of its precepts were later abandoned, it had a lasting influence on French cooking.

Fundamentally, however, French food is a regionally based cuisine and many French dishes are called after their place of origin, from *entrecôte à la bordelaise* to *sole à la normande* to *boeuf à la bourguignonne.* Eating your way around France

France is a strong agricultural nation and grows wonderful local produce, from beans to cherries and apricots to red currants. They are sold in daily and weekly markets all over France, such as this one closing up after a busy morning in Périgueux. The land also supports a good dairy industry with much of the milk used in cheeses. Cafés, like this Marseilles one, are a French institution.

7

Every town in France has a market selling local and seasonal produce such as asparagus and eggs, and artisan-made bread, cheese and wines. Here, bread is sold at a Provence market and vegetables are temptingly displayed in a Paris market. George Mulot's pâtisserie in Paris is a feast for the eyes, while Honfleur (center photograph) is one of France's many fishing ports.

8

reveals regional differences that are still very distinct, and most restaurants cook not only dishes of the region, but those of the town or village. This is a result not only of tradition, but also of an enduring respect for local produce, *les produits du terroir*. Each area of France grows or produces food uniquely suited to its terrain and climate, such as chickens from Bresse, walnuts from Grenoble, butter from Normandy and mustard from Dijon. Nowadays, there is more crossover between the provinces, and the best, not just the local, vegetables can be found in the markets, but the notion of regional specialties still underlies French cooking.

This respect for ingredients extends also to eating fruit and vegetables only at the height of their season. Recipes change to reflect the best that each month has to offer, and every month seasonal fruits and vegetables are eagerly awaited, like the summer melons of Provence or the autumn walnuts and winter truffles of the Dordogne.

The French have also gone to great lengths to protect their ingredients and traditional methods of food preparation. The strict *appellation d'origine contrôlée* (AOC) system that they use to keep their cheese and wines as authentic as possible is also being extended to an increasing number of other important and regionally based food products, such as Puy lentils and carrots from Créances.

The French love food and though many traditions have changed—an office worker is just as likely to grab a quick sandwich on the run as enjoy a four-course lunch—as a foundation of French culture eating and drinking remain remarkably important. One of the great joys of France is starting the morning with a *petit déjeuner* of a fresh croissant and a *café au lait*. Lunch is still the main meal of the day for many, though dinner may be equally substantial, and with many shops and work places closed between 12:30 and 3:30, it can extend to three or four courses with wine.

Despite the emergence of the *hypermarché,* specialty food shops and weekly markets are integral to the French way of life. There is a *boulangerie* in every village; meat is purchased at a *boucherie*; while a *charcuterie* specializes in pork products and delicatessen items and a *pâtisserie* in baked goods. Markets are usually held weekly, and in some areas you can follow the same stallholders from town to town through the week. Even Paris has its neighborhood markets, and there are also specialty markets, such as the garlic market in Aix-en-Provence in July and the foie gras market in the winter in Sarlat in Périgord.

THE FOOD OF THE NORTH

Paris is a world culinary center, where neighborhood markets sell fantastic produce from all over France. Much of the city's reputation lies with its restaurants, a legacy of the revolution when private chefs had to find a new living. Parisians are legendarily discerning about their food and it is here you find the real home of the baguette, the country's most refined pâtisseries and its finest cheese shops.

Brittany is traditionally a fishing and farming region with outstanding seafood, including native oysters, and wonderful early fruits and vegetables. Sweet crêpes and savory buckwheat galettes are found throughout the region. Its sea salt, *sel de guerande*, is used all over France.

Normandy's rich pastures are home to some of France's greatest cheeses: Camembert, Pont l'Evêque and Livarot; along with crème fraîche, butter and apples—three classic ingredients in French cuisine. There are also pré-salé lamb (raised in salt marshes), mussels, oysters, cider and calvados.

Known as "the Garden of France," the Loire Valley produces fruit, vegetables and white wines. Wild mushrooms are grown in the caves of Saumur and regional dishes include rillettes, andouillettes and tarte Tatin. The region also produces fine goat cheeses, including Crottin de Chavignol. Poitou-Charentes on the Atlantic Coast has some of France's best oyster beds near Marennes and is the home of Charentais melons, unsalted butter and Cognac.

Nord-Pas-de-Calais along the coast includes Boulogne-sur-mer, France's biggest fishing port. Inland the washed-rind Maroilles cheese, andouillettes and Flemish beers, used for cooking in dishes such as *carbonnade à la flamande*, can be found. Picardie has vegetables, fruit and pré-salé lamb.

Champagne-Ardennes is a rural region, with Champagne famous not just for its wine, but also for cheeses such as Brie and Chaource. In the rugged north, the game forests of Ardennes have created a tradition of charcuterie. Jambon d'Ardennes and pâtés d'Ardennes are world famous.

Bordering Germany, Alsace-Lorraine's mixed heritage is reflected in its cuisine. Its charcuterie is used in quiche lorraine, *choucroute garnie*, *tarte flambée* and *baeckenoffe* (stew). Meat dishes *à la lorraine* are served with red cabbage cooked in wine, while Alsace's baking has Germanic influences with pretzels, rye bread and kugelhopf.

Paris has a wonderful choice of food with the finest produce brought to the capital from all over France. It is known for its baguettes, upscale *traiteurs* (take-out food shops) and sidewalk cafés. Cabbage is used in many local Alsace-Lorraine dishes, while oysters, apples and soft cheeses are eaten all over Normandy and Brittany, such as in these waterfront cafés in Honfleur.

Lyon's Quai Saint Antoine market in the center of this gastronomic city sells everything from eggs and scallions to potatoes and charcuterie. Limousin is a meat-rearing area and home to wild mushrooms. Mild red onions grow in Burgundy, pears are a Savoie specialty and chickens from Bresse have AOC status. Cheeses from the Alps are among France's best.

12

THE FOOD OF THE EAST AND CENTER

Central France is made up of the regions of Auvergne and Limousin. With very cold winters, the cuisine of these areas tends to be hearty and potatoes and cabbages are heavily used for dishes such as *aligot* and *potée auvergnate* (one-pot pork and cabbage stew). Limousin is famous for its beef, lamb, pork and veal and Auvergne for its game and tiny green Puy lentils. The area also produces Cantal and Saint Nectaire cheeses, as well as blue cheeses such as Bleu d'Auvergne and Fourme d'Ambert. Auvergne is known for its bottled mineral waters, including Vichy and Volvic.

Burgundy is world famous for its red and white wines with the wine industry centered around the town of Beaune. Burgundian dishes tend to be rich, full of flavor and a perfect match for the area's wines. Wine is also an important part of the region's cooking, and *à la bourguignon* usually means cooked in red wine. Beef bourguignon, coq au vin, Bresse chicken cooked with cream and wild morels, snails filled with garlic herb butter and slices of *jambon persillé* (ham and parsley set in aspic) are all Burgundian classics. Dijon is synonymous with mustard and is also the home of *pain d'épices* (spicy gingerbread) and kir—white wine mixed with *crème de cassis* from local black currants.

One of France's great gastronomic capitals, Lyon is home to great restaurants, including Paul Bocuse's, as well as many simple *bouchons* (traditionally working-class cafés) and brasseries all over the city. Considered to be the charcuterie center of France, Lyon is renowned for its andouillettes, cervelas and rosette sausages, served at *bouchons* along with *salade lyonnaise*, pike quenelles, *poulet au vinaigre* (chicken stewed in vinegar), potato gratins, the fresh herb cheese *cervelle de canut* (silk-weavers' brains) and *pots* (one pint bottles) of local Beaujolais or Côtes du Rhône. The surrounding countryside produces excellent fruit and vegetables, as well as AOC chickens from Bourg-en-Bresse.

The East of France rises up into the French Alps and is made up of three regions, Franche-Comté in the north and Savoie and Dauphiné in the south. These mountain regions have great cheese-making traditions, and in the summer *alpages* cheeses such as Reblochon are still made from the milk of animals taken up to the high meadows. Tomme de Savoie, Beaufort and Comté are other mountain cheeses, and dishes include fondues and raclettes. Potatoes are found all over the Center and East, but it is Dauphiné that gives its name to the famous *gratin dauphinois*.

THE FOOD OF THE SOUTH AND SOUTHWEST

Bordeaux is associated with great wines and the *grands crus* of Médoc and Saint Emilion are world famous, as are dessert wines from Sauternes. Red wine is used in cooking and these dishes are usually known as *à la bordelaise*, such as *entrecôte à la bordelaise*. Oysters from the Atlantic beds at Arcachon and pré-salé lamb from Pauillac are specialties.

Goose and duck confit and foie gras are the Dordogne and Lot's most famous exports along with the black truffles and walnuts of Périgord. Black truffles and foie gras are used as a garnish in many southwest dishes and these dishes are sometimes known as *à la périgourdine*. Walnuts are used in *salade aux noix* and in oils, and prunes are grown at Agen.

Gascony is a largely rural area that produces Armagnac and is famous, along with the Dordogne, for its foie gras, duck and goose confit, pâtés and terrines and for the use of goose fat in its cooking. Home made and local specialties can be tasted at *fermes auberges* (farmhouse restaurants).

The southwest Basque country close to Spain flavors its food with spicy *piment d'Espelette*, dried red chiles, which are also often used in the salting mixture for the local Bayonne ham. Tuna are caught off the Atlantic coast, and the tradition of baking, such as making *gâteau basque*, is strong.

The flavors of Provence are those of the Mediterranean: olives, olive oil, garlic, eggplant, zucchini, tomatoes and *herbes de provence,* along with melons from Cavaillon, strawberries and peaches. Provençal cuisine includes the strong flavors of aïoli, anchoïade and tapenade; pissaladière and pistou from the Italian-bordering Côte d' Azur; simple broiled fish and the classic bouillabaisse; red rice from the Camargue and honey and candied fruit.

Close to Spain, Languedoc-Roussillon is home to the famous Roquefort blue cheese, which is aged in caves. Along the coast, anchovies are conserved and the area uses salt cod in dishes such as *brandade de morue*. There is fresh seafood from the Mediterranean and *bourride* is Languedoc's bouillabaisse. Inland, there is hearty cassoulet from Carcassonne, Castelnaudary and Toulouse, sausages from Toulouse and pink garlic from Tarn.

Corsica, closer to Italy and Sardinia than France, has a tradition of Italian charcuterie, pasta and polenta. *Stufato* is a classic rich beef stew, where the sauce is served over pasta.

Many great wines have been aged in Bordeaux's cellars, such as this one at Château Lafite-Rothschild. Tapenade, olives and garlic are the tastes of the South, while figs, lemons and tomatoes grow well in the hot climate. In Marseilles, tiny snails are sold alongside fish on the harbor front. Black truffles are a winter specialty in the Dordogne and fougasse is a bread from Provence.

15

SOUPS

FRENCH ONION SOUP

THE ORIGINS OF THIS ONION SOUP ARE UNCLEAR, SOME CLAIMING IT TO BE A LYONNAIS INVENTION AND OTHERS CREDITING IT TO PARIS. THERE IS ALSO MUCH DISPUTE OVER HOW THE DISH SHOULD BE MADE: WHEN TO ADD THE BREAD AND WHETHER THE ONIONS ARE COARSELY SLICED OR PURÉED.

Lyon is certainly the area of France most associated with the onion: "à la lyonnaise" means a dish containing onions.

3 tablespoons butter
1 1/2 lb. onions, finely sliced
2 garlic cloves, finely chopped
1/3 cup all-purpose flour
8 cups beef or chicken stock
1 cup white wine
1 bay leaf
2 thyme sprigs
12 slices stale baguette
4 oz. Gruyère, finely grated

SERVES 6

MELT the butter in a heavy-bottomed saucepan and add the onions. Cook over low heat, stirring occasionally, for 25 minutes, or until the onions are a deep golden brown and begin to caramelize.

ADD the garlic and flour and stir continuously for 2 minutes. Gradually blend in the stock and the wine, stirring all the time, and bring to a boil. Add the bay leaf and thyme and season. Cover the saucepan and simmer for 25 minutes. Remove the bay leaf and thyme and check the seasoning. Preheat the broiler.

TOAST the baguette slices, then divide among six warmed soup bowls and ladle the soup over the top. Sprinkle with the grated cheese and broil until the cheese melts and turns a light golden brown. Serve immediately.

CAULIFLOWER SOUP

2 tablespoons butter
1 onion, finely chopped
1/2 celery stalk, finely chopped
1 1/4 lb. cauliflower, broken into florets
1 3/4 cups chicken stock
1 1/4 cups milk
1 bay leaf
1 thyme sprig
1/2 cup whipping cream
freshly grated nutmeg
2 tablespoons chopped chives

SERVES 4

MELT the butter in a large saucepan and add the onion and celery. Cook over low heat until the vegetables are softened but not browned. Add the cauliflower, stock, milk, bay leaf and thyme and bring to a boil. Cover the saucepan, reduce the heat and simmer for 20 minutes, or until the cauliflower is tender.

ALLOW the soup to cool, then remove the bay leaf and thyme. Purée the soup until smooth in a blender or food processor and return to the clean saucepan. Bring to a boil, stirring constantly, add the cream and reheat without boiling. Season with salt, white pepper and nutmeg. Serve garnished with chives.

CAULIFLOWER SOUP

CHICKEN CONSOMMÉ

STOCK

2 lb. chicken carcasses, halved
6 oz. chicken legs
1 carrot, chopped
1 onion, chopped
1 celery stalk, chopped
2 parsley sprigs
20 black peppercorns
1 bay leaf
1 thyme sprig

CLARIFICATION MIXTURE

2 chicken drumsticks
1 carrot, finely chopped
1 leek, finely chopped
1 celery stalk, finely chopped
10 black peppercorns
1 parsley sprig, chopped
2 tomatoes, chopped
2 egg whites, lightly beaten

sea salt
1 small carrot, julienned
1/2 small leek, white part only,
    julienned

SERVES 4

TO MAKE the stock, remove any skin and fat from the chicken carcasses and legs and place in a large heavy-bottomed saucepan with 12 cups cold water. Bring to a boil and skim any fat that floats to the surface. Add the remaining ingredients and simmer for 1 1/2 hours, skimming occasionally. Strain the stock (you should have about 6 cups) and return to the clean saucepan.

TO MAKE the clarification mixture, remove the skin and meat from the chicken drumsticks and discard the skin. Chop the meat finely (you will need about 5 oz.) and mix with the carrot, leek, celery, peppercorns, parsley, tomatoes and egg white. Add 3/4 cup of the warm stock to loosen the mixture.

ADD the clarification mixture to the strained stock and whisk in well. Bring to a gentle simmer. As the mixture simmers the clarification ingredients will bind with any impurities and form a "raft." As the raft rises, gently move it with a wooden spoon to one side of the saucepan away from the main movement of the simmering stock (this will make it easier to ladle out the stock later). Simmer for 1 hour, or until the stock is clear.

LADLE OUT the chicken stock, taking care not to disturb the raft, and strain through a fine sieve lined with damp cheesecloth. Place sheets of paper towel over the top of the consommé and then quickly lift away to remove any remaining fat. Season with coarse sea salt (or other iodine-free salt, as iodine will cloud the soup).

JUST BEFORE serving, reheat the consommé. Place the julienned vegetables in a saucepan of boiling water and cook for 2 minutes until just tender. Drain well, spoon into warmed soup bowls and pour the consommé over the top.

Clarity is the hallmark of a good consommé. This soup uses a clarification mixture that forms a "raft," to which all the impurities cling. The stock is then strained through fine cheesecloth, leaving a beautifully transparent liquid.

CRAB BISQUE

ORIGINALLY BISQUES WERE MADE WITH POULTRY AND GAME BIRDS (IN PARTICULAR PIGEONS) AND WERE MORE OF A STEW. TODAY THEY HAVE EVOLVED INTO RICH VELVETY SOUPS AND TEND TO USE CRUSTACEANS. YOU CAN RESERVE SOME OF THE CRAB MEAT OR CLAWS FOR A GARNISH.

You will need a large saucepan or stockpot for making crab bisque—the crab shells take up a lot of room in the saucepan.

2 lb. live crabs
3 tablespoons butter
1/2 carrot, finely chopped
1/2 onion, finely chopped
1 celery stalk, finely chopped
1 bay leaf
2 thyme sprigs
2 tablespoons tomato paste
2 tablespoons brandy
1/2 cup dry white wine
4 cups fish stock
1/3 cup rice
1/4 cup heavy cream
1/4 teaspoon cayenne pepper

SERVES 4

PUT the crabs in the freezer for 1 hour. Remove the top shell and bony tail flap from the underside of each crab, remove the gills from both sides of the crab, then remove the grit sac. Detach the claws and legs.

HEAT the butter in a large saucepan. Add the vegetables, bay leaf and thyme and cook over moderate heat for 3 minutes, without allowing the vegetables to color. Add the crab claws, legs and body and cook for 5 minutes, or until the crab shells turn red. Add the tomato paste, brandy and white wine and simmer for 2 minutes, or until reduced by half.

ADD the stock and 2 cups water and bring to a boil. Reduce the heat and simmer for 5 minutes. Remove the shells and reserve the claws. Finely crush the shells with a mortar and pestle (or in a food processor with a little of the soup).

RETURN the crushed shells to the soup with the rice. Bring to a boil, reduce the heat, cover the saucepan and simmer for 30 minutes, or until the rice is very soft.

STRAIN the bisque into a clean saucepan through a fine sieve lined with damp cheesecloth, pressing down firmly on the solids to extract all the cooking liquid. Add the cream and season with salt and cayenne, then gently reheat to serve. Ladle into warmed soup bowls and garnish, if you like, with the crab claws or some of the meat.

LEEK AND POTATO SOUP

LEEK AND POTATO SOUP CAN BE SERVED HOT OR CHILLED. IN ITS HOT FORM THE DISH IS TRADITIONALLY FRENCH. THE CHILLED VERSION, VICHYSSOISE, WAS THOUGHT TO HAVE BEEN FIRST SERVED AT THE RITZ-CARLTON HOTEL IN NEW YORK BY A FRENCH CHEF FROM VICHY.

3 tablespoons butter
1 onion, finely chopped
3 leeks, white part only, sliced
1 celery stalk, finely chopped
1 garlic clove, finely chopped
1/2 lb. potatoes, chopped
3 cups chicken stock
3/4 cup whipping cream
2 tablespoons chopped chives

SERVES 6

MELT the butter in a large saucepan and add the onion, leeks, celery and garlic. Cover the saucepan and cook, stirring occasionally, over low heat for 15 minutes, or until the vegetables are softened but not browned. Add the potatoes and stock and bring to a boil.

REDUCE the heat and simmer, covered, for 20 minutes. Allow to cool a little before puréeing in a blender or food processor. Return to the clean saucepan.

BRING the soup gently back to a boil and stir in the cream. Season with salt and white pepper and reheat without boiling. Serve hot or well chilled, garnished with chives.

Do not rush the initial cooking of the leeks. The long cooking time over low heat is what gives them their sweet flavor.

WATERCRESS SOUP

2 tablespoons butter
1 onion, finely chopped
1/2 lb. potatoes, diced
2 1/2 cups chicken stock
2 lb. watercress, trimmed and chopped
1/2 cup whipping cream
1/2 cup milk
freshly grated nutmeg
2 tablespoons chopped chives

SERVES 4

MELT the butter in a large saucepan and add the onion. Cover the saucepan and cook over low heat until the onion is softened but not browned. Add the potatoes and chicken stock and simmer for 12 minutes, or until the potatoes are tender. Add the watercress and cook for 1 minute.

REMOVE FROM the heat and allow the soup to cool a little before pouring into a blender or food processor. Blend until smooth and return to the clean saucepan.

BRING the soup gently back to a boil and stir in the cream and milk. Season with nutmeg, salt and pepper and reheat without boiling. Serve garnished with chives.

WATERCRESS SOUP

A pavement café in Marseille.

Basil is more usually associated with Italy than with France but, in fact, the herb originated not in Italy, but in India. It was introduced to Europe in the sixteenth century and is often used in southern French cooking as a perfect match for Provençal tomatoes and olive oil. It can be bought in pots or bunches.

SOUPE AU PISTOU

PISTOU IS A PROVENÇAL MIXTURE OF GARLIC, BASIL AND PARMESAN MIXED TOGETHER WITH OLIVE OIL FROM THE SOUTH OF FRANCE. SIMILAR TO ITALIAN PESTO, IT IS THE TRADITIONAL ACCOMPANIMENT TO THIS SPRING VEGETABLE SOUP AND IS ADDED AT THE TABLE.

1 1/4 cups dried white beans, such as cannellini, navy or flageolet
2 teaspoons olive oil
1 onion, finely chopped
2 garlic cloves, crushed
1 celery stalk, chopped
3 carrots, diced
bouquet garni
4 potatoes, diced
1/4 lb. small green beans, chopped
2 cups chicken stock
3 tomatoes
4 zucchini, diced
1 1/2 cups vermicelli, broken into pieces
1 cup peas, fresh or frozen

PISTOU
6 garlic cloves
1 1/3 cups basil leaves
1 cup Parmesan, grated
3/4 cup olive oil

SERVES 4

SOAK the dried beans in cold water overnight, then drain, put in a saucepan and cover with cold water. Bring to a boil, then lower the heat and simmer for 1 hour, or until the beans are tender. Drain well.

TO MAKE the pistou, put the garlic, basil and Parmesan in a food processor or a mortar and pestle and process or pound until finely mashed. Slowly add the olive oil, with the motor running if you are using the food processor or pounding constantly with the mortar and pestle, and mix thoroughly. Cover with plastic wrap and set aside.

HEAT the olive oil in a large saucepan, add the onion and garlic and cook over low heat for 5 minutes until softened but not browned. Add the celery, carrots and bouquet garni and cook for 10 minutes, stirring occasionally. Add the potatoes, green beans, chicken stock and 7 cups water and simmer for 10 minutes.

SCORE a cross in the top of each tomato. Plunge into boiling water for 20 seconds, then drain and peel the skin away from the cross. Chop the tomatoes finely, discarding the cores. Add to the soup with the zucchini, dried beans, vermicelli and peas and cook for 10 minutes or until tender (if you are using frozen peas, add them at the last minute just to heat through). Season and serve with pistou on top.

BOURRIDE

THIS RICH FISH SOUP CAN BE SERVED IN A VARIETY OF WAYS. THE BREAD CAN BE PUT IN A DISH WITH THE FISH PILED ON TOP AND THE SOUP LADLED OVER, OR THE BROTH MAY BE SERVED WITH CROUTONS AND THE FISH EATEN SEPARATELY WITH BOILED POTATOES AS A MAIN COURSE.

GARLIC CROUTONS
1/2 stale baguette, sliced
1/4 cup olive oil
1 garlic clove, halved

AÏOLI
2 egg yolks
4 garlic cloves, crushed
3–5 teaspoons lemon juice
1 cup olive oil

STOCK
1/4 teaspoon saffron threads
4 cups dry white wine
1 leek, white part only, chopped
2 carrots, chopped
2 onions, chopped
2 long pieces orange zest
2 teaspoons fennel seeds
3 thyme sprigs
5 lb. whole firm white fish such as
    monkfish, sea bass, cod, perch,
    or sole, filleted, skinned and cut
    into 1 1/2 inch pieces (reserve the
    trimmings)
3 egg yolks

SERVES 4

PREHEAT the oven to 315°F. Brush the bread with oil and bake for 10 minutes until crisp. Rub one side of each slice with garlic.

TO MAKE the aïoli, put the egg yolks, garlic and 3 teaspoons of the lemon juice in a mortar and pestle or food processor and pound or mix until light and creamy. Add the oil, drop by drop from the tip of a teaspoon, whisking constantly until it begins to thicken, then add the oil in a very thin stream. (If you're using a processor, pour in the oil in a thin stream with the motor running.) Season, add the remaining lemon juice and, if necessary, thin with a little warm water. Cover and refrigerate.

TO MAKE the stock, soak the saffron threads in a tablespoon of hot water for 15 minutes. Put the saffron, wine, leek, carrots, onions, orange zest, fennel seeds, thyme and fish trimmings in a large saucepan with 4 cups water. Cover and bring to a boil, then simmer for 20 minutes, skimming occasionally. Strain into a clean saucepan, pressing the solids with a wooden spoon to extract all the liquid. Bring the stock to a gentle simmer, add half the fish and poach for 5 minutes. Remove and keep warm while you cook the rest of the fish, then remove them from the saucepan and bring the stock back to a boil. Boil for 5 minutes, or until slightly reduced, and remove from the heat.

PUT HALF the aïoli and the egg yolks in a bowl and mix until smooth. Whisk in a ladleful of hot stock, then gradually add 5 ladlefuls, stirring constantly. Pour back into the saucepan holding the rest of the stock and whisk over low heat for 3–5 minutes, or until the soup is hot and slightly thicker (don't let it boil or it will curdle). Season with salt and pepper.

TO SERVE, put two garlic croutons in each bowl, top with a few pieces of fish and ladle over the hot soup. Serve the remaining aïoli separately.

Use slightly stale bread for the croutons. Rubbing with the cut side of the garlic will give them a mild flavor. Buy whole fish and cut them up yourself, keeping the trimmings. A flavorsome stock, made with fresh trimmings, is the basis of a good fish soup.

Keeping the garlic cloves whole, rather than chopping them, gives a much sweeter flavor.

GARLIC SOUP

GARLIC SOUPS ARE SERVED THROUGHOUT FRANCE. IN PROVENCE, A SIMPLE SOUP OF GARLIC, HERBS AND OLIVE OIL IS KNOWN AS *AÏGO BOUÏDO*. THE SOUTHWEST VERSION, MADE WITH GOOSE FAT, IS CALLED *LE TOURAIN*. THIS SOUP IS GIVEN MORE SUBSTANCE WITH POTATO TO THICKEN IT.

2 bulbs of garlic, about 30 cloves, cloves separated
1/2 cup olive oil
4 oz. bacon, finely chopped
1 baking potato, diced
6 cups chicken stock or water
bouquet garni
3 egg yolks

CHEESE CROUTONS
1/2 baguette or 1 ficelle, sliced
13/4 oz. Gruyère, grated

SERVES 4

SMASH the garlic with the flat side of a knife and peel. Heat 1 tablespoon of the oil in a large heavy-bottomed saucepan and cook the bacon over moderate heat for 5 minutes without browning. Add the garlic and potato and cook for 5 minutes until softened. Add stock and bouquet garni, bring to a boil and simmer for 30 minutes, or until the potato starts to dissolve into the soup.

PUT the egg yolks in a large bowl and pour in the remaining oil in a thin stream, whisking until thickened. Gradually whisk in the hot soup. Strain back into the saucepan, pressing to extract all the liquid, and heat gently without boiling. Season.

TO MAKE the cheese croutons, preheat the broiler and lightly toast the bread on both sides. Sprinkle with the cheese and broil until melted. Place a few croutons in each warm bowl and ladle the soup over the top, or serve the croutons on the side.

CABBAGE SOUP

CABBAGE SOUP

31/2 oz. dried white beans
4 oz. bacon, cubed
3 tablespoons butter
1 carrot, sliced
1 onion, chopped
1 leek, white part only, roughly chopped
1 turnip, peeled and chopped
bouquet garni
5 cups chicken stock
3/4 lb. cabbage, finely shredded

SERVES 4

SOAK the beans overnight in cold water. Drain, put in a saucepan and cover with cold water. Bring to a boil and simmer for 5 minutes, then drain. Put the bacon in the same saucepan, cover with water and simmer for 5 minutes. Drain and pat dry with paper towels.

MELT the butter in a large heavy-bottomed saucepan, add the bacon and cook for 5 minutes, without browning. Add the beans, carrot, onion, leek and turnip and cook for 5 minutes. Add the bouquet garni and chicken stock and bring to a boil. Cover and simmer for 30 minutes. Add the cabbage, uncover and simmer for 30 minutes, or until the beans are tender. Remove the bouquet garni before serving and season to taste.

HORS D'OEUVRES
AND APPETIZERS

AÏOLI

OFTEN REFERRED TO AS "PROVENCE BUTTER," AÏOLI IS A SIMPLE BUT SUPERB GARLIC-FLAVORED MAYONNAISE. IT IS SERVED WITH A SELECTION OF CRUDITÉS OR HOT VEGETABLES, POACHED CHICKEN, SNAILS OR FISH, AND IT CAN ALSO BE ADDED TO FISH SOUPS.

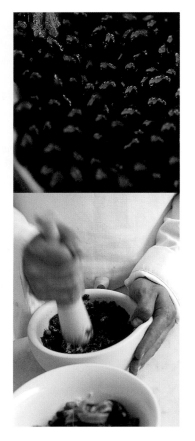

A mortar and pestle are ideal for making tapenade, which should be a fairly rough paste. The name comes from *tapenado*, the Provençal word for caper.

4 egg yolks
8 garlic cloves, crushed
1/2 teaspoon salt
2 tablespoons lemon juice
2 cups olive oil

CRUDITÉS
6 baby carrots, trimmed, but with
   green tops left on
6 asparagus spears, trimmed and
   blanched
6 green beans, trimmed and
   blanched
6 button mushrooms, halved
1 yellow pepper, seeded and cut
   into strips
1 red pepper, seeded and cut into
   strips
6 cauliflower florets
1 fennel bulb, cut into strips

SERVES 6

PUT the egg yolks, garlic, salt and half the lemon juice in a mortar and pestle or food processor and pound or mix until light and creamy. Add the oil, drop by drop from the tip of a teaspoon, whisking constantly until it begins to thicken, then add the oil in a very thin stream. (If you're using a processor, pour in the oil in a thin stream with the motor running.) Season, add the remaining lemon juice and, if necessary, thin with a little warm water.

ARRANGE the crudités around a large platter and serve the aïoli in a bowl in the center. You can keep the aïoli sealed in a sterilized jar in the refrigerator. It will last for up to 3 weeks.

TAPENADE

2 cups black olives, pitted
3 tablespoons capers, rinsed
8 anchovies
1 garlic clove, crushed
3/4 cup olive oil
1 tablespoon lemon juice
2 teaspoons Dijon mustard
1 teaspoon chopped thyme
1 tablespoon chopped parsley

SERVES 6

POUND TOGETHER the olives, capers, anchovies and garlic, either using a mortar and pestle or a food processor. Add the olive oil, lemon juice, mustard and herbs and pound or process again until you have a fairly rough paste.

SERVE with bread or crudités for dipping. Can be kept, covered, in the refrigerator for several days.

TAPENADE

LEEKS A LA GRECQUE

A LA GRECQUE REFERS TO THE GREEK STYLE OF COOKING, USING OLIVE OIL, LEMON, HERBS AND SPICES. THESE INGREDIENTS THAT ARE SO READILY FOUND IN THE DUSTY GREEK HILLSIDES ARE EQUALLY AT HOME IN THE MORE VERDANT LANDSCAPE OF FRANCE.

1/4 cup extra virgin olive oil
2 tablespoons white wine
1 tablespoon tomato paste
1/4 teaspoon sugar
1 bay leaf
1 thyme sprig
1 garlic clove, crushed
4 coriander seeds, crushed
4 peppercorns
8 small leeks, trimmed
1 teaspoon lemon juice
1 tablespoon chopped parsley

SERVES 4

PUT the oil, wine, tomato paste, sugar, bay leaf, thyme, garlic, coriander seeds, peppercorns and 1 cup water in a large non aluminum frying pan. Bring to a boil, cover and simmer for 5 minutes.

ADD the leeks in a single layer and bring just to a simmer. Reduce the heat, cover the frying pan again and cook for 20–30 minutes, or until the leeks are tender (pierce with a fine skewer). Take out the leeks and put them in a serving dish.

ADD the lemon juice to the cooking liquid and boil rapidly until the liquid is slightly syrupy. Remove the bay leaf, thyme and peppercorns. Season with salt and pour over the leeks. Serve the leeks cold, sprinkled with chopped parsley.

MUSHROOMS A LA GRECQUE

2 tomatoes
1/3 cup extra virgin olive oil
1/4 cup white wine
2 shallots, finely chopped
1 garlic clove, crushed
6 coriander seeds, lightly crushed
1 bay leaf
1 thyme sprig
1 lb. button mushrooms
2 teaspoons lemon juice
pinch of sugar
1 tablespoon chopped parsley

SERVES 4

SCORE a cross in the top of each tomato. Plunge into boiling water for 20 seconds, then drain and peel the skin away from the cross. Chop the tomatoes, discarding the cores.

PUT the oil, wine, tomatoes, shallots, garlic, coriander seeds, bay leaf, thyme and 1 cup water in a non aluminum saucepan. Bring to a boil, cover and simmer for 10 minutes. Uncover the saucepan, add the mushrooms and simmer for another 10 minutes, stirring occasionally. Take out the mushrooms with a slotted spoon and put them in a serving dish.

BOIL the cooking liquid rapidly until you have only about 1 cup left. Remove the bay leaf and thyme. Add the lemon juice and season with salt, pepper and the sugar. Pour the liquid over the mushrooms and allow to cool. Serve the mushrooms cold, sprinkled with chopped parsley.

MUSHROOMS A LA GRECQUE

Pound the anchoïade mixture to a coarse paste and then add a little extra olive oil to give it a spreadable consistency.

ASPARAGUS WITH HOLLANDAISE SAUCE

24 asparagus spears

HOLLANDAISE SAUCE
2 egg yolks
2 teaspoons lemon juice
1/3 cup unsalted butter, cut into
   cubes

SERVES 4

WASH the asparagus and remove the woody ends (hold each spear at both ends and bend it gently—it will snap at its natural breaking point). Cook the asparagus in a frying pan of simmering salted water for 4 minutes, or until just tender. Drain, then cool under cold running water.

TO MAKE the hollandaise sauce, put the egg yolks and lemon juice in a saucepan over very low heat. Whisk continuously, adding the butter piece by piece until the sauce thickens. Do not overheat or the eggs will scramble. Season.

(ALTERNATIVELY, put the eggs yolks, salt and pepper in a blender and mix together. Heat the lemon juice and butter together until boiling and then, with the motor running, pour onto the yolks in a steady stream.)

ARRANGE a few asparagus spears on each plate and spoon the hollandaise over the top.

ANCHOÏADE

COLLIOURE ON THE SOUTH COAST IS THE HOME OF ANCHOVY FISHING IN FRANCE AND IT IS FROM THE SOUTH THAT THIS PUNGENT ANCHOVY PASTE HAILS. IT CAN BE SERVED AS A DIP, STIRRED INTO DRESSINGS AND STEWS, OR SPREAD ON BREAD, FISH AND CHICKEN AND THEN BROILED.

ANCHOÏADE

2³/₄ oz. anchovy fillets in oil
2 garlic cloves
14 black olives, pitted
1 small tomato
1 teaspoon thyme leaves
3 teaspoons chopped parsley
olive oil
8 slices baguette

SERVES 4

PUT the anchovies (with their oil), garlic, olives, tomato, thyme, 1 teaspoon chopped parsley and a generous grinding of black pepper in a mortar and pestle or food processor and pound or mix until you have a coarse paste. Add a little extra olive oil if the paste is too thick—it should have a spreadable consistency.

PREHEAT the broiler and toast the baguette slices on both sides until golden brown. Spread the anchoïade over the baguette and sprinkle with the remaining parsley.

FRANCE'S BOULANGERIES are named after *boules,* the round balls of dough found in bakeries. Every village in France must by law have a shop that sells bread and in most villages the boulangerie will bake bread twice daily. If there is no boulangerie, the general village shop will display a *"depôt de pain"* sign showing that it sells bread brought to the "depot" daily. A boulangerie may also double-up as a patisserie

BREAD

BREAD IS AN ESSENTIAL PART OF FRENCH LIFE. EATEN WITH EVERY MEAL, BREAD IS BOUGHT DAILY, OR EVEN TWICE DAILY, AND BY LAW, EVERY VILLAGE IN FRANCE MUST HAVE A SHOP MAKING OR SELLING BREAD.

Breads are sold not only by the loaf (*la pièce*) but also by weight, perpetuating the tradition of buying just enough bread for each meal or day. Boulangeries bake twice daily so that people can have the freshest bread possible, especially since a baguette made of just wheat flour, yeast and salt begins to go stale after only a few hours.

Bread has been the staple of the French diet since the Middle Ages. The first loaves were large and coarse, made from a mix of flours and unsalted because of the high cost of salt. Not until the seventeenth century was white bread invented when a method for removing bran was discovered.

THE BAGUETTE

The baguette is seen as a symbol of France, but many Frenchmen see it instead as a symbol of Paris. Invented in the nineteenth century and based on Viennese bread, it was made from white flour and a sourdough starter, then rolled up into a slim, light loaf with lots of crust. Paris, always a great consumer of bread due to its place in the center of the Beauce wheat plains, immediately took to the new loaf, though it was not until the twentieth century that it became truly popular in rural France. The best baguettes have a crisp, golden outside, with the score marks rising above the crust.

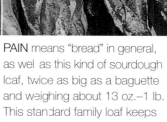

COURONNE a ring loaf with a dense texture and hard crust. The name means crown or wreath and the hole means you can thread your arm through it when you are out shopping.

PAIN D'ÉPICES a specialty of Dijon, this spiced gingerbread is flavored with honey, aniseed, ginger and cinnamon. Though called a bread, it is more of a cake and can keep for weeks.

PAIN means "bread" in general, as well as this kind of sourdough loaf, twice as big as a baguette and weighing about 13 oz.–1 lb. This standard family loaf keeps for longer than a baguette.

PAIN POILÂNE a crusty wood-fired sourdough loaf produced by the Poilâne family at their bakery in Paris. Exported world-wide, it is so well known that it has become a type of its own.

PAIN DE CAMPAGNE a rustic country-style loaf usually made with white, whole wheat and rye flours. This one is a sourdough version from Provence, but they vary from baker to baker.

PAIN AUX NOIX walnut bread made with whole wheat and white flours and flavored with chopped walnuts. Very good toasted and eaten with cheese.

MÉTURE a round yeasted corn bread that is a favorite of the Basque country. It is baked in a round metal dish and has a crust that cracks as it rises.

PAIN AUX OLIVES made by rolling olive paste into bread dough to give a scrolled effect. Some olive breads have whole or chopped olives kneaded into the dough instead.

PAIN AUX HERBES bread flavored with herbs. The herbs used may be fresh or dried and can be an individual flavor or a mix, such as fines herbes or herbes de Provence.

PAIN AU CHOCOLAT a rich butter croissant dough wrapped around one or two sticks of chocolate and baked. Usually eaten warm at breakfast.

CROISSANTS made with fresh butter, croissants should have a light texture. The dough is yeast-risen, incorporating layers of butter that make the pastry flaky.

PAIN AUX RAISINS yeasted butter dough rolled up with raisins to form a snail shape. It is baked and then heavily glazed with icing or preserves.

FOUGASSE a flat bread very common in the South and made with olive oil. It can be sweet or flavored with savory items like bacon. The sweet version from Provence is served at Christmas.

BRIOCHE a sweet yeasted bread that is made with butter and eggs and has an almost cake-like texture. This classic top-knot shape is known as a *brioche à tête* or Parisian brioche.

PAIN AU LEVAIN a classic sourdough loaf made with a starter of naturally occurring yeasts and risen overnight to improve its flavor. Also known as a *pain à l'ancienne*.

BAGUETTE this classic French loaf makes up about 80% of bread sold in France. Baguettes get stale very quickly so they are baked two or three times a day to be fresh for each meal.

CROISSANT AUX AMANDES these croissants are filled with almond paste and sprinkled with chopped or sliced almonds. They are eaten at breakfast or as a snack.

FICELLE meaning "string," a ficelle is a long narrow loaf like a baguette but about half the weight and thinner.

TOURTON a baguette-type loaf where two long pieces of dough are joined together to get the maximum amount of crust. The shape makes it easy to carry looped over your arm.

PAIN DE SEIGLE a rye bread made of rye and wheat flours. Traditional to France's mountain areas, it is often eaten with oysters and *fruits de mer*. This is an organic version.

PETIT PAIN the name given to anything small enough to eat as a roll. They vary from being a mini baguette to a small brioche or soft white milk roll.

PAIN AUX CÉRÉALES a multigrain bread usually containing about five different grains. Sometimes the number of grains is included in the name.

BOULE meaning "ball," these are the loaves that gave the *boulangerie* its name. Generally made with wheat flour.

BÂTARD a traditional white loaf weighing about 1 lb. with an irregular appearance. Bâtard means "bastard" and it s sold by the loaf and by weight.

and all boulangeries bake croissants, brioche and *pain au chocolat* to be eaten with a *café au lait* for a simple French breakfast. Bread is also handmade by small artisan producers and sold in markets, along with specialties such as the pastries being eaten as a snack *(le goûter)* by these two girls in a market in Provence, and also traditional breads such as the *pain au levain* sold from this van in a Lyon market.

TYPES OF BREADS

Although the elegant baguette is still France's most popular bread, the more rustic and nutritious *pain de campagne* is growing in popularity, as are other loaves made from barley and rye. These country-style breads often use a *levain* (sourdough starter) rather than yeast. Sourdough breads have a long production time, but they do keep for a few days rather than going stale quickly like baguettes. These loaves may also be baked in a wood-fired oven, which adds a smoky taste.

A real baguette is actually a certain weight and size (about 28 inches in length and 8 oz. in weight) and not all long loaves are baguettes. A ficelle is thinner and lighter and a flûte is midway between the two, though all are made in the same way. A long, thin *pain au levain* (sourdough bread) may also be labelled as a baguette, and although strictly it is not, the shape is now so recognizable that the name covers many things.

THE SOURDOUGH BREADS shown here are made by the French *levain* system, using a living sourdough starter in which the yeasts that cause the bread to rise are organic. The starter ferments for at least a few days to give the bread its tangy taste.

CELERY ROOT REMOULADE

juice of 1 lemon
2 celery roots, trimmed and peeled
2 tablespoons capers
5 cornichons, chopped
2 tablespoons finely chopped
  parsley

MUSTARD MAYONNAISE
2 egg yolks
1 tablespoon white wine vinegar or
  lemon juice
1 tablespoon Dijon mustard
1/2 cup light olive oil

SERVES 4

PLACE 4 cups cold water in a large bowl and add half the lemon juice. Roughly grate the celery roots and then place in the acidulated water. Bring a saucepan of water to a boil and add the remaining lemon juice. Drain the celery roots and add to the water. After 1 minute, drain and cool under running water. Pat dry with paper towels.

TO MAKE the mustard mayonnaise, put the egg yolks, vinegar or lemon juice and mustard in a bowl or food processor and whisk together. Add the oil, drop by drop from the tip of a teaspoon, whisking constantly until it begins to thicken, then add the oil in a very thin stream. (If you're using a processor, pour in the oil in a thin stream with the motor running.) Season and, if necessary, thin with a little warm water.

TOSS the celery roots with the mayonnaise, capers, cornichons and parsley. Serve with bread.

Once the mayonnaise has started to thicken, you can add the oil in a thin stream, whisking constantly.

POTATO SALAD

POTATO VARIETIES CONTAIN VARYING AMOUNTS OF STARCH, MAKING THEM EITHER "WAXY" OR "MEALY." WAXY OR ALL-PURPOSE VARIETIES, SUCH AS DESIREE OR YUKON GOLD, ARE LOWER IN STARCH AND HOLD THEIR SHAPE WHEN COOKED, MAKING THEM BETTER FOR SALADS.

4 large waxy potatoes, cubed
3 celery stalks
1 red pepper
1 tablespoon olive oil
1/3 cup mayonnaise (page 286)
juice of 1 lemon
1 1/2 tablespoons chopped parsley

SERVES 4

PUT the potatoes in a large saucepan, cover with cold water and cook for 15 minutes, or until just tender (don't allow them to over-cook). Refresh under cold water and drain.

STRING the celery stalks and cut them into very small cubes. Cut the pepper in half, remove the seeds and dice finely.

PUT the potatoes, celery and pepper in a bowl, add the olive oil, mayonnaise, lemon juice and parsley and toss well. Season well before serving.

POTATO SALAD

RAW OYSTERS

24 oysters in their shells
1 shallot, finely chopped
2 tablespoons red wine vinegar
1 lemon, cut into wedges

SERVES 4

SHUCK the oysters by holding each one, rounded side down, in a cloth in your left hand. Using an oyster knife, carefully wiggle the point of the knife between the two shells and, keeping the blade flat, run the knife across the top shell to sever the muscle. Pull off the top shell and loosen the oyster from the bottom shell, being careful not to lose any liquid. Nestle the opened oysters on a bed of crushed ice or rock salt on a large platter (this will keep them steady).

MIX the shallot with the red wine vinegar and some black pepper in a small bowl. Put this in the center of the platter and arrange the lemon wedges around the oysters. Serve with slices of rye bread and butter.

RAW OYSTERS

OYSTERS MORNAY

24 oysters in their shells
3 tablespoons butter
1 shallot, finely chopped
1/4 cup all-purpose flour
1 1/2 cups milk
pinch of nutmeg
1/2 bay leaf
2 tablespoons Gruyère, grated
1/4 cup Parmesan, grated, plus a
  little extra for broiling

SERVES 6

SHUCK the oysters, reserving all the liquid. Strain the liquid into a saucepan. Rinse the oysters to remove any bits of shell. Wash and dry the shells.

MELT 2 tablespoons of the butter in another saucepan, add the shallot and cook, stirring, for 3 minutes. Stir in the flour to make a roux and stir over very low heat for 3 minutes without allowing the roux to brown. Remove from the heat and add the milk gradually, stirring after each addition until smooth. Return to the heat, add the nutmeg and bay leaf and simmer for 5 minutes. Strain through a fine sieve into a clean saucepan.

HEAT the oyster liquid in the saucepan to a simmer (add a little water if you need more liquid). Add the oysters and poach for 30 seconds, then take them out with a slotted spoon and put them back into their shells. Stir the cooking liquid into the sauce. Add the cheeses and remaining butter and stir until they have melted into the sauce. Season with salt and pepper. Preheat the broiler.

SPOON a little sauce over each oyster, sprinkle with Parmesan and place under the hot broiler for a couple of minutes, or until golden brown.

To store oysters, wrap them in a damp cloth and refrigerate in the salad compartment for up to 3 days. Eat oysters that have been shucked immediately.

ARTICHOKES VINAIGRETTE

THIS IS THE CLASSIC WAY TO SERVE ARTICHOKES: BE SURE TO BUY THE BEST ONES AVAILABLE. SMALLER ARTICHOKES CAN ALSO BE PREPARED IN THIS FASHION, BUT CUT THEM INTO QUARTERS AND SERVE WITH THE DRESSING RATHER THAN LEAVING WHOLE AND REMOVING THE LEAVES ONE BY ONE.

juice of 1 lemon
4 globe artichokes

VINAIGRETTE
5 tablespoons olive oil
2 scallions, finely chopped
2 tablespoons white wine
2 tablespoons white wine vinegar
1/4 teaspoon Dijon mustard
pinch of sugar
1 tablespoon finely chopped
   parsley

SERVES 4

TO PREPARE the artichokes, bring a large saucepan of salted water to a boil and add the lemon juice. Break the stems from the artichokes, pulling out any strings at the same time, and then trim the bottoms flat. Add the artichokes to the water and put a small plate on top of them to keep them submerged. Cook at a simmer for 25–30 minutes, or until a leaf from the bottom comes away easily. (The bottom will be tender when pierced with a skewer.) Cool quickly under cold running water, then drain upside down on a baking sheet.

TO MAKE the vinaigrette, heat 1 tablespoon of the oil in a small saucepan, add the scallions and cook over low heat for 2 minutes. Allow to cool a little, then add the white wine, vinegar, mustard and sugar and gradually whisk in the remaining oil. Season well with salt and pepper and stir in half the parsley.

PLACE an artichoke on each plate and gently pry it open a little. Spoon the dressing over the top, allowing it to drizzle into the artichoke and around the plate. Pour the remaining dressing into a small bowl for people to dip the leaves. Sprinkle each artichoke with a little parsley.

EAT the leaves one by one, dipping them in the vinaigrette and scraping the flesh off the leaves between your teeth. When you reach the middle, pull off any really small leaves and then use a teaspoon to remove the furry choke. Once you've removed the choke, you can get to the tender bottom or "heart" of the artichoke.

Whisking the remaining oil into the vinaigrette.

Hollow out the vegetables with a spoon and brush the edges with a little oil before filling with the ground meat stuffing.

PETITS FARCIS

THIS WONDERFUL DISH FROM PROVENCE MAKES GOOD USE OF THE REGION'S ABUNDANCE OF GARDEN PRODUCE AND THE STUFFING CAN INCLUDE ANY HERBS, MEAT OR CHEESES AT HAND. SERVE HOT OR COLD WITH BREAD FOR A SIMPLE SUMMER LUNCH.

2 small eggplants, halved
  lengthwise
2 small zucchini, halved lengthwise
4 tomatoes
2 small red peppers, halved
  lengthwise and seeded
4 tablespoons olive oil
2 red onions, chopped
2 garlic cloves, crushed
1/2 lb. ground pork
1/2 lb. ground veal
1/4 cup tomato paste
1/3 cup white wine
2 tablespoons chopped parsley
1/2 cup Parmesan, grated
1 cup fresh bread crumbs

SERVES 4

PREHEAT the oven to 350°F. Grease a large roasting pan with oil. Use a spoon to hollow out the centers of the eggplants and zucchini, leaving a border around the edge. Chop the flesh finely.

CUT the tops from the tomatoes (don't throw away the tops). Use a spoon to hollow out the centers, catching the juice in a bowl, and chop the flesh roughly. Arrange the vegetables, including the red peppers, in the roasting pan. Brush the edges of the eggplants and zucchini with a little of the oil. Pour 1/2 cup water into the roasting pan.

HEAT HALF the oil in a large frying pan. Cook the onions and garlic for 3 minutes, or until they have softened. Add the ground meat and stir for 5 minutes until the meat browns, breaking up any lumps with the back of a fork. Add the chopped eggplants and zucchini and cook for another 3 minutes. Add the tomato pulp and juice, tomato paste and wine. Cook, stirring occasionally, for 10 minutes.

REMOVE the frying pan from the heat and stir in the parsley, Parmesan and bread crumbs. Season well with salt and pepper. Spoon the mixture into the vegetables. Place the tops back on the tomatoes. Sprinkle the vegetables with the remaining oil and bake for 45 minutes or until the vegetables are tender.

MILLEFEUILLE OF LEEKS AND POACHED EGGS

MILLEFEUILLE MEANS "A THOUSAND LEAVES" AND REFERS TO THE MANY LAYERS OF THE PUFF PASTRY. YOU CAN EITHER USE THE RECIPE IN THIS BOOK OR 11 OZ. STORE-BOUGHT PUFF PASTRY. MAKE SURE YOU USE THE FRESHEST EGGS YOU CAN FIND.

1/2 batch puff pastry (page 281)
1 egg, lightly beaten
3 leeks, white part only
2 tablespoons butter
4 eggs

BEURRE BLANC
2 shallots, finely chopped
1 tablespoon butter
3 tablespoons white wine
3/4 cup chicken stock
3/4 cup unsalted butter, chilled and diced

SERVES 4

PREHEAT the oven to 375°F. Roll out the pastry on a lightly floured surface to make a 9 1/2 x 5 inch rectangle. Chill for 10 minutes and then cut into four equal triangles. Trim the edges so they are straight. Place the triangles on a damp baking sheet, lightly brush with the beaten egg and bake for 15 minutes, or until puffed and golden brown. Slice the triangles in half horizontally and use a spoon to remove any uncooked dough from the inside.

CUT the leeks in half and then into thin julienne strips. Melt the butter in a frying pan, add the leeks and cook, stirring, for 10 minutes or until they are tender. Season with salt.

TO POACH the eggs, bring a saucepan of water to a boil. Crack an egg into a ramekin, reduce the heat and slide the egg into the simmering water. Poach for 3 minutes, then remove carefully with a slotted spoon and drain on paper towels. Poach all the eggs in the same way.

TO MAKE the beurre blanc, fry the shallots gently in the butter until they are tender but not browned. Add the wine and bubble in the frying pan until reduced by half. Add the stock and continue cooking until reduced by a third. Add the butter, piece by piece, whisking continuously until the sauce thickens—take care not to overheat. You may need to move the frying pan on and off the heat to keep the temperature even. Season the beurre blanc with salt and white pepper.

ARRANGE the bottom triangles of pastry on a serving dish, top each one with a spoonful of warm leek, then a poached egg and a little beurre blanc. Cover with the pastry tops and serve with the beurre blanc drizzled around or on the side.

Cook the julienned leeks in the butter until they are tender. When making the beurre blanc, take care not to overheat the sauce or the butter will melt too quickly and not form an emulsion.

Spoon the choux pastry around the edge of the baking dish and bake until well risen. To remove the bone from the trout, simply lift off the top fillet and then pull the bone away cleanly.

SMOKED TROUT GOUGÈRE

FOR A GOUGÈRE, CHOUX PASTRY IS TRADITIONALLY PIPED INTO A CIRCULAR OR OVAL SHAPE AND FILLED WITH A SAVORY MIXTURE. IF YOU PREFER, THE PASTRY CAN ALSO BE MADE INTO SMALL CHOUX BUNS, SPLIT OPEN AND THE FILLING SPOONED INTO THE CENTERS.

1/4 cup butter
1 cup all-purpose flour, sifted twice
1/4 teaspoon paprika
3 large eggs, beaten
3/4 cup Gruyère, grated

FILLING
3/4 lb. smoked trout
3 cups watercress, trimmed
2 tablespoons butter
1/4 cup all-purpose flour
1 1/4 cups milk

SERVES 4

PREHEAT the oven to 400°F and put a baking sheet on the top shelf to heat up.

MELT the butter with 3/4 cup water in a saucepan, then bring it to a rolling boil. Remove from the heat and sift in all the flour and the paprika. Return to the heat and beat continuously with a wooden spoon to make a smooth shiny paste that comes away from the side of the pan. Cool for a few minutes. Beat in the eggs one at a time, until shiny and smooth—the mixture should drop off the spoon but not be too runny. Stir in two-thirds of the cheese.

SPOON the dough round the edge of a shallow, lightly greased baking dish. Put this in the oven on the hot baking sheet and cook for 45–50 minutes, or until the choux is well risen and browned.

MEANWHILE, to make the filling, peel the skin off the trout and lift off the top fillet. Pull out the bone. Break the trout into large flakes. Wash the watercress and put in a large saucepan with just the water clinging to the leaves. Cover the saucepan and steam for 2 minutes, or until it has just wilted. Drain, cool and squeeze with your hands to get rid of the excess liquid. Roughly chop the watercress.

MELT the butter in a saucepan, stir in the flour to make a roux and cook, stirring, for 3 minutes over a very low heat without allowing the roux to brown. Remove from the heat and add the milk gradually, stirring after each addition until smooth. Return to the heat and simmer for 3 minutes. Stir in the smoked trout and watercress and season well.

SPOON the trout filling into the center of the cooked choux pastry and return to the oven for 10 minutes, then serve immediately.

PROVENÇAL TART

PASTRY
2 cups all-purpose flour
²/₃ cup butter, diced
1 egg yolk, beaten

2 tablespoons olive oil
1 large white onion, finely chopped
10 tomatoes (or 2 x 14¹/₂ oz. cans diced tomatoes)
1 teaspoon tomato paste
2 garlic cloves, finely chopped
1 tablespoon roughly chopped oregano, plus a few whole leaves to garnish
1 red pepper
1 yellow pepper
6 anchovies, halved
12 pitted olives
drizzle of olive oil

SERVES 6

TO MAKE the pastry, sift the flour into a bowl, add the butter and rub in with your fingertips until the mixture resembles bread crumbs. Add the egg yolk and a little cold water (about 2–3 teaspoons) and mix with a flexible bladed knife until the dough just starts to come together. Bring the dough together with your hands and shape into a ball. Wrap in plastic wrap and put in the refrigerator to rest for at least 30 minutes.

HEAT the oil in a frying pan, add the onion, cover and cook over very low heat for 20 minutes, stirring often, until softened but not browned.

SCORE a cross in the top of each tomato. Plunge into boiling water for 20 seconds, then drain and peel the skin away from the cross. Chop the tomatoes, discarding the cores. Add the tomatoes, tomato paste, garlic and oregano to the frying pan and simmer, uncovered, for 20 minutes, stirring occasionally. Once the tomato is soft and the mixture has become a paste, allow to cool.

ROLL OUT the pastry to fit a 13¹/₂ x 10¹/₂ inch shallow baking sheet. Prick the pastry gently all over, without piercing right through. Cover the pastry with plastic wrap and chill for 30 minutes. Preheat the broiler.

CUT the peppers in half, remove the seeds and membrane and place, skin side up, under the hot broiler until the skin blackens and blisters. Allow to cool before peeling away the skin. Cut the peppers into thin strips.

REDUCE the oven to 400°F. Line the pastry shell with a crumpled piece of waxed paper and fill with baking beads (use dried beans or rice if you don't have beads). Blind bake the pastry for 10 minutes, remove the paper and beads and bake for another 3–5 minutes, or until the pastry is just cooked but still very pale. Reduce the oven to 350°F.

SPREAD the tomato mixture over the pastry, then scatter with peppers. Arrange the anchovies and olives over the top. Brush with olive oil and bake for 25 minutes. Scatter with oregano leaves to serve.

Simmer the filling until the tomato is so soft that it forms a paste.

PISSALADIÈRE

PISSALADIÈRE TAKES ITS NAME FROM *PISSALAT*, PURÉED ANCHOVIES. IT CAN VARY IN TS TOPPING FROM ONIONS AND ANCHOVIES TO ONIONS, TOMATOES AND ANCHOVIES OR SIMPLY ANCHOVIES PURÉED WITH GARLIC. TRADITIONAL TO NICE, IT CAN BE MADE WITH A BREAD OR PASTRY BASE.

3 tablespoons butter
1 tablespoon olive oil
3 lb. onions, thinly sliced
2 tablespoons thyme leaves
1 batch bread dough (page 277)
1 tablespoon olive oil
16 anchovies, halved engthwise
24 pitted olives

SERVES 6

MELT the butter with the olive oil in a saucepan and add the onions and half the thyme. Cover the saucepan and cook over low heat for 45 minutes, stirring occasionally, until the onion is softened but not browned. Season and cool. Preheat the oven to 400°F.

ROLL OUT the bread dough to roughly fit a greased 13¹/₂ x 10¹/₂ inch shallow baking sheet. Brush with olive oil, then spread with the onions.

LAY the anchovies in a lattice pattern over the onions and arrange the olives in the lattice diamonds. Bake for 20 minutes, or until the dough is cooked and lightly browned. Sprinkle with the remaining thyme leaves and cut into squares. Serve hot or warm.

Spread the softened onions over the bread base and then arrange the anchovies over the top in the traditional lattice pattern.

TARTE FLAMBÉE

TARTE FLAMBÉE IS THE ALSATIAN VERSION OF THE PIZZA. IT IS COOKED QUICKLY AT A VERY HIGH TEMPERATURE IN A WOOD-FIRED OVEN AND TAKES ITS NAME FROM THE FACT THAT THE EDGE OF THE DOUGH OFTEN CAUGHT FIRE IN THE INTENSE HEAT OF THE OVEN.

2 tablespoons olive oil
2 white onions, sliced
¹/₂ cup cream cheese or farmer's cheese
³/₄ cup crème fraîche
6¹/₂ oz. piece of bacon, cut into small strips
1 batch bread dough (page 277)

SERVES 6

PREHEAT the oven to 450°F. Heat the olive oil in a saucepan and fry the onions until softened but not browned. Beat the cream or farmer's cheese with the crème fraîche and then add the onions and bacon and season well.

ROLL OUT the bread dough into a rectangle about ¹/₈ inch thick—the dough needs to be quite thin, like a pizza—and place on a greased baking sheet. Fold the edge of the dough over to make a slight rim. Spread the topping over the dough, right up to the rim, and bake for 10–15 minutes, or until the dough is crisp and cooked and the topping browned. Cut into squares to serve.

TARTE FLAMBÉE

EGGS & CHEESE

Once the crêpe starts to come away from the side of the pan, turn it over.

HAM, MUSHROOM AND CHEESE CRÊPES

1 batch crêpe batter (page 282)
1 tablespoon butter
1³/4 cups mushrooms, sliced
2 tablespoons whipping cream
1¹/4 cups Gruyère, grated
²/3 cup ham, chopped

SERVES 6

HEAT a large crêpe or frying pan and grease with a little butter or oil. Pour in enough batter to coat the bottom of the frying pan in a thin even layer and pour out any excess. Cook over moderate heat for about a minute, or until the crêpe starts to come away from the side of the frying pan. Turn the crêpe and cook on the other side for 1 minute or until lightly golden. Stack the crêpes on a plate, with pieces of waxed paper between them, and cover with plastic wrap while you cook the rest of the batter to make six large crêpes.

PREHEAT the oven to 350°F. Heat the butter in a frying pan, add the mushrooms, season well and cook, stirring, for 5 minutes, or until all the liquid from the mushrooms has evaporated. Stir in the cream, cheese and ham.

LAY one crêpe on a board or work surface. Top with a sixth of the filling and fold the crêpe into quarters. Place it on a baking sheet and then fill and fold the remaining crêpes. Bake for 5 minutes then serve immediately.

CERVELLE DE CANUT

CERVELLE DE CANUT IS A LYONNAIS DISH. THE NAME MEANS "SILK WEAVERS' BRAINS" (APPARENTLY SILK WEAVERS WERE CONSIDERED TO BE QUITE STUPID). DEPENDING ON THE TYPE OF CHEESE THAT YOU USE, THE DISH CAN BE EITHER SMOOTH AND CREAMY OR MORE COARSE.

1 lb. curd cheese or farmer's cheese
2 tablespoons olive oil
1 garlic clove, finely chopped
2 tablespoons chopped chervil
4 tablespoons chopped parsley
2 tablespoons chopped chives
1 tablespoon chopped tarragon
4 shallots, finely chopped

SERVES 8

BEAT the curd cheese or farmer's cheese with a wooden spoon, then add the olive oil and garlic and beat it into the cheese. Add the herbs and shallots and mix together well. Season and serve with pieces of toast or bread, perhaps after dessert as you would cheese and crackers.

CERVELLE DE CANUT

OMELET AUX FINES HERBES

THE OMELET IS WONDERFULLY ACCOMMODATING TO PERSONAL TASTE—IT CAN BE FOLDED, ROLLED OR LEFT FLAT, COOKED ON ONE SIDE OR BOTH. THIS FOLDED OMELET IS TRADITIONALLY *BAVEUSE* (CREAMY) IN THE MIDDLE AND COOKED ONLY ON ONE SIDE BEFORE BEING FOLDED.

1 tablespoon butter
2 shallots, finely chopped
1 garlic clove, crushed
2 tablespoons chopped parsley
2 tablespoons chopped basil
1/2 tablespoon chopped tarragon
2 tablespoons heavy cream
8 eggs, lightly beaten
oil

SERVES 4

MELT the butter in a frying pan and cook the shallots and garlic over low heat until tender. Stir in the herbs and then pour into a bowl. Mix in the cream and eggs and season well.

HEAT A LITTLE oil in a nonstick frying pan. Pour a quarter of the batter into the frying pan and cook gently, constantly pulling the set egg around the edge of the frying pan into the center, until the omelet is set and browned underneath and the top is just cooked. Fold the omelet into three and slide it out of the frying pan onto a plate with the seam underneath. Serve hot, for someone else to eat, while you cook up the remaining three omelets.

When the omelet is set and browned underneath, fold it in three so the inside stays creamy.

CROQUE MONSIEUR

5 tablespoons unsalted butter
4 tablespoons all-purpose flour
3/4 cup milk
1/2 teaspoon Dijon mustard
1 egg yolk
grated nutmeg
12 slices white bread
6 slices ham
1 cup Gruyère, grated

SERVES 6

MELT 3 tablespoons of the butter in a saucepan, add the flour and stir over low heat for 3 minutes. Slowly add the milk and mustard, whisking constantly. Allow to simmer until the mixture has thickened and reduced by about a third. Remove from the heat and stir in the egg yolk. Season with salt, pepper and nutmeg and allow to cool completely.

PLACE HALF of the bread slices on a baking sheet. Top each piece of bread with a slice of ham, then with some of the sauce, then Gruyère and finally with another piece of bread. Melt half of the remaining butter in a large frying pan and fry the sandwiches on both sides until they are golden brown, adding the remaining butter when you need it. Cut each sandwich in half to serve.

CROQUE MONSIEUR

Grate the cheese for soufflés finely so that it melts quickly without forming bubbles of oil.

Round zucchini are used in the same way as the more common long variety.

ZUCCHINI SOUFFLÉ

SOUFFLÉS HAVE DEVELOPED A REPUTATION AS UNPREDICTABLE CREATIONS, BUT THEY ARE NOT HARD TO MAKE. THE SECRET LIES IN BEATING THE EGG WHITES TO THE RIGHT STIFFNESS AND SERVING THE SOUFFLÉ STRAIGHT FROM OVEN TO TABLE. YOU COULD USE BROCCOLI INSTEAD OF ZUCCHINI.

1 tablespoon butter, melted
1 1/2 tablespoons dried
  bread crumbs
3/4 lb. zucchini, chopped
1/2 cup milk
2 tablespoons butter
1/4 cup all-purpose flour
2/3 cup Gruyère or Parmesan, finely
  grated
3 scallions, finely chopped
4 eggs, separated

SERVES 4

BRUSH a 6-cup soufflé dish with the melted butter and then put the bread crumbs in the dish. Rotate the dish to coat the side completely with bread crumbs. Pour out the excess bread crumbs.

COOK the zucchini in boiling water for 8 minutes until tender. Drain and then put the zucchini in a food processor with the milk and mix until smooth. Alternatively, mash the zucchini with the milk and then press it through a sieve with a wooden spoon. Preheat the oven to 350°F.

MELT the butter in a heavy-bottomed saucepan and stir in the flour to make a roux. Cook, stirring, for 2 minutes over low heat without allowing the roux to brown. Remove from the heat and add the zucchini purée, stirring until smooth. Return to the heat and bring to a boil. Simmer, stirring, for 3 minutes, then remove from the heat. Pour into a bowl, add the cheese and scallions and season well. Mix until smooth, then beat in the egg yolks until smooth again.

WHISK the egg whites in a clean dry bowl until they form soft peaks. Spoon a quarter of the egg white onto the soufflé mixture and quickly but lightly fold it in to loosen the mixture. Lightly fold in the remaining egg white. Pour into the soufflé dish and run your thumb around the inside rim of the dish, about 3/4 inch into the soufflé mixture (try not to wipe off the butter and bread crumbs). This ridge helps the soufflé to rise without sticking.

BAKE for 45 minutes, or until the soufflé has risen and wobbles slightly when tapped. Test with a skewer through a crack in the side of the soufflé—the skewer should come out clean or slightly moist. If the skewer is slightly moist, by the time the soufflé makes it to the table it will be cooked in the center. Serve immediately.

BLUE CHEESE SOUFFLÉ

1 tablespoon butter, melted
2 tablespoons butter
1/4 cup all-purpose flour
1 cup milk
1/2 cup blue cheese, mashed
4 egg yolks
grated nutmeg
5 egg whites

SERVES 4

PREHEAT the oven to 400°F. Cut a strip of waxed paper long enough to fold around a 5-cup soufflé dish, then fold in half and tie around the dish so it sticks 1 inch above the top. Brush the inside of the dish and the waxed paper collar with the melted butter and put the dish on a baking sheet.

MELT the butter in a heavy-bottomed saucepan and stir in the flour to make a roux. Cook, stirring, for 2 minutes over low heat without allowing the roux to brown. Remove from the heat and add the milk gradually, stirring after each addition until smooth. Return to the heat and bring to a boil. Simmer, stirring, for 3 minutes, then remove from the heat.

STIR the cheese into the sauce until it melts (it might separate but keep stirring—it will correct itself). Beat in the yolks, one at a time, beating well after each addition. Season with nutmeg, salt and pepper and pour into a large mixing bowl.

WHISK the egg whites in a clean dry bowl until they form soft peaks. Spoon a quarter of the egg white onto the soufflé mixture and quickly but lightly fold it in to loosen the mixture. Lightly fold in the remaining egg white. Pour into the soufflé dish.

BAKE for 20–25 minutes, or until the soufflé has risen and wobbles slightly when tapped. Test with a skewer through a crack in the side of the soufflé—the skewer should come out clean or slightly moist. If the skewer is slightly moist, by the time the soufflé makes it to the table it will be cooked in the center. Serve immediately.

Cook the roux for a couple of minutes without browning, then turn off the heat before adding the milk gradually. Removing the saucepan from the heat before adding each ingredient prevents the sauce from becoming lumpy.

MOUNTAIN CHEESES Each spring in the French Alps, herds of cows begin their annual transhumance from the winter lowlands to the *alpages,* the highland pastures. The farmers live in chalets while their herds eat the grass, herbs and flowers that will result in the rich, high-fat milk needed to produce cheeses such as *reblochon* and *beaufort d'alpage*, aged in cellars below their chalets.

CHEESE

FRANCE PROUDLY PRODUCES OVER 500 VARIETIES OF CHEESES, MANY OF THEM AMONG THE WORLD'S BEST, AND A REFLECTION OF THE STRENGTH OF REGIONAL TRADITIONS THAT HAD GENERAL DE GAULLE FAMOUSLY ASKING HOW ANYONE COULD GOVERN A COUNTRY WITH SO MANY CHEESES.

THE APPELLATION D'ORIGINE CONTRÔLÉE (AOC)

The AOC is granted to quality cheeses produced in a specified region following established production methods. AOC cheeses can be distinguished by a stamp and often by wording on the package such as *Fabrication traditionnelle au lait cru avec moulé à la louche* on AOC camembert.

CHEESEMAKERS

Fermier cheeses are farmhouse cheeses, using milk from the farmer's herd and traditional methods. *Artisanal* cheeses come from independent farmers using their own or others' milk. *Coopérative* cheeses are made at a dairy with milk coming from cooperative members. *Industriel* cheeses are produced in factories. Many *artisanal* and *fermier* cheesemakers have made traditional cheeses for generations, often in small quantities and sold just within their region. Only a few AOC or well-known cheeses reach a wider audience. Some cheese, such as camembert, is produced by *fermier, coopérative* and *industriel* methods with very different qualities.

MILK FOR CHEESE

French cheeses are made from cow's, goat's and sheep's milk, with ewe's milk being the strongest in flavor. Milk is pasteurized or *lait cru* (raw), which produces more complex flavors as the cheese develops. All *fermier* cheeses are made of *lait cru* and it is compulsory for some AOC cheeses.

CAMEMBERT is made at Isigny Ste Mère in Normandy using *industriel* methods but following AOC guidelines to the letter. First a starter is added to the milk and left overnight. The milk is heated to no more than 98°F, rennet added and the milk left to coagulate. Five portions of curds are ladled into perforated plastic molds (*moulé à la louche*), with time between each "pass" to evenly distribute the fat. The whey is

CAMEMBERT DE NORMANDIE this AOC cheese is produced in Normandy from unpasteurized milk. The rind is covered in white mold and it has a yellow creamy pâte. A table or cooking cheese.

BRIE DE MEAUX France's most famous brie, this unpasteurized AOC cheese from the Île-de-France is usually sold half ripe. When very ripe, its white surface reddens. A good table cheese.

LIVAFOT this washed-rind AOC cheese from Normandy is known as "the Colonel" due to stripes of grass that bind its shape. A table cheese eaten very ripe, it has a spicy taste and pungent smell.

MIMOLETTE/BOULE DE LILLE produced like Dutch Edam, the name comes from mi-mou, "half-soft," but it is usually eaten very hard, after up to 2 years of aging. Use in cooking or eat with beer.

NEUFCHÂTEL a classic soft, white-rinded AOC cheese from Normandy, that comes in shapes such as a heart, log or square. A table cheese whose rind can be eaten, it is good with bread.

MORBIER this mild cheese from Franche-Comté is cut by a dark line, originally ash separating two layers of milk from two milkings, but now just decorative. A table cheese or melted on bread.

BRILLAT-SAVARIN created in the 1930s and named after a French food writer, this mild, triple-cream cheese, with its very high butterfat content, is made mainly around Normandy.

CARRÉ DE L'EST made in Alsace, Champagne-Ardennes and Lorraine, this soft cheese comes with an extremely sticky orange washed-rind. Here it has been washed in plum eau de vie.

MUNSTER/MUNSTER-GÉROMÉ this washed-rind AOC cheese from Alsace, Lorraine and Franche-Comté has a pungent smell and is traditionally eaten with potatoes, cumin and wine.

CHAOURCE this AOC cheese is produced in Bourgogne and Champagne and is eaten when only 2 or 3 weeks old. It is a table cheese with a white mold rind and light creamy pâte.

BEAUFORT a large, round AOC mountain cheese from the Rhône-Alpes. A Gruyère-type table cheese with a concave surface, it is also used in fondue. Beaufort d'alpage is particularly flavorsome.

FLEUR DU MAQUIS this aromatic goat cheese from Corsica is covered with chile, juniper and wild herbs and is named after the "maquis," the scrubby landscape of the island.

CHÈVRE FERMIER an artisan-made goat's-milk cheese. There are many different types, but this version is very fresh and has a mild flavor and aroma. Eat on its own or with bread.

MAROILLES this square AOC cheese from the North has a washed rind that darkens with age to a distinctive red. The pâte is soft and sweet and it is eaten with beer or used in cooking.

GRUYÈRE DE SAVOIE a hard cheese from the Frache-Comté and Savoie. Gruyère refers to the variety of cheese, of which there are many types. Good for grating and cooking.

ABONDANCE a firm, aged mountain cheese from the Alps, made from the milk of Abondance cows. The curds are pressed twice and salted, which gives a dense texture and a fruity taste.

TOMME DE SAVOIE the generic name for a type of cow's milk cheese made in the Savoie. They have a hard rind but an elastic, mellow tasting pâte inside. A table and cooking cheese.

POULIGNY-SAINT-PIERRE an AOC goat's-milk cheese, covered with a blue mold that develops as the cheese ages (this one is young). It has a strong taste and aroma.

OSSAU-IRATY-BREBIS PYRÉNÉES this AOC cheese is made with ewe's milk during the summer when sheep are in the mountain pastures. A table and grating cheese.

EMMENTAL a cooked, nutty cheese based on the Swiss version, with a pale, holey pâte. The Emmental Grand Cru has a red label guaranteeing its quality. A table and cooking cheese.

ROQUEFORT a strong, creamy AOC blue cheese, which must ripen in the caves of Cambalou. Cut the cheese with a warm knife to prevent it from crumbling. A table and cooking cheese.

CHAUMES an orange washed-rind cheese produced with milk from several areas. The pâte is semi-soft and the flavor very mild. A table cheese that broils well, it is similar to Port Salut.

REBLOCHON a Savoie AOC mountain cheese made from milk from the cow's rich second milking. A good table cheese, it has an orange rind, white mold, walnut flavor and creamy pâte.

CANTAL an AOC cheese from the mountains of Auvergne, sold as a young, sweet, white cheese or matured with a dark yellow rind and strong taste. A table and cooking cheese.

GOAT'S MILK CHEESES are produced all over France, with some of the most famous found in the Loire Valley, including the *crottin de Chavignon*, Provence and Corsica. Goat cheeses were traditionally made seasonally, with the best cheeses produced in the spring from rich milk. Some are dusted with ash to encourage a mold to appear, while others are decorated with herbs or soaked in oil.

TYPES OF CHEESES

Cheeses can be categorized into families, and looking at the rind and the texture of the *pâte* (inside) of a cheese can help you determine its category and therefore roughly its taste.

FRESH CHEESE (fromage frais, chèvre frais) cheeses with no rind (because they haven't been ripened). A mild or slightly acidic taste and a high moisture content.

PÂTE FLEURIE (Camembert, Brie) soft cheeses with an edible white rind. These uncooked, unpressed (drained naturally) cheeses are high in moisture, causing white molds to form a rind. A creamy, melting pâte and sometimes a mushroom taste.

PÂTE LAVÉE (Munster and Livarot) soft cheeses with washed rinds. These uncooked, unpressed high-moisture cheeses develop a cat's-fur mold when ripening, which is washed away in a process that encourages sticky orange bacteria to ripen the cheese from the outside in. They often have a smooth, elastic pâte, piquant taste and pungent aroma.

FROMAGES DE CHÈVRE goat cheeses. These uncooked, unpressed cheeses have a slightly wrinkled rind and fresh taste when young, while older cheeses are more wrinkly, often with a blue mold (sometimes encouraged by dusting with ash) and a more intense, nutty, "goat" flavor.

PÂTE PERSILLÉE (Roquefort, Bleu d'Auvergne) blue cheeses. A penicillium is introduced into the cheeses, which in some cases, via airholes, spreads into blue veins. These uncooked, unpressed cheeses tend to have a sharp flavor and aroma.

PÂTE PRESSÉE (Cantal, Port-du-Salut) semi-hard cheeses with a supple rind that hardens with age. These uncooked cheeses are pressed so the dry cheese matures slowly to produce a well-developed mellow taste. They are washed to seal the rind and molds are brushed off as the cheese ripens, or sealed in plastic or wax to stop the rind forming. The pâte varies from supple to hard if aged.

PÂTE CUITE (Beaufort, Emmental) hard mountain cheeses with a thick rind, depending on their age. These are cheeses whose curds have been finely cut, cooked and pressed and can be matured for a long time. They often have a fruity or nutty flavor and, with little moisture, a high fat content.

drained, then the cheeses removed from the molds, salted and sprayed with mold and moved to drying rooms for two weeks while the white mold grows. Finally, the cheeses are wrapped in waxed paper and put in a wooden box to continue to age. There is up to four weeks of maturing (*affinage*) in the box, with many locals preferring the cheese when it is *moitié affiné* (half mature), with the heart not yet creamy.

Add the eggs and scramble lightly into the piperade. The eggs will continue to cook after they are removed from the heat.

PIPERADE

THIS TRADITIONAL BASQUE DISH IS A DELICIOUS MELDING OF RATATOUILLE AND EGGS. THE NAME IS DERIVED FROM *"PIPER,"* MEANING RED PEPPER IN THE LOCAL DIALECT. THE EGGS CAN EITHER BE COOKED MORE LIKE AN OMELET OR SCRAMBLED TOGETHER AS DONE HERE.

2 tablespoons olive oil
1 large onion, thinly sliced
2 red peppers, seeded and cut into strips
2 garlic cloves, crushed
1 1/2 lb. tomatoes
pinch of cayenne pepper
8 eggs, lightly beaten
1 tablespoon butter
4 thin slices of ham, such as Bayonne

SERVES 4

HEAT the oil in a large heavy-bottomed frying pan and cook the onion for 3 minutes, or until it has softened. Add the pepper and garlic, cover and cook for 8 minutes to soften—stir frequently and don't allow it to brown.

SCORE a cross in the top of each tomato. Plunge into boiling water for 20 seconds, then drain and peel the skin away from the cross. Chop the tomatoes, discarding cores. Spoon the chopped tomatoes and cayenne over the pepper, cover the frying pan and cook for another 5 minutes.

UNCOVER the frying pan and increase the heat. Cook for 3 minutes or until the juices have evaporated, shaking the frying pan often. Season well with salt and pepper. Add the eggs and scramble into the mixture until they are cooked.

HEAT the butter in a small frying pan and fry the ham. Arrange on the piperade and serve at once.

EGGS EN COCOTTE

EGGS EN COCOTTE

1 tablespoon butter, melted
1/2 cup heavy cream
4 button mushrooms, finely chopped
1/4 cup ham, finely chopped
1/3 cup Gruyère, finely chopped
4 eggs
1 tablespoon finely chopped herbs such as chervil, parsley, chives

SERVES 4

PREHEAT the oven to 400°F and put a baking sheet on the top shelf. Grease four ramekins with melted butter. Pour half the cream into the ramekins and then put a quarter of the mushrooms, ham and cheese into each. Break an egg into each ramekin. Mix the remaining cream with the herbs and pour over the top.

BAKE for 15–20 minutes on the hot baking sheet, depending on how runny you like your eggs. Remove from the oven while still a little runny as the eggs will continue to cook. Season well and serve immediately with crusty toasted bread.

EGGS EN CROUSTADE

A CROUSTADE IS A HOLLOWED-OUT PIECE OF BREAD THAT HAS BEEN FRIED OR BAKED TO MAKE A FIRM
LITTLE SHELL FOR FILLINGS. CROUSTADES PROVIDE THE PERFECT BASE FOR POACHED EGGS. FOR A
NEATER FINISH, TRIM EACH EGG INTO A CIRCLE TO FIT THE WELL.

Use the freshest eggs you can find for poaching, so that the whites don't spread too much in the water. If you can't guarantee their freshness, add a little vinegar to the water to keep the whites together.

CROUSTADES
1 stale unsliced loaf white bread
3 tablespoons butter, melted
1 garlic clove, crushed

HOLLANDAISE SAUCE
2 egg yolks
2 teaspoons lemon juice
6 tablespoons unsalted butter, cut
   into cubes

4 eggs
1 teaspoon finely chopped parsley

SERVES 4

TO MAKE the croustades, preheat the oven to 350°F. Cut four $1^{1}/_{4}$-inch thick slices from the bread and remove the crusts. Cut each piece of bread into a $3^{1}/_{2}$-inch square, then use a $2^{1}/_{2}$-inch round cutter to cut a circle in the center of the bread, without cutting all the way through. Use a knife to scoop out the bread from the center to form a neat hollow.

MIX TOGETHER the melted butter and garlic and brush all over the bread. Place on a baking sheet and bake for 8 minutes, or until crisp and lightly golden. Keep warm.

TO MAKE the hollandaise sauce, put the egg yolks and lemon juice in a saucepan over very low heat. Whisk continuously, adding the butter piece by piece until the sauce thickens. Do not overheat or the eggs will scramble. Season with salt and pepper. The sauce should be of pouring consistency—if it is too thick, add 1–2 tablespoons of hot water to thin it.

(ALTERNATIVELY, put the eggs yolks, salt and pepper in a blender and mix together. Heat the lemon juice and butter together until boiling and then, with the motor running, pour onto the yolks in a steady stream.)

TO POACH the eggs, bring a saucepan of water to a boil. Crack an egg into a small bowl, reduce the heat and slide the egg into the simmering water. Poach for 3 minutes, then remove carefully with a slotted spoon and drain on paper towels. Poach the other three eggs. Trim off the uneven ends of the egg white to make a circle.

GENTLY PLACE an egg into each croustade. Pour over a little hollandaise sauce and sprinkle with parsley. Serve at once with extra hollandaise.

Cook the onions for the tart slowly to bring out the sweetness.

FLAMICHE

ONION TART

1 batch tart pastry (page 278)
3 tablespoons butter
1¹/₄ lb. onions, finely sliced
2 teaspoons thyme leaves
3 eggs
1¹/₄ cups heavy cream
¹/₂ cup Gruyère, grated
grated nutmeg

SERVES 6

PREHEAT the oven to 350°F. Line a 9-inch fluted loose-bottomed tart pan with the pastry. Line the pastry shell with a crumpled piece of waxed paper and baking beads (use dried beans or rice if you don't have beads). Blind bake the pastry for 10 minutes, remove the paper and beads and bake for another 3–5 minutes, or until the pastry is just cooked but still very pale.

MEANWHILE, melt the butter in a small frying pan and cook the onions, stirring, for 10–15 minutes or until tender and lightly browned. Add the thyme leaves and stir well. Allow to cool. Whisk together the eggs and cream and add the cheese. Season with salt, pepper and nutmeg.

SPREAD the onions into the pastry shell and pour the egg mixture over the top. Bake for 35–40 minutes, or until golden brown. Allow to rest in the pan for 5 minutes before serving.

FLAMICHE

A SPECIALTY OF THE PICARDIE REGION, FLAMICHE IS MADE BOTH AS AN OPEN TART AND A CLOSED PIE. YOU WILL USUALLY COME ACROSS IT WITH A LEEK FILLING, AS HERE, BUT IT CAN ALSO BE MADE WITH ONIONS, PUMPKIN OR SQUASH.

1 batch tart pastry (page 278)
1 lb. leeks, white part only, finely sliced
3 tablespoons butter
6 oz. Maroilles (soft cheese), Livarot or Port-Salut, chopped
1 egg
1 egg yolk
¹/₄ cup heavy cream
1 egg, lightly beaten

SERVES 6

PREHEAT oven to 350°F and put a baking sheet on the top shelf. Use three-quarters of the pastry to line a 9-inch fluted loose-bottomed tart pan.

COOK the leeks for 10 minutes in boiling salted water, then drain. Heat the butter in a frying pan, add the leeks and cook, stirring, for 5 minutes. Stir in the cheese. Pour into a bowl and add the egg, egg yolk and cream. Season and mix well.

POUR the filling into the pastry shell and smooth. Roll out the remaining pastry to cover the pie. Pinch the edges together and trim. Cut a hole in the center and brush egg over the top. Bake for 35–40 minutes on the baking sheet until browned. Leave in the pan for 5 minutes before serving.

QUICHE LORRAINE

TRADITIONALLY SERVED ON MAY DAY TO CELEBRATE THE START OF SPRING, QUICHE LORRAINE IS A
REGIONAL DISH FROM NANCY IN LORRAINE AND IS MADE USING BACON, ANOTHER SPECIALTY OF THE
AREA. THIS FOLLOWS THE ORIGINAL RECIPE, WHICH WAS MADE WITHOUT CHEESE.

1 batch tart pastry (page 278)
2 tablespoons butter
10 oz. bacon, diced
1 cup heavy cream
3 eggs
grated nutmeg

SERVES 8

PREHEAT the oven to 400°F. Line a 10-inch fluted
loose-bottomed tart pan with the pastry. Line the
pastry shell with a crumpled piece of waxed paper
and baking beads (use dried beans or rice if you
don't have beads). Blind bake the pastry for
10 minutes, remove the paper and beads and
bake for another 3–5 minutes, or until the pastry
is just cooked but still very pale. Reduce the
heat to 350°F.

MELT the butter in a small frying pan and cook
the bacon until golden. Drain on paper towels.

MIX TOGETHER the cream and eggs and season
with salt, pepper and nutmeg. Scatter the bacon
into the pastry shell, then pour in the egg mixture.
Bake for 30 minutes, or until the filling is set. Allow
to rest in the pan for 5 minutes before serving.

Blind bake, then fill the pastry shell
on the oven shelf, so you don't
have to worry about spillages.

BLUE CHEESE QUICHE

1 cup walnuts
1 batch tart pastry (page 278)
3/4 cup blue cheese, mashed
1/3 cup milk
3 eggs
2 egg yolks
3/4 cup heavy cream

SERVES 8

PREHEAT the oven to 400°F. Toast the walnuts on
a baking sheet for 5 minutes, then chop. Line a
10-inch fluted loose-bottomed tart pan with the
pastry. Line the pastry shell with a crumpled piece
of waxed paper and baking beads (use dried
beans or rice if you don't have beads). Blind bake
the pastry for 10 minutes, remove the paper and
beads and bake for another 3–5 minutes, or until
the pastry is just cooked but still very pale.
Reduce the heat to 350°F.

MIX TOGETHER the blue cheese, milk, eggs, egg
yolks and cream and season. Pour into the pastry
shell and sprinkle with the walnuts. Bake for
25–30 minutes, or until the filling is just set. Allow
to rest in the pan for 5 minutes before serving.

BLUE CHEESE QUICHE

PÂTÉS & TERRINES

Gently fry the onion and garlic before adding the chicken livers and thyme. Once the livers have changed color, add the brandy.

CHICKEN LIVER PÂTÉ

1 lb. chicken livers
1/3 cup brandy
6 tablespoons unsalted butter
1 onion, finely chopped
1 garlic clove, crushed
1 teaspoon chopped thyme
1/4 cup heavy cream
4 slices white bread

SERVES 6

TRIM the chicken livers, cutting away any discolored spots and veins. Rinse them, pat dry with paper towels and cut in half. Place in a small bowl with the brandy, cover and let sit for a couple of hours. Drain the livers, reserving the brandy.

MELT half of the butter in a frying pan, add the onion and garlic and cook over low heat until the onion is soft and transparent. Add the livers and thyme and stir over moderate heat until the livers change color. Add the reserved brandy and simmer for 2 minutes. Cool for 5 minutes.

PLACE the livers and liquid in a food processor and whiz until smooth. Add the remaining butter, cut into pieces, and process again until smooth. (Alternatively, roughly mash the livers with a fork, then push them through a sieve and mix with the melted butter.) Pour in the cream and process until incorporated.

SEASON the pâté and spoon into an earthenware dish or terrine, smoothing the surface. Cover and refrigerate until firm. If the pâté is to be kept for more than a day, chill it and then pour clarified butter over the surface to seal.

TO MAKE Melba toasts, preheat the broiler and cut the crusts off the bread. Toast the bread on both sides, then slice horizontally with a sharp serrated knife to give you eight pieces. Carefully toast the uncooked side of each slice and then cut it into two triangles. Serve with the pâté.

TERRINE DE CAMPAGNE

THIS IS THE DISH THAT YOU WILL FIND IN RESTAURANTS IF YOU ORDER *PÂTÉ MAISON*. IT IS OFTEN SERVED WITH PICKLED VEGETABLES AND COARSE COUNTRY BREAD. TERRINE DE CAMPAGNE FREEZES VERY WELL IF YOU HAVE SOME LEFT OVER OR WANT TO MAKE IT IN ADVANCE.

1 lb. 6 oz. lean pork, cut into cubes
6^1/$_2$ oz. pork belly, cut into strips
6^1/$_2$ oz. chicken livers, trimmed
3^1/$_2$ oz. bacon, chopped
1^1/$_2$ teaspoons sea salt
^{1}/$_2$ teaspoon black pepper
pinch of grated nutmeg
8 juniper berries, lightly crushed
3 tablespoons brandy
2 shallots, finely chopped
1 large egg, lightly beaten
sprig of bay leaves
8 thin bacon slices

SERVES 8

PUT the lean pork, pork belly, chicken livers and chopped bacon in a food processor and roughly chop into small dice (you will need to do this in two or three batches). Alternatively, finely dice the meat with a sharp knife.

PUT the diced meat in a large bowl and add the sea salt, pepper, nutmeg, juniper berries and brandy. Mix carefully and allow to marinate in the refrigerator for at least 6 hours or overnight.

PREHEAT the oven to 350°F. Lightly butter an 8 x 2^3/$_4$ x 3^1/$_2$ inch terrine or loaf pan. Add the shallots and egg to the marinated meat and carefully mix together.

PUT a sprig of bay leaves in the bottom of the terrine and then line with the bacon slices, leaving enough hanging over the sides to cover the top. Spoon the filling into the terrine and fold the ends of the bacon over the top. Cover the top with a layer of well-buttered waxed paper and then wrap the whole terrine in a layer of aluminum foil.

PLACE the terrine in a large baking dish and pour water into the baking dish to come halfway up the sides of the terrine. Bake in this bain-marie for 1^1/$_2$ hours, or until the pâté is shrinking away from the sides of the terrine.

TAKE the terrine out of the bain-marie and allow the pâté to cool, still wrapped in the paper and foil. Once cold, drain off the excess juices and refrigerate for up to a week. You may find that a little moisture has escaped from the pâté—this is quite normal and prevents it from drying out. Run a knife around the inside of the terrine to loosen the pâté and then turn out onto a board and serve in slices.

The free-range chicken and egg stall at a Lyon market.

PORK RILLETTES

PORK RILLETTES

OFTEN KNOWN AS *RILLETTES DE TOURS*, THIS SPECIALTY OF THE LOIRE VALLEY IS THE FRENCH VERSION OF POTTED MEAT. SPREAD ON TOAST OR BREAD AND SERVE WITH A GLASS OF WINE, OR STIR A SPOONFUL INTO SOUPS AND STEWS TO ADD FLAVOR.

$1^1/_2$ lb. pork neck or belly, rind and
   bones removed
5 oz. pork back fat
$^1/_3$ cup dry white wine
3 juniper berries, lightly crushed
1 teaspoon sea salt
2 teaspoons dried thyme
$^1/_2$ teaspoon ground nutmeg
$^1/_4$ teaspoon ground allspice
pinch of ground cloves
1 large garlic clove, crushed

SERVES 8

PREHEAT the oven to 275°F. Cut the meat and fat into short strips and put in a casserole with the rest of the ingredients. Mix together thoroughly and cover. Bake for 4 hours, by which time the pork should be soft and surrounded by liquid fat.

PUT the meat and fat into a sieve placed over a bowl to collect the fat. Shred the warm meat with two forks. Season if necessary. Pack the meat into a 3-cup dish or terrine and allow to cool. Strain the hot fat through a sieve lined with damp cheesecloth.

ONCE the pork is cold, pour the fat over it (you may need to melt the fat first if it has solidified as it cooled). Cover and refrigerate for up to a week. Serve at room temperature.

DUCK RILLETTES

$1^1/_4$ lb. pork belly, rind and bones
   removed
6–8 duck legs
$^1/_2$ cup dry white wine
1 teaspoon sea salt
$^1/_4$ teaspoon black pepper
$^1/_2$ teaspoon ground nutmeg
$^1/_4$ teaspoon ground allspice
1 large garlic clove, crushed

SERVES 8

PREHEAT the oven to 275°F. Cut the pork belly into small pieces and put in a casserole with the rest of the ingredients and 1 cup water. Mix together thoroughly and cover with a lid. Bake for 4 hours, by which time the meat should be soft and surrounded by liquid fat.

PUT the meat and fat into a sieve placed over a bowl to collect the fat. Remove the meat from the duck legs and shred all the warm meat with two forks. Season if necessary. Pack the meat into a 3-cup dish or terrine and allow to cool. Strain the fat through a sieve lined with damp cheesecloth.

ONCE the meat is cold, pour the fat over it (you may need to melt the fat first if it has solidified as it cooled). Cover and refrigerate for up to a week. Serve at room temperature.

Use two forks to shred the meat.

DUCK RILLETTES

SALMON TERRINE

IF YOU CAN FIND WILD SALMON IT WILL GIVE A MUCH BETTER FLAVOR THAN FARMED. A MILD SMOKED SALMON IS BETTER THAN A REALLY SMOKY ONE—SOME SMOKED SALMON VARIETIES CAN BE SO STRONG THEY MAKE THEIR PRESENCE FELT THROUGHOUT THE WHOLE TERRINE.

1 lb. 6 oz. salmon fillet, skinned and
  al small bones removed
4 eggs
2¼ cups heavy cream
⅓ cup finely chopped chervil
1 lb. button mushrooms
1 teaspoon lemon juice
2 tablespoons butter
1 tablespoon grated onion
2 tablespoons white wine
10 large spinach leaves
10 oz. smoked salmon, thinly sliced

LEMON MAYONNAISE
1 tablespoon lemon juice
grated zest of 1 lemon
1 cup mayonnaise (page 286)

SERVES 8

Line the terrine with the salmon, leaving the slices hanging over the sides. Once the terrine is filled, fold the salmon over to cover the top.

PREHEAT the oven to 325°F. Purée the salmon fillet and eggs in a food processor until smooth. Push through a fine sieve into a glass bowl. (Alternatively, mash with a fork and push through a fine sieve.) Place the bowl over iced water, then gradually mix in the cream. Stir in the chervil and season. Cover and put in the refrigerator.

DICE the mushrooms and toss with the lemon juice to prevent discoloring. Melt the butter in a frying pan and cook the onion, stirring, for 2 minutes. Add the mushrooms and cook for 4 minutes. Add the wine and cook until it has evaporated. Season and remove from the heat.

DIP the spinach leaves in boiling water, then remove them carefully with a slotted spoon and lay them flat on paper towels.

BRUSH an 8 x 2¾ x 3½ inch terrine or loaf pan with oil and line the bottom with waxed paper. Line the bottom and sides with the smoked salmon, leaving enough hanging over the sides to cover the top. Spoon in enough salmon mixture to half-fill the terrine. Lay half the spinach over the salmon mixture, then spread with the mushrooms and another layer of spinach. Cover with the remaining salmon mixture, fold over the smoked salmon and cover with a piece of buttered waxed paper.

PLACE the terrine in a large baking dish and pour water into the baking dish to come halfway up the side of the terrine. Bake in this bain-marie for 45–50 minutes, or until a skewer inserted into the terrine comes out clean. Leave for 5 minutes before unmolding onto a serving plate. Peel off the waxed paper, cover and chill the terrine.

TO MAKE the lemon mayonnaise, stir the lemon juice and zest through the mayonnaise and serve with slices of salmon terrine.

VEGETABLE TERRINE WITH HERB SAUCE

1¹/₂ lb. carrots, cut into chunks
8 large Swiss chard or spinach
    leaves (or 16 smaller)
12 asparagus spears
2 small zucchini
16 green beans, trimmed
1 cup crème fraîche
6 teaspoons powdered gelatin
16 cherry tomatoes, halved

HERB SAUCE
1 tablespoon finely chopped parsley
1 tablespoon finely chopped chervil
1 tablespoon finely shredded basil
grated zest of 1 small lemon
1¹/₄ cups crème fraîche

SERVES 8

COOK the carrots in boiling water for 25 minutes or until tender, then drain and cool. Dip the chard leaves in boiling water, then remove carefully with a slotted spoon and lay flat on paper towels.

LIGHTLY OIL an 8 x 2³/₄ x 3¹/₂ inch terrine or loaf pan. Line with a layer of plastic wrap, leaving enough hanging over the sides to cover the top. Then line the pan with the chard leaves, making sure there are no gaps and leaving enough hanging over the sides to cover the top.

TRIM the asparagus spears at the thicker ends so they fit the length of the terrine. Slice each zucchini in half lengthwise, then each half into four lengthwise. Steam the asparagus, zucchini and beans for 6 minutes, or until tender to the point of a knife. Drain and refresh in cold water so they keep their color. Pat dry with paper towels.

PURÉE the carrots with the crème fraîche in a food processor, or mash and push through a sieve, and season well. Put 2 tablespoons water in a small bowl and sprinkle with the gelatin. Let sit for 5 minutes until spongy, then put the bowl over a pan of simmering water until melted. Add to the carrot purée and mix well.

SPOON a quarter of the carrot purée into the terrine, then arrange six asparagus spears on top, all pointing in the same direction. Arrange the zucchini on top in one flat layer. Smooth over another quarter of carrot purée, then a layer of tomatoes, cut sides up. Spoon over another layer of carrot purée and then the beans. Arrange the rest of the asparagus on top and finally the remaining carrot purée. Fold over the overhanging chard leaves and plastic wrap to cover the top. Put in the refrigerator overnight. Unmold onto a plate, peel off the plastic wrap and cut into slices.

TO MAKE the herb sauce, fold the herbs and lemon zest into the crème fraîche and season well. Serve with the vegetable terrine.

Take a little time to trim the vegetables to the same size and arrange the layers as neatly and evenly as you can.

PÂTÉ EN CROÛTE

THE WORD "PÂTÉ" MEANING CRUST, WAS TRADITIONALLY ONLY USED WHEN REFERRING TO THIS DISH.
THESE DAYS, THE WORDS PÂTÉ AND TERRINE ARE USED INTERCHANGEABLY AND PÂTÉ IS SYNONYMOUS
WITH ALL KINDS OF MEAT AND SEAFOOD PASTES, NOT JUST THOSE WITH A PASTRY CRUST.

1¹/4 lb. veal scallopine slices, finely
    diced
¹/2 lb. lean pork, finely diced
6¹/2 oz. bacon, finely diced
large pinch of ground cloves
large pinch of allspice
finely grated zest of 1 lemon
2 tablespoons brandy
2 bay leaves
1 tablespoon butter
1 large garlic clove, crushed
1 onion, finely chopped
6¹/2 oz. wild or chestnut
    mushrooms, finely chopped
3 tablespoons finely chopped
    parsley
1 batch puff pastry (page 281)
1 egg, lightly beaten

SERVES 8

MIX TOGETHER the veal, pork, bacon, cloves, allspice, lemon zest and brandy. Stir well, tuck the bay leaves into the mixture, then cover and allow to marinate in the refrigerator for at least 6 hours or preferably overnight.

MELT the butter in a frying pan and add the garlic and onion. Cook over low heat for 10 minutes, then add the mushrooms and cook for another 10 minutes, until they are softened and the liquid from the mushrooms has evaporated. Stir in the parsley and allow to cool.

REMOVE the bay leaves from the marinated meat. Add the cold mushroom mixture to the raw meat, season well and mix together thoroughly.

PREHEAT the oven to 400°F. Roll out the pastry on a lightly floured surface into a 15-inch square, trim the edges and keep for decoration. Pile the meat mixture onto the middle of the pastry, shaping it into a rectangle about 12 inches long. Brush the edges of the pastry with a little beaten egg. Fold the pastry over the meat as if you were wrapping a package. Place on a baking sheet, seam side down.

DECORATE the package with shapes cut from the pastry scraps and brush all over with beaten egg. Cook on the middle shelf of the oven for 15 minutes, then reduce the temperature to 350°F and cook for 1–1¹/4 hours, or until the filling is cooked and the pastry golden brown. Cool completely before serving in slices with pickles.

Pâté for sale at a Provence market.

SEAFOOD

Cut down each side of the underside of the lobster tail and peel back the shell.

A busy Provence port.

POACHED SEAFOOD WITH HERB AÏOLI

THE BEST WAY TO APPROACH THIS RECIPE IS AS A GUIDE—AS WITH ALL SEAFOOD COOKING, YOU SHOULD ALWAYS ASK YOUR FISHMONGER'S ADVICE AS TO WHAT'S THE BEST CATCH THAT DAY. DON'T FORGET TO PROVIDE FINGERBOWLS.

2 raw lobster tails
12 mussels
1/2 lb. scallops on their shells
1 lb. shrimp
1 cup dry white wine
1 cup fish stock
pinch of saffron threads
1 bay leaf
4 black peppercorns
4 x 2 oz. salmon fillets

HERB AÏOLI
4 egg yolks
4 garlic cloves, crushed
1 tablespoon chopped basil
4 tablespoons chopped flat-leaf
  parsley
1 tablespoon lemon juice
3/4 cup olive oil

lemon wedges

SERVES 4

REMOVE the lobster meat from the tail by cutting down each side of the underside with scissors and peeling back the middle piece of shell. Scrub the mussels and remove their beards, discarding any that are open and don't close when tapped on the work surface. Remove the scallops from their shells and pull away the white muscle and digestive tract around each one, leaving the roes intact. Clean the scallop shells and keep them for serving. Peel and devein the shrimp, leaving the tails intact, and butterfly them by cutting them open down the backs.

TO MAKE the herb aïoli, put the egg yolks, garlic, basil, parsley and lemon juice in a mortar and pestle or food processor and pound or mix until light and creamy. Add the oil, drop by drop from the tip of a teaspoon, pounding constantly until the mixture begins to thicken, then add the oil in a very thin stream. (If you're using a processor, pour in the oil in a thin stream with the motor running.)

PUT the wine, stock, saffron, bay leaf and peppercorns in a frying pan and bring to a very slow simmer. Add the lobster and poach for 5 minutes then remove, cover and keep warm.

POACH the remaining seafood in batches: the mussels and scallops will take about 2 minutes to cook and open (discard any mussels that have not opened after this time). The shrimp will take 3 minutes and the salmon a little longer, depending on the thickness. (Keep the poaching liquid to use as soup stock.) Cut the lobster into thick medallions, put the scallops back on their shells and arrange the seafood on a large platter with the aïoli in a bowl in the center. Serve with lemon wedges.

CRAB SOUFFLÉS

1 tablespoon butter, melted
2 cloves
1/4 small onion
1 bay leaf
6 black peppercorns
1 cup milk
1 tablespoon butter
1 shallot, finely chopped
2 tablespoons all-purpose flour
3 egg yolks
1 lb. cooked crab meat
pinch of cayenne pepper
5 egg whites

SERVES 6

PREHEAT the oven to 400°F. Brush six 1/2-cup ramekins with the melted butter.

PRESS the cloves into the onion, then put in a small saucepan with the bay leaf, peppercorns and milk. Gently bring to a boil, then remove from the heat and allow to infuse for 10 minutes. Strain the milk.

MELT the butter in a heavy-bottomed saucepan, add the shallot and cook, stirring, for 3 minutes until softened but not browned. Stir in the flour to make a roux and cook, stirring, for 3 minutes over low heat without allowing the roux to brown.

REMOVE from the heat and add the infused milk gradually, stirring after each addition until smooth. Return to the heat and simmer for 3 minutes, stirring continuously. Beat in the egg yolks, one at a time, beating well after each addition. Add the crab meat and stir over the heat until the mixture is hot and thickens again (do not let it boil). Pour into a large heatproof bowl, then add the cayenne and season well.

WHISK the egg whites in a clean dry bowl until they form soft peaks. Spoon a quarter of the egg white onto the soufflé mixture and quickly but lightly fold it in to loosen the mixture. Lightly fold in the remaining egg white. Pour into the ramekins and then run your thumb around the inside rim of each ramekin. This ridge helps the soufflés to rise evenly without sticking.

PUT the ramekins on a baking sheet and bake for 12–15 minutes, or until the soufflés are well risen and wobble slightly when tapped. Test with a skewer through a crack in the side of a soufflé—the skewer should come out clean or slightly moist. If the skewer is slightly moist, by the time the soufflés make it to the table they will be cooked in the center. Serve immediately.

Fold a quarter of the egg white into the soufflé mixture to loosen it up before you add the rest.

Unloading the catch in Marseille.

The Quai des Belges, Marseille.

COQUILLES SAINT JACQUES MORNAY

SCALLOPS IN FRANCE ARE NAMED AFTER SAINT JAMES. THEIR SHELLS WERE ONCE WORN BY PILGRIMS WHO FOUND THEM AS THEY WALKED ALONG THE SPANISH COAST ON THEIR PILGRIMAGE TO A CATHEDRAL IN SPAIN DEDICATED TO THE SAINT.

Poach the scallops in court bouillon first, so that they are thoroughly cooked before they are broiled. The heat of the broiler alone isn't enough to cook them.

COURT BOUILLON
1 cup white wine
1 onion, sliced
1 carrot, sliced
1 bay leaf
4 black peppercorns

24 scallops on their shells
3 tablespoons butter
3 shallots, finely chopped
3 tablespoons all-purpose flour
1²/₃ cups milk
1 cup Gruyère, grated

SERVES 6

TO MAKE the court bouillon, put the wine, onion, carrot, bay leaf, peppercorns and 2 cups water into a deep frying pan, bring to a boil and simmer for 20 minutes. Strain the court bouillon and return to the clean frying pan.

REMOVE the scallops from their shells and pull away the white muscle and digestive tract from each one, leaving the roes intact. Clean the shells and keep for serving.

BRING the court bouillon to a gentle simmer, add the scallops and poach over low heat for 2 minutes. Remove the scallops from the court bouillon, drain and return to their shells. Pour away the court bouillon.

MELT the butter in a heavy-bottomed saucepan, add the shallots and cook, stirring, for 3 minutes. Stir in the flour to make a roux and cook, stirring, for 3 minutes over low heat without allowing the roux to brown.

REMOVE from the heat and add the milk gradually, stirring after each addition until smooth. Return to the heat and simmer, stirring, for about 3 minutes, until the sauce has thickened. Remove from the heat and stir in the cheese until melted. Season with salt and pepper. Preheat the broiler. Spoon the sauce over the scallops and place under the broiler until golden brown. Serve immediately.

GARLIC SHRIMP

24 large shrimp
6 garlic cloves, crushed
1–2 small red chiles, very finely chopped
1 cup olive oil
4 tablespoons butter
2 tablespoons chopped parsley

SERVES 4

PEEL and devein the shrimp, leaving the tails intact. Preheat the oven to 425°F. Sprinkle the garlic and chiles into four cast iron or gratin dishes. Divide the oil and butter among the dishes.

PUT the dishes on a baking sheet in the oven and heat for about 6 minutes, or until the butter has melted.

DIVIDE the shrimp among the dishes (put them in carefully, without splashing yourself with hot oil) and bake for 7 minutes, or until the shrimp are pink and tender. Sprinkle with parsley and serve immediately with crusty bread.

SNAILS WITH GARLIC BUTTER

THERE ARE MANY VARIETIES OF EDIBLE SNAIL, WITH THE MOST COMMON BEING *PETITS GRIS* OR THE SLIGHTLY LARGER *ESCARGOTS DE BOURGOGNE*, ALSO KNOWN AS THE ROMAN SNAIL. CANNED SNAILS ARE SOLD ALONG WITH THEIR SHELLS AND ARE EASIER TO USE THAN FRESH ONES.

Simmer the snails and then allow to cool in the poaching liquid.

1 cup white wine
1 cup chicken stock
3 tarragon sprigs
24 canned snails, well drained
24 snail shells
2 garlic cloves, crushed
2 tablespoons finely chopped basil leaves
2 tablespoons finely chopped parsley
2 tablespoons finely chopped tarragon leaves
2/3 cup butter, at room temperature

SERVES 4

PUT the wine, stock, tarragon and 1/2 cup water in a small saucepan and boil for 2 minutes. Add the snails and simmer for 7 minutes. Remove from the heat and allow to cool in the poaching liquid. Drain and place a snail in each shell. Preheat the oven to 400°F.

MIX TOGETHER the garlic, basil, parsley and tarragon. Mix in the butter and season well.

PUT a little garlic butter into each shell and arrange them on a snail plate or baking sheet covered with a layer of rock salt. Bake for 7–8 minutes, or until the butter melts and the snails are heated through. Serve immediately with crusty bread to mop up the garlic butter.

SNAILS WITH GARLIC BUTTER

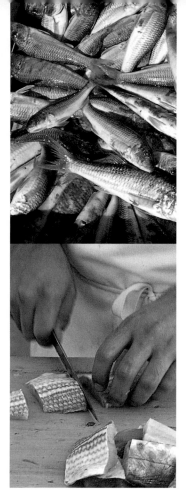

Leaving the skin on the fish is traditional as originally whole fish would have been used for this dish. The skin also helps the pieces hold together while the soup is cooking.

Fishermen selling their morning's catch on the Quai des Belges, in the old port of Marseille.

BOUILLABAISSE

BOUILLABAISSE IS THE MOST FAMOUS FRENCH FISH SOUP AND IS ASSOCIATED WITH THE SOUTH OF THE COUNTRY, PARTICULARLY MARSEILLE. AS A FISHERMAN'S MEAL IT IS OFTEN MADE WITH WHOLE FISH, ESPECIALLY *RASCASSE* (SCORPION FISH). USING FILLETS IS MUCH SIMPLER.

ROUILLE
1 small red pepper
1 slice white bread, crusts removed
1 red chile
2 garlic cloves
1 egg yolk
1/3 cup olive oil

SOUP
18 mussels
3 lb. firm white fish fillets such
   as red mullet, bass, snapper,
   monkfish, rascasse (scorpion
   fish), John Dory or eel, skin on
2 tablespoons oil
1 fennel bulb, thinly sliced
1 onion, chopped
1 1/2 lb. ripe tomatoes
5 cups fish stock or water
pinch of saffron threads
bouquet garni
2-inch piece of orange zest

SERVES 6

TO MAKE the rouille, preheat the broiler. Cut the pepper in half, remove the seeds and membrane and place, skin side up, under the hot broiler until the skin blackens and blisters. Allow to cool before peeling away the skin. Roughly chop the pepper.

SOAK the bread in 3 tablespoons water, then squeeze dry with your hands. Put the pepper, chile, bread, garlic and egg yolk in a mortar and pestle or food processor and pound or mix together. Gradually add the oil in a thin stream, pounding or mixing until the rouille is smooth and has the texture of thick mayonnaise. Cover and refrigerate the rouille until needed.

TO MAKE the soup, scrub the mussels and remove their beards. Discard any mussels that are already open and don't close when tapped on the work surface. Cut the fish into bite-size pieces.

HEAT the oil in a large saucepan and cook the fennel and onion over medium heat for 5 minutes, or until golden.

SCORE a cross in the top of each tomato. Plunge into boiling water for 20 seconds, then drain and peel the skin away from the cross. Chop the tomatoes, discarding the cores. Add to the pan and cook for 3 minutes. Stir in the stock, saffron, bouquet garni and orange zest, bring to a boil and boil for 10 minutes. Remove the bouquet garni and either push the soup through a sieve or purée in a blender. Return to the cleaned pan, season well and bring back to a boil.

REDUCE the heat to a simmer and add the fish and mussels. Cook for 5 minutes or until the fish is tender and the mussels have opened. Throw out any mussels that haven't opened in this time. Serve the soup with rouille and bread. Or take out the fish and mussels and serve separately.

LOBSTER THERMIDOR

LOBSTER THERMIDOR WAS CREATED FOR THE FIRST NIGHT CELEBRATIONS OF A PLAY CALLED "THERMIDOR" IN PARIS IN 1894. TRADITIONALLY THE LOBSTER IS CUT IN HALF WHILE ALIVE, BUT FREEZING IT FIRST IS MORE HUMANE.

2 live lobsters
1 cup fish stock
2 tablespoons white wine
2 shallots, finely chopped
2 teaspoons chopped chervil
2 teaspoons chopped tarragon
1/2 cup butter
2 tablespoons all-purpose flour
1 teaspoon dry mustard
1 cup milk
2/3 cup Parmesan, grated

SERVES 4

Fry the lobster in butter until it is lightly browned, but take care not to overcook it or it will toughen. Spoon the lobster and sauce into the cleaned shells for serving.

PUT the lobsters in the freezer an hour before you want to cook them. Bring a large pan of water to a boil, drop in the lobsters and cook for 10 minutes. Drain and cool slightly before cutting off the heads. Cut the lobster tails in half lengthwise. Use a spoon to ease the lobster meat out of the shells and cut it into bite-size pieces. Rinse the shells, pat dry and keep for serving.

PUT the stock, wine, shallot, chervil and tarragon into a small saucepan. Boil until reduced by half and then strain.

MELT 4 tablespoons of the butter in a heavy-bottomed saucepan and stir in the flour and mustard to make a roux. Cook, stirring, for 2 minutes over low heat without allowing the roux to brown.

REMOVE from the heat and add the milk and the reserved stock mixture gradually, stirring after each addition until smooth. Return to the heat and stir constantly until the sauce boils and thickens. Simmer, stirring occasionally, for 3 minutes. Stir in half the Parmesan. Season with salt and pepper.

HEAT the remaining butter in a frying pan and fry the lobster over moderate heat for 2 minutes until lightly browned—take care not to overcook. Preheat the broiler.

DIVIDE HALF the sauce among the lobster shells, top with the lobster meat and then finish with the remaining sauce. Sprinkle with the remaining Parmesan and place under the broiler until golden brown and bubbling. Serve immediately.

Carefully remove the flesh from the lobster tails by cutting away the underside of the shells. Cook the tails by simmering on top of the sauce. To finish off, stir the lobster roe and livers into the sauce for a rich flavor.

LOBSTER A L'AMÉRICAINE

4 live lobsters
4 tablespoons olive oil
1 onion, finely chopped
4 shallots, finely chopped
1 carrot, finely chopped
1 celery stalk, finely chopped
1 garlic clove, crushed
1 lb. ripe tomatoes
2 tablespoons tomato paste
1/2 cup white wine
2 tablespoons brandy
1 cup fish stock
bouquet garni
4 tablespoons butter, softened
3 tablespoons chopped parsley

SERVES 4

PUT the lobsters in the freezer an hour before you want to use them. Cut off the lobster heads and remove the claws. Heat the oil in a large frying pan and cook the lobster heads, tails and claws in batches over moderate heat until the lobster turns bright red and the flesh begins to shrink away from the shell.

ALLOW TO cool slightly before cutting the lobster heads in half and scraping out the red roe (coral) and the yellowy livers. Keep these to add flavor to the sauce.

CUT DOWN each side of the underside of the tail, then remove the center piece of shell and carefully remove the meat from the tail.

ADD the onion and shallot to the saucepan with the lobster claws and head shells. Cook over moderate heat for 3 minutes, or until a golden brown, then add the carrot, celery and garlic and cook for 5 minutes, or until soft.

SCORE a cross in the top of each tomato. Plunge into boiling water for 20 seconds, then drain and peel the skin away from the cross. Chop the tomatoes, discarding the cores. Add the tomatoes, tomato paste, wine, brandy, fish stock and bouquet garni to the pan and bring to a boil.

ARRANGE the meat from the lobster tails on top of the sauce, cover and simmer for 5 minutes, or until the lobster is cooked.

REMOVE the tail meat, heads and claws from the sauce, cover and keep warm. Continue cooking the sauce until it has reduced by half.

MIX the reserved roe and livers with the softened butter and stir this into the sauce with the parsley. Season with salt and pepper and remove the bouquet garni. Slice the tail meat into medallions and divide among four plates. Spoon the sauce over the lobster and decorate with the claws to serve if you like.

MOULES À LA MARINIÈRE

GROWN ON WOODEN POSTS ALL ALONG THE COAST OF FRANCE, MUSSELS ARE REGIONAL TO MANY AREAS BUT ARE PARTICULARLY ASSOCIATED WITH BRITTANY, NORMANDY AND THE NORTH-EAST. THIS IS ONE OF THE SIMPLEST WAYS TO SERVE THEM.

4 lb mussels
3 tablespoons butter
1 large onion, chopped
1/2 celery stalk, chopped
2 garlic cloves, crushed
1²/₃ cups white wine
1 bay leaf
2 thyme sprigs
3/4 cup heavy cream
2 tablespoons chopped parsley

SERVES 4

SCRUB the mussels and remove their beards. Discard any that are already open and don't close when tapped on the work surface. Melt the butter in a large saucepan and cook the onion, celery and garlic, stirring occasionally, over a moderate heat until the onion is softened but not browned.

ADD the wine, bay leaf and thyme to the saucepan and bring to a boil. Add the mussels, cover the saucepan tightly and simmer over a low heat for 2–3 minutes, shaking the saucepan occasionally. Use tongs to remove the mussels as they open, putting them into a warm dish. Throw away any mussels that haven't opened after 3 minutes.

STRAIN the liquid through a fine sieve into a clean saucepan, leaving behind any grit or sand. Bring to a boil and boil for 2 minutes. Add the cream and reheat the sauce without boiling. Season well. Serve the mussels in individual bowls with the liquid poured over. Sprinkle with the parsley and serve with plenty of bread.

Wash the mussels, taking care to discard any that are already open and don't close when tapped.

BROILED SARDINES

8 sardines
2 tablespoons olive oil
3 tablespoons lemon juice
1/2 lemon, halved and thinly sliced
lemon wedges

SERVES 4

SLIT the sardines along their bellies and remove the innards. Rinse well and pat dry. Use scissors to cut out the gills.

MIX TOGETHER the oil and lemon juice and season generously with salt and black pepper. Brush the inside and outside of each fish with the oil, then place a few lemon slices into each cavity.

PUT the sardines onto a preheated griddle and cook, basting frequently with the remaining oil, for about 2–3 minutes on each side until cooked through. They can also be cooked under a very hot broiler. Serve with lemon wedges.

BROILED SARDINES

LANGOUSTINES AU CURRIE

24 langoustines (Dublin Bay
prawns)
2 tablespoons butter
1 teaspoon oil
1 tablespoon whisky

SAUCE
1 tablespoon butter
1 tablespoon whisky
1 cup chicken stock
1 teaspoon curry powder
1 cup heavy cream

SERVES 4

TWIST the heads off the langoustines and peel, by cutting down both sides of the underside of the tail and pulling back the flap. Keep the last section of shell and tail attached. Reserve the shells and heads.

TO MAKE the sauce, heat the butter in a saucepan, add the langoustine heads and shells and cook for 4 minutes. Add the whisky, chicken stock, curry powder and $1/4$ cup water and allow to boil until the sauce has reduced by half. Stir in the cream and keep boiling until the sauce has reduced by a third. Season and then strain.

TO COOK the langoustines, heat the butter and oil in a large frying pan, add the langoustines and cook for 3 minutes on each side. Add the whisky and flambé by lighting the pan with your gas flame or a match (stand back when you do this and keep a pan lid handy for emergencies). The flames will last a short time. Put the langoustines on a plate and pour the sauce over the top.

Peel the langoustines, leaving the tails attached. Use the trimmings to add flavor to the sauce.

SOLE MEUNIÈRE

THIS CLASSIC RECIPE, SERVED IN SOME OF THE WORLD'S TOP RESTAURANTS, IS ACTUALLY A QUICK AND EASY STAPLE SUPPER IN FRANCE. MEUNIÈRE MEANS "MILLERS' STYLE," PROBABLY REFERRING TO THE FLOUR FOR DUSTING. YOU CAN USE SOLE FILLETS IF YOU PREFER.

4 sole, gutted and dark skin
removed
3 tablespoons all-purpose flour
$3/4$ cup clarified butter
2 tablespoons lemon juice
4 tablespoons chopped parsley
lemon wedges

SERVES 4

PAT the fish dry with paper towels, removing the heads if you prefer, and then dust lightly with the flour and season. Heat $1/2$ cup of the butter in a frying pan large enough to fit all four fish, or use half the butter and cook the fish in two batches.

PUT the fish in the pan, skin side up, and cook for 4 minutes on each side or until a golden brown. Lift the fish out onto warm plates and drizzle with the lemon juice and parsley. Add the remaining butter to the pan and heat until it browns to make a *beurre noisette*. Pour over the fish (it will foam as it mixes with the lemon juice) and serve with lemon wedges.

SOLE MEUNIÈRE

MARSEILLES OLD PORT is still a thriving fishing port, even though the main fish market has now moved undercover. Fishing here is very much a local and family industry and *"Pêche le nuit, vendu le matin"* (fish the night, sell in the morning) is the saying—though in reality the men go out in the early morning, not all night. The fishing boats arrive back at the Quay des Belges at about ten in the morning, when their

SEAFOOD

BORDERED ON THREE SIDES BY WATER, THE CHOICE OF

SEAFOOD AVAILABLE IN FRANCE IS PROBABLY UNSURPASSABLE,

AND THE FRENCH CERTAINLY KNOW HOW TO EAT IT—THIS IS A

COUNTRY FAMOUS FOR ITS WONDERFUL FISH DISHES.

The seafood comes from the Mediterranean to the south, the Bay of Biscay and the Atlantic to the west and the English Channel to the northwest, as well as freshwater fish from rivers and lakes. What is not available in home waters is snapped up elsewhere, with long-distance trawlers fishing as far away as the waters of Newfoundland and Iceland.

FISH MARKETS

The fishing fleets bring their catch into *criées,* or wholesale markets, where the seafood is auctioned early in the morning and then distributed to the towns and cities before daybreak. The most important of these markets is at the channel port of Boulogne, which services Paris, and also the fishing ports of Brittany and Normandy. Some of the daily catch may also be sold on the wharf, where fishermen bring their boats alongside and sell fish that are still alive from containers running with sea water. Away from the coast, *poissonneries* and supermarkets sell fish.

REGIONAL SPECIALTIES

In the Northwest, oysters, scallops, Dublin Bay prawns, clams and whelks can all be found on Brittany and Normandy's *plateau de fruits de mer,* riches from an area that has some of France's most important fishing ports.

SEA BASS (*Loup de mer*) both caught wild and farmed in France, this is considered a fish for special occasions. It keeps its shape well when cooked whole and has only a few small bones.

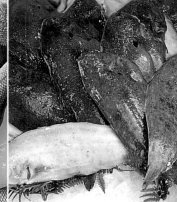

DOVER SOLE (*Sole*) used in many French recipes such as *sole normande*, Dover sole is superb broiled, but expensive. It can be substituted with any flat fish such as lemon sole or brill.

CONGER EEL (*Congre*) a seawater eel with a meaty texture and flavor. Tail cutlets are bony and usualy made into soup, but middle or neck cut sections are good for baking and roasting.

SCORPION FISH (*Rascasse*) considered to be an essential ingredient of *bouillabaisse*, this fish has sweet flesh. It is used in soups because it has an excellent flavor and firm flesh.

DUELIN BAY PRAWNS (*Langoustines*) small lobsters that can be bought live and cooked in boiling water, or basted in oil and garlic and broiled. A good addition to a seafood platter.

CARPET SHELL CLAMS (*Palourde*) smallish in size, these clams are very tender and can be eaten raw or steamed until the shells open, then sprinkled with lemon juice or garlic butter.

ANCHOVIES (*Anchois*) fished in spring, fresh anchovies are best broiled or fried and eaten with lemon. Their oily flesh does not keep well though, so they are often canned.

RED MULLET (*Rouget*) a prized fish in the Mediterranean, where two varieties are found. It is traditionally cooked with its liver intact, and its delicate flesh is best grilled with rosemary.

SEA BREAM (*Saupe*) a very wide category of fish including many varieties. Pictured is a *salema*, but the most prized is a *daurade*. Sea breams are all very good baked or broiled.

MACKEREL (*Maquereau*) (pictured centre) an oily and rich fish that goes well with sharp-tasting fruit sauces and tomato. Cheap and easy-to-use, mackerel broils or grills very well.

TUNA (*Thon*) several varieties are caught worldwide, varying in size from 2–1 500 lb. Tuna flesh should not be oily looking and is very good just seared like steak.

MONKFISH (*Lotte*) an ugly fish usually sold as a tail because this is where the meat is (in France known as a *gigot* [leg of lamb] for its shape). The tail must be skinned, then broiled or roasted.

LOBSTER (*Homard*) there are two species, an American and European, with the European considered finer. Lobsters are usually dark-coloured when alive, then turn red when cooked.

SKATE (*Raie*) also called rays, these fish have no real bones or scales. All species can be used interchangeably. It is the sweet "wings" that are eaten, classically with a burnt butter sauce.

MUSSELS (*Moules*) grown on poles or ropes along France's coast. Buy live ones, discarding any open ones that do not close when tapped. Use small varieties for dishes like *moules marinière*.

FRITURE a mixture of small fish used for deep-frying. The smallest can be cooked whole without cleaning and eaten intact. When they are bigger, they are sold under their names.

WHELKS (*Bulots/Escargots de mer*) like a pointed snail, whelks are seawater shellfish. *Murex* are the most common variety in the south of France and are served as part of a seafood platter.

SPINY LOBSTER (*Langouste*) also called a crawfish or rock lobster, it differs from other lobsters in having no claws. Can be boiled, broiled or sautéed and used interchangeably with lobster.

OYSTERS (*Huîtres*) in France, *huîtres creuses* are crinkly Portuguese oysters while *huîtres plates* are rounder natives. The best French oysters are from Belon in Brittany and Marennes.

SQUID (*Encornet*) buy whole or as cleaned bodies or rings. Remove the insides, head and eyes before cooking, then broil or grill quickly, or stuff and braise slowly with wine and herbs.

WARTY VENUS CLAMS (*Praire*) these tasty clams have a ridged shell and can be eaten raw, steamed, cooked in wine and herbs or dipped in mayonnaise.

SEA URCHINS (*Oursins*) the tiny orange/yellow roe is all that is eaten—cut away the top with a pair of long scissors and scoop out. Eat raw or serve with scrambled eggs.

OCTOPUS (*Poulpe*) a whole octopus needs to be cleaned and skinned, then tenderized by beating. The flesh can be stewed, braised or broiled and goes well with lemon and herbs.

POISSONS DES ROCHES a mixture of rockfish sold as a kind of soup mix. Rockfish have bony bodies that are really only suitable for being cooked whole in soups and then eaten off the bones.

catch is unloaded, still wriggling, into blue trays. Usually a family member sells the catch while the fishermen clean up their boats and mend nets. As well as individual fish, mixtures of small fish are sold for frying and bonier fish for soup. The seafood, including octopus, is carried away live in plastic bags, though each stall also has a knife and chopping block, and fish can be gutted and filleted before being sold.

Brittany fleets fish for sardines and tuna, and the area also claims *lobster à l'américaine* as its own, while Normandy is famous for its *moules marinière*, stewy *marmite dieppoise* and its Dover sole, cooked as *sole normande*.

The center of the fishing industry in the North is Boulogne, which has wonderful local sole and mussels, as well as fishing boats bringing in catches from the Mediterranean to the Atlantic. Inland, freshwater trout, prepared "*au bleu*," is a specialty of Alsace-Lorraine. In the Southwest there are Atlantic tuna from the Basque ports and oysters from Bordeaux.

Sardines and anchovies are a southern favorite from Languedoc-Roussillon on the Spanish border, while Provence's Mediterranean catch, from rascasse, chapon, mullet, conger eel, sea bass to bream, is transformed into wonderful dishes such as *bouillabaisse* and *bourride*.

SOLE NORMANDE

12 shrimp
2 cups dry white wine
12 oysters, shucked
12 small button mushrooms
4 sole fillets
1 cup cream
1 truffle, thinly sliced
1 tablespoon chopped parsley

SERVES 4

PEEL and devein the shrimp. Put the wine in a deep frying pan and bring to a boil. Add the oysters to the wine and poach for 2–3 minutes, then remove with a slotted spoon, drain and keep warm. Poach the shrimp in the wine for 3 minutes, or until pink and cooked through. Take out and keep warm. Poach the mushrooms for 5 minutes, then take out and keep warm. Add the sole fillets to the poaching liquid and cook for 5 minutes, or until cooked through. Remove to a serving dish, cover and keep warm.

ADD the cream to the poaching liquid and bring to a boil. Boil until the sauce has reduced by half and thickened enough to coat the back of a spoon. Season with salt and pepper.

PUT a sole fillet on each plate and scatter with the shrimp, oysters and mushrooms, then pour the sauce over the top. Sprinkle with the sliced truffle and parsley and serve immediately

Slash the fish in the thickest part of the body so they cook quickly and evenly and the basting liquid runs through the flesh.

GRILLED RED MULLET WITH HERB SAUCE

4 x 6 oz. red mullet
3 tablespoons lemon juice
3 tablespoons olive oil

HERB SAUCE
4 cups spinach leaves
3 tablespoons olive oil
1 tablespoon white wine vinegar
1 tablespoon chopped parsley
1 tablespoon chopped chives
1 tablespoon chopped chervil
1 tablespoon finely chopped capers
2 anchovy fillets, finely chopped
1 hard-boiled egg, finely chopped

SERVES 4

PREHEAT a griddle or barbecue. Make a couple of deep slashes in the thickest part of each fish. Pat the fish dry and sprinkle inside and out with salt and pepper. Drizzle with a little lemon juice and olive oil and cook on the griddle or barbecue for 4–5 minutes each side, or until the fish flakes when tested with the tip of a knife. Baste with the lemon juice and oil during cooking.

TO MAKE the sauce, wash the spinach and put it in a large saucepan with just the water clinging to the leaves. Cover the saucepan and steam the spinach for 2 minutes, or until just wilted. Drain, cool and squeeze with your hands to get rid of the excess liquid. Finely chop. Mix with the oil, vinegar, herbs, capers, anchovies and egg in a food processor or mortar and pestle. Spoon the sauce on a plate and place the fish on top to serve.

GRILLED RED MULLET WITH HERB SAUCE

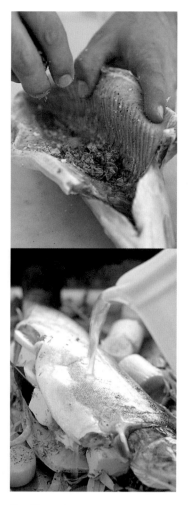

Stuffing the trout allows the flavors to permeate the flesh. Use the vegetables as a rack for the fish to lie on.

BAKED TROUT WITH FENNEL AND CAPERS

PURISTS LIKE THEIR TROUT COOKED WITH A MINIMUM OF FUSS, PERHAPS DRESSED WITH A LITTLE BUTTER AND LEMON. THE FENNEL AND CAPERS, HOWEVER, COMPLEMENT THE TROUT PERFECTLY, THEIR FLAVORS PERMEATING THE DELICATE FLESH OF THE FISH DURING BAKING.

2 fennel bulbs, with fronds
1 leek, white part only, thickly sliced
1 large carrot, cut into sticks
2 tablespoons olive oil
2 tablespoons capers, rinsed and patted dry
1 shallot, finely chopped
1 x 2¾ lb. brown or rainbow trout, or 4 x 10 oz. trout, gutted and fins removed
1 or 2 bay leaves
2 tablespoons butter, cut into 4 cubes
4 slices lemon
¾ cup fish stock
¼ cup dry vermouth
2 tablespoons heavy cream
2 tablespoons chopped chervil

SERVES 4

PREHEAT the oven to 400°F. Cut off the fronds from the fennel bulbs and finely chop them. Thinly slice the bulbs and place in a roasting pan with the leek and carrot. Drizzle a tablespoon of olive oil over the vegetables, add salt and pepper and then toss well to coat them in the oil and seasoning. Bake on the middle shelf of the oven for 20 minutes.

MEANWHILE, mix the chopped fennel fronds with the capers and shallot. Season the inside of the trout and fill with the fennel and caper stuffing. Put the bay leaf, cubes of butter and the lemon slices inside the fish too. Mix together the fish stock and vermouth.

REMOVE the vegetables from the oven, stir well and reduce the oven temperature to 275°F. Lay the trout over the vegetables and pour the stock and vermouth over the fish. Season the trout and drizzle with the remaining tablespoon of olive oil. Cover the top of the pan with aluminum foil and return to the oven for 1 hour 15 minutes or until the fish is cooked through. The flesh should feel flaky through the skin and the inside will look opaque and cooked. Transfer the fish to a large serving platter.

TRANSFER the roasting pan of vegetables to the stove top and heat for a couple of minutes, until the juices bubble and reduce. Now add the cream and cook for 1 minute, then stir in the chervil and season to taste. Spoon the vegetables around the fish on the platter, pour over a little of the juice and serve the rest separately in a gravy boat.

MARMITE DIEPPOISE

THIS RICH SOUPY STEW OF SHELLFISH AND FISH GIVES AWAY ITS ORIGINS IN THE NORMANDY REGION BY ITS USE OF CIDER AND CREAM. TRADITIONALLY TURBOT AND SOLE ARE USED. BUT THE SALMON ADDS A SPLASH OF COLOR.

16 mussels

12 large shrimp

1³/4 cups cider or dry white wine

3 tablespoons butter

1 garlic clove, crushed

2 shallots, finely chopped

2 celery stalks, finely chopped

1 large leek, white part only, thinly sliced

3 cups small chestnut mushrooms, sliced

1 bay leaf

10 oz. salmon fillet, skinned and cut into chunks

13 oz. sole fillet, skinned and cut into thick strips widthwise

1¹/4 cups heavy cream

3 tablespoons finely chopped parsley

SERVES 6

SCRUB the mussels and remove their beards. Throw away any that are already open and don't close when tapped on the work surface. Peel and devein the shrimp.

POUR the cider or white wine into a large saucepan and bring to a simmer. Add the mussels, cover the saucepan and cook for 3–5 minutes, shaking the saucepan every now and then. Place a fine sieve over a bowl and put the mussels into the sieve. Transfer the mussels to a plate, throwing away any that haven't opened in the cooking time. Strain the cooking liquid again through the sieve, leaving behind any grit or sand.

ADD the butter to the cleaned saucepan and melt over moderate heat. Add the garlic, shallots, celery and leek and cook for 7–10 minutes, or until the vegetables are just soft. Add the mushrooms and cook for another 4–5 minutes, until softened. While the vegetables are cooking, remove the mussels from their shells.

ADD the strained liquid to the vegetables in the saucepan, add the bay leaf and bring to a simmer. Add the salmon, sole and shrimp and cook for 3–4 minutes until the fish is opaque and the shrimp have turned pink. Stir in the cream and cooked mussels and simmer gently for 2 minutes. Season to taste and stir in the parsley.

Put the cooked mussels into a sieve and throw away any that haven't opened. Make a sauce of the vegetables and poaching liquid, then add the seafood to cook quickly at the end.

Salt cod on sale in a Paris market.

BRANDADE DE MORUE

THIS RICH GARLICKY PURÉE IS TRADITIONALLY MADE WITH *MORUE*, SALT COD PRESERVED BY THE SALT RATHER THAN BY DRYING. SALT COD IS ALSO SOLD AS BACALAO, ITS SPANISH NAME. YOU WILL HAVE TO PREPARE TWO DAYS IN ADVANCE, BECAUSE OF THE TIME NEEDED TO SOAK THE COD.

1½ lb. piece salt cod (also known as *morue*)
1¼ cups olive oil
2 garlic cloves, crushed
1¼ cups whipping cream
2 tablespoons lemon juice

SERVES 4

PUT the salt cod in a shallow bowl and cover with cold water. Refrigerate for 1 or 2 days, changing the water every 8 hours, to soak the salt out of the fish.

DRAIN the cod and rinse again. Put in a saucepan and cover with 8 cups water. Bring to a simmer and cook for 10 minutes (do not boil or the salt cod will toughen). Drain and rinse again.

REMOVE the skin and bones from the cod. Use a fork to flake the cod into small pieces. Make sure there are no small bones left in the cod, then finely chop in a food processor or with a sharp knife. (It will have a fibrous texture.)

HEAT ¼ cup of the oil in a heavy-bottomed frying pan and cook the garlic over a low heat for 3 minutes without coloring. Add the cod and stir in a spoonful of the remaining oil. Beat in a spoonful of cream and continue adding the oil and cream alternately, beating until the mixture is smooth and has the consistency of fluffy mashed potato. Add the lemon juice and season with pepper (you won't need to add any salt). Serve warm or cold with bread or toast. Keep in the refrigerator for up to 3 days and warm through with a little extra cream before serving.

Add the cream and oil alternately, beating until the brandade has a fluffy consistency.

PIKE QUENELLES

PIKE QUENELLES ARE A SPECIALTY OF THE LYON REGION. QUENELLES ARE SMALL OVAL BALLS OF CHOPPED FISH OR MEAT, USUALLY COOKED BY POACHING. THEY CAN BE A LITTLE TRICKY TO MAKE— THE KEY LIES IN KEEPING THE MIXTURE CHILLED. IF PIKE IS UNAVAILABLE, SOLE WORKS WELL ALSO.

14 oz. pike fillet, bones and skin
   removed
2 tablespoons finely chopped
   parsley
³/₄ cup milk
¹/₂ cup all-purpose flour
2 large eggs, lightly beaten
²/₃ cup butter, softened and cubed
2 large egg whites
³/₄ cup heavy cream
4 cups fish stock

SAUCE
3 tablespoons butter
¹/₃ cup all-purpose flour
1²/₃ cup milk
¹/₃ cup heavy cream
large pinch of grated nutmeg
¹/₂ cup Gruyère, grated

SERVES 6

Dairy herd in the Alpine foothills.

POUND the fish to a paste in a mortar and pestle, or purée in a food processor. Transfer to a mixing bowl, stir in the parsley, cover and refrigerate.

PUT the milk in a saucepan and bring just to a boil. Take the saucepan off the heat and add all the flour. Return to a gentle heat and beat in the flour, then take the saucepan off the heat and allow to cool. Using electric beaters or a wooden spoon, gradually add the eggs, beating after each addition. Add the butter, piece by piece, then stir the mixture into the fish purée, cover and chill.

WHEN the mixture is very cold, put the bowl inside a larger bowl filled with ice cubes. Gradually and alternately, add the egg whites and cream, beating after each addition. Season generously, cover and chill again.

TO MAKE the sauce, melt the butter in a saucepan, then stir in the flour to make a roux. Cook, stirring constantly, for 2 minutes without allowing the roux to brown. Remove from the heat and gradually add the milk, stirring after each addition until smooth. Return to the heat and bring to a boil. Simmer for 2 minutes, add the cream and season with nutmeg, salt and pepper.

USING TWO tablespoons, mold the fish mixture into 30 egg shapes (quenelles) and put onto a buttered baking sheet and put in the refrigerator for 20 minutes. Heat the fish stock in a large frying pan until barely simmering and gently lower the quenelles into the liquid in batches. Poach for 5–7 minutes, or until the quenelles rise to the surface and feel firm to the touch. At no stage should the poaching liquid boil. Use a slotted spoon to gently place the quenelles into six lightly buttered gratin dishes. Preheat the broiler. Pour the sauce over the quenelles and sprinkle with the cheese. Broil until brown and bubbling.

Pound the fish to a paste and then stir in the parsley.

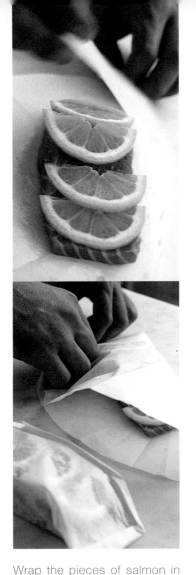

Wrap the pieces of salmon in large circles of parchment paper as this will seal in the flavors while they bake.

SALMON EN PAPILLOTE WITH HERB SAUCE

4 x 6 oz. salmon fillets, skinned
1 tablespoon butter, melted
8 thin slices of lemon, halved

HERB SAUCE
1/4 cup fish stock
1/3 cup dry white wine
2 shallots, finely chopped
1 cup heavy cream
4 tablespoons finely chopped herbs
    such as chervil, chives, parsley,
    tarragon or sorrel

SERVES 4

PREHEAT the oven to 400°F.

REMOVE ANY bones from the salmon fillets: you may need to use tweezers to do this. Cut out four 12-inch parchment paper circles. Fold each circle in half, then open out again and brush with melted butter. Place a salmon fillet on one half of each paper circle, lay four half slices of lemon on top, season, then fold the other half of the paper over the fish to enclose it. Seal the packages by folding the two edges of parchment paper tightly together. Put on a baking sheet and bake for 10–15 minutes (depending on the thickness of the salmon), or until the fish is firm to the touch.

TO MAKE the herb sauce, put the stock, wine and shallots in a saucepan and simmer until the mixture has reduced to a syrup (you should have about 5 tablespoons of liquid left). Add the cream and bubble for a few minutes to thicken slightly. Season and gently stir in the herbs. Serve each diner a package to unwrap at the table with the herb sauce in a separate bowl.

SKATE WITH BLACK BUTTER

COURT BOUILLON
1 cup white wine
1 onion, sliced
1 carrot, sliced
1 bay leaf
4 black peppercorns

4 x 1/2 lb. skate wings, skinned
1/3 cup unsalted butter
1 tablespoon chopped parsley
1 tablespoon capers, rinsed,
    squeezed dry and chopped

SERVES 4

TO MAKE the court bouillon, put the wine, onion, carrot, bay leaf, peppercorns and 4 cups water into a large deep frying pan, bring to a boil and simmer for 20 minutes. Strain the court bouillon and return to the cleaned frying pan.

ADD the skate and simmer for 10 minutes, or until it flakes when tested with the point of a knife. Take out the fish, drain, cover and keep warm.

HEAT the butter in a frying pan and cook over moderate heat for 2 minutes until it turns brown to make a *beurre noisette*. Remove from the heat and stir in the parsley, capers, salt and pepper.

POUR the sauce over the top of the fish and serve immediately. You can remove the fillet from each side of the fish first, if you prefer.

SKATE WITH BLACK BUTTER

POULTRY, MEAT & GAME

COQ AU VIN

A DISH ALLEGEDLY PREPARED BY CAESAR WHEN BATTLING THE GAULS, WHO SENT HIM A SCRAWNY CHICKEN AS A MESSAGE OF DEFIANCE. CAESAR COOKED IT IN WINE AND HERBS AND INVITED THEM TO EAT, THUS DEMONSTRATING THE OVERWHELMING SOPHISTICATION OF THE ROMANS.

2 x 3¹/₄ lb. chickens
1 bottle red wine
2 bay leaves
2 thyme sprigs
8 oz. bacon, diced
4 tablespoons butter
20 pickling or pearl onions
8 oz. button mushrooms
1 teaspoon oil
¹/₄ cup all-purpose flour
4 cups chicken stock
¹/₂ cup brandy
2 teaspoons tomato paste
1 ¹/₂ tablespoons softened butter
1 tablespoon all-purpose flour
2 tablespoons chopped parsley

SERVES 8

Cooking the chicken with the skin on keeps the flesh moist.

CUT EACH chicken into eight pieces by removing both legs and cutting between the joint of the drumstick and the thigh. Cut down either side of the backbone and remove backbone. Turn the chickens over and cut through the cartilage down the center of the breastbone. Cut each breast in half, leaving the wing attached to the top half.

PUT the wine, bay leaves, thyme and some salt and pepper in a bowl and add the chickens. Cover and allow to marinate, preferably overnight.

BLANCH the bacon in boiling water, then drain, pat dry and sauté in a frying pan until a golden brown. Remove onto a plate. Melt a quarter of the butter in the pan, add the onions and sauté until browned. Take out and set aside.

MELT another quarter of the butter, add the mushrooms, season with salt and pepper and sauté for 5 minutes. Remove and set aside.

DRAIN the chickens, reserving the marinade, and pat them dry. Season. Add the remaining butter and the oil to the frying pan, add chickens and sauté until a golden brown. Stir in the flour.

TRANSFER the chickens to a large saucepan or casserole and add the stock. Pour the brandy into the frying pan and boil, stirring, for 30 seconds to deglaze the pan. Pour over the chickens. Add the marinade, onions, mushrooms, bacon and tomato paste. Cook over moderate heat for 45 minutes, or until the chickens are cooked through.

IF the sauce needs thickening, take out the chickens and vegetables and bring the sauce to a boil. Mix together the butter and flour to make a *beurre manié* and whisk into the sauce. Boil, stirring, for 2 minutes until thickened. Add the parsley and return the chickens and vegetables to the sauce.

CHICKEN WITH FORTY CLOVES OF GARLIC

THIS SOUNDS FRIGHTENINGLY OVERPOWERING BUT, AS ANYONE WHO HAS EVER ROASTED GARLIC KNOWS, THE CLOVES MELLOW AND SWEETEN IN THE OVEN UNTIL THE CREAMY FLESH THAT IS SQUEEZED FROM THE SKINS IS QUITE DIFFERENT FROM THE RAW CLOVE.

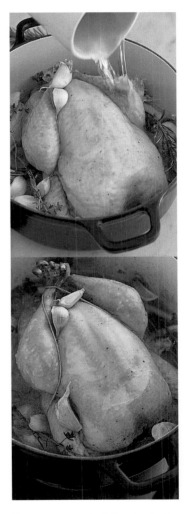

2 celery stalks, including leaves
2 rosemary sprigs
4 thyme sprigs
4 flat-leaf parsley sprigs
1 x 3¹/₄ lb. chicken
40 garlic cloves, unpeeled
2 tablespoons olive oil
1 carrot, roughly chopped
1 small onion, cut into 4 wedges
1 cup white wine
1 baguette, cut into slices
small herb sprigs, to garnish

SERVES 4

PREHEAT the oven to 400°F. Put a chopped celery stalk and 2 sprigs each of the rosemary, thyme and parsley into the chicken cavity. Add 6 cloves of garlic. Tie the legs together and tuck the wing tips under.

BRUSH the chicken liberally with some of the oil and season well. Scatter about 10 more garlic cloves over the bottom of a large casserole. Put the remaining sprigs of herbs, chopped celery, carrot and onion in the casserole.

PUT the chicken in the casserole. Scatter the remaining garlic cloves around the chicken and add the remaining oil and the wine. Cover and bake for 1 hour 20 minutes, or until the chicken is tender and the juices run clear when the thigh is pierced with a skewer.

TO SERVE, carefully remove the chicken from the casserole. Strain off the juices into a small saucepan. Use tongs to pick out the garlic cloves from the strained mixture. Spoon off the fat from the juices and boil for 2–3 minutes to reduce and thicken a little.

CUT the chicken into serving portions, pour over some of the juices and scatter with the garlic. Toast the baguette slices, then garnish the chicken with herb sprigs and serve with the bread to be spread with the soft flesh squeezed from the garlic.

Use a casserole into which the chicken and vegetables fit snugly so that the flavors mingle well.

CHICKEN CHASSEUR

CHASSEUR MEANS "HUNTER" AND IS USED FOR DISHES INCLUDING MUSHROOMS, SHALLOTS, TOMATOES, WINE AND BRANDY. THE NAME PROBABLY REFERS TO THE FACT THAT THIS WAS ORIGINALLY A RECIPE FOR COOKING GAME.

1 x 3^{1}/$_{4}$ lb. chicken
1 tablespoon oil
4 tablespoons butter
2 shallots, finely chopped
^{1}/$_{4}$ lb. button mushrooms, sliced
1 tablespoon all-purpose flour
^{1}/$_{2}$ cup white wine
2 tablespoons brandy
2 teaspoons tomato paste
^{3}/$_{4}$ cup chicken stock
2 teaspoons chopped tarragon
1 teaspoon chopped parsley

CROUTONS
2 slices bread
olive oil

SERVES 4

CUT the chicken into eight pieces by removing both legs and cutting between the joint of the drumstick and the thigh. Cut down either side of the backbone and remove backbone. Turn the chicken over and cut through the cartilage down the center of the breastbone. Cut each breast in half, leaving the wing attached to the top half.

HEAT the oil in a frying pan or saucepan and add half the butter. When the foaming subsides, add the chicken and sauté in batches on both sides until browned. Put on a plate and keep warm. Pour the excess fat out of the pan.

MELT the remaining butter in the pan, add the shallots and cook gently until softened but not browned. Add the mushrooms and cook, covered, over moderate heat for 3 minutes.

ADD the flour and cook, stirring constantly, for 1 minute. Stir in the white wine, brandy, tomato paste and stock. Bring to a boil, stirring constantly, then reduce the heat and add the tarragon. Season.

RETURN the chicken to the pan, cover and simmer for 30 minutes, or until the chicken is tender and cooked through. Sprinkle with parsley to serve.

TO MAKE the croutons, trim the crusts from the bread and cut the bread into moon shapes with a cookie cutter. Heat the olive oil in a frying pan and fry the bread until a golden brown. Drain the croutons on paper towels and serve hot with the chicken.

TARRAGON CHICKEN

TARRAGON HAS A DELICATE, BUT DISTINCTIVE, LICORICE FLAVOR AND IS ONE OF THE HERBS THAT GOES INTO THE FRENCH *FINES HERBES* MIXTURE. IT IS KNOWN AS A PARTICULARLY GOOD PARTNER FOR CHICKEN, WITH A TARRAGON CREAM SAUCE MAKING A CLASSIC COMBINATION.

1¹/₂ tablespoons chopped tarragon
1 small garlic clove, crushed
3 tablespoons butter, softened
1 x 3¹/₄ lb. chicken
2 teaspoons oil
¹/₂ cup chicken stock
2 tablespoons white wine
1 tablespoon all-purpose flour
1 tablespoon tarragon leaves
¹/₂ cup heavy cream

SERVES 4

PREHEAT the oven to 400°F. Mix together the chopped tarragon, garlic and half the butter. Season with salt and pepper and place inside the cavity of the chicken. Tie the legs together and tuck the wing tips under.

HEAT the remaining butter with the oil in a large casserole over low heat and brown the chicken on all sides. Add the chicken stock and wine. Cover the casserole and bake in the oven for 1 hour 20 minutes, or until the chicken is tender and the juices run clear when the thigh is pierced with a skewer. Remove the chicken draining all the juices back into the casserole. Cover with aluminum foil and a kitchen towel and allow the chicken to rest.

SKIM a tablespoon of the surface fat from the cooking liquid and put it in a small bowl. Skim the remainder of fat from the surface and throw this away. Add the flour to the reserved fat and mix until smooth. Whisk quickly into the cooking liquid and stir over moderate heat until the sauce boils and thickens.

STRAIN the sauce into a clean saucepan and add the tarragon leaves. Simmer for 2 minutes, then stir in the cream and reheat without boiling. Season with salt and pepper. Carve the chicken and spoon the sauce over the top to serve.

Brown the chicken to seal before adding the stock and wine.

Buying cooked chickens and meat from a market rotisserie.

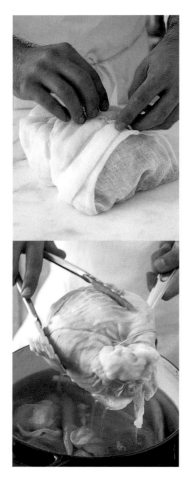

Cook the chicken wrapped in cheesecloth to keep its shape.

POULE AU POT

WHEN HENRY IV WISHED THAT ALL HIS SUBJECTS HAVE A CHICKEN FOR THEIR POT EVERY SUNDAY, THIS WAS PRESUMABLY THE MEAL HE HAD IN MIND. THE CHICKEN IS COOKED SIMPLY, SO IT IS IMPERATIVE TO USE A FREE-RANGE BIRD FOR THE BEST FLAVOR.

1 x 3^1/$_4$ lb. chicken
1 carrot, roughly chopped
^{1}/$_2$ onion, halved
1 celery stalk, roughly chopped
1 garlic clove
4 parsley sprigs
2 bay leaves
8 black peppercorns
8 juniper berries
2 ham bones
1 teaspoon salt
12 baby carrots
8 baby leeks
8 baby turnips
12 small new potatoes

SERVES 4

SEASON the chicken and wrap it up in cheesecloth, securing with string. Put into a large saucepan. Tie the carrots, onion, celery, garlic, parsley, bay leaves, peppercorns and juniper berries in another piece of cheesecloth and add to the saucepan. Add the ham bones and salt, cover with cold water and bring to a simmer. Cook over very low heat for 40 minutes.

TRIM the baby vegetables, add to saucepan and cook for 10 more minutes. Take out the chicken and drain on a wire rack over a baking sheet. Cook the vegetables for another 10 minutes. Remove the skin from the chicken and carve, then serve with the vegetables. Strain the cooking liquid, discarding the ham bones, and serve as a broth to start the meal or freeze for soup stock.

POULET RÔTI

3 tablespoons butter, softened
1 x 3^1/$_4$ lb. chicken
1 tarragon or rosemary sprig
1^1/$_4$ cups chicken stock

SERVES 4

PREHEAT the oven to 400°F. Place half the butter inside the chicken with the tarragon or rosemary. Rub the chicken with the remaining butter and season. Tie the legs together and tuck the wing tips under. Put in a roasting pan, breast side down, and add the stock.

COVER the chicken loosely with aluminum foil and roast for 30 minutes, basting occasionally. Uncover, turn the chicken and roast for another 30–40 minutes, or until a golden brown and the juices run clear when the thigh is pierced with a skewer.

REMOVE the chicken from the pan, cover with aluminum foil and a kitchen towel and allow to rest. Put the pan on the stove top and skim off most of the fat. Boil rapidly until the juices reduce and become syrupy. Strain and serve with the chicken.

POULET RÔTI

POULET VALLÉE D'AUGE

THIS IS ONE OF THE CLASSIC DISHES OF NORMANDY AND BRITTANY, THE APPLE-GROWING REGIONS OF FRANCE. IF YOU HEAR IT REFERRED TO AS *POULET AU CIDRE*, THIS MEANS THE CHICKEN HAS BEEN COOKED IN CIDER RATHER THAN STOCK.

1 x 3¼ lb. chicken
2 eating apples
1 tablespoon lemon juice
4 tablespoons butter
½ onion, finely chopped
½ celery stalk, finely chopped
1 tablespoon all-purpose flour
⅓ cup Calvados or brandy
1½ cups chicken stock
⅓ cup crème fraîche

SERVES 4

CUT the chicken into eight pieces by removing both legs and cutting between the joint of the drumstick and the thigh. Cut down either side of the backbone and remove backbone. Turn the chicken over and cut through the cartilage down the center of the breastbone. Cut each breast in half, leaving the wing attached to the top half.

PEEL and core the apples. Finely chop half of one apple and cut the rest into 12 wedges. Toss the apple in the lemon juice.

HEAT half the butter in a large frying pan. Add the chicken pieces, skin side down, and cook until golden. Turn over and cook for another 5 minutes. Remove the chicken and pour off the fat.

HEAT 1 tablespoon more butter in the same frying pan, add the onion, celery and chopped apples and fry over moderate heat for 5 minutes without browning.

REMOVE from the heat. Sprinkle the flour over the vegetables and stir in. Add the Calvados and return to the heat. Gradually stir in the chicken stock. Bring to a boil, return the chicken to the saucepan, cover and simmer gently for 15 minutes, or until the chicken is tender and cooked through.

MEANWHILE, heat the remaining butter in a small frying pan. Add the apple wedges and fry over moderate heat until browned and tender. Remove from the pan and keep warm.

REMOVE the chicken from the pan and keep warm. Skim the excess fat from the cooking liquid. Add the crème fraîche, bring to a boil and boil for 4 minutes, or until the sauce is thick enough to lightly coat the back of a wooden spoon. Season and pour over the chicken. Serve with the apple wedges.

Fry the chopped apple with the chicken and its sauce to give flavor and then fry the apple wedges separately.

DUCK BREASTS WITH CASSIS AND RASPBERRIES

"MAGRET" IS THE FRENCH NAME FOR DUCK BREAST, THE LEANEST PORTION OF THE DUCK. *MAGRET DE CANARD* IS USUALLY SERVED PINK WITH A VERY CRISPY SKIN. YOU CAN USE FROZEN RASPBERRIES FOR THIS RECIPE, BUT MAKE SURE THEY ARE THOROUGHLY DEFROSTED.

4 x 6 oz. duck breasts
2 teaspoons sea salt
2 teaspoons ground cinnamon
4 teaspoons Demerara sugar
1 cup red wine
1/2 cup crème de cassis
1 tablespoon cornstarch or
   arrowroot
1/2 lb. raspberries

SERVES 4

SCORE the duck breasts through the skin and fat but not all the way through to the meat. Heat a frying pan and fry the duck breasts, skin side down, until the skin browns and the fat runs out. Lift the breasts out of the frying pan and pour off most of the fat.

MIX TOGETHER the sea salt, cinnamon and Demerara sugar. Sprinkle over the skin of the duck breasts, then press in with your hands. Season with black pepper. Reheat the frying pan and cook the duck breasts, skin side up, for 10–15 minutes. Take them out of the frying pan and allow to rest on a carving board. Preheat the broiler.

MEANWHILE, mix together the red wine and cassis in a pitcher. Pour about 1/3 cup of the liquid into a small bowl and mix in the cornstarch or arrowroot, then pour this back into the pitcher.

POUR the excess fat out of the frying pan keeping about 2 tablespoons. Return the frying pan to the heat and pour in the red wine and cassis. Simmer for 2–3 minutes, stirring constantly, until the sauce has thickened. Add the raspberries and simmer for another minute to warm the fruit through. Check the seasoning.

BROIL the duck breasts, skin side up, for a minute, or until the sugar starts to caramelize. Slice the duck breasts thinly, pour a little sauce over the top and serve the rest separately in a gravy boat.

DUCK A L'ORANGE

DUCK CAN BE FATTY, WHICH IS WHY IT SHOULD BE PRICKED ALL OVER AND COOKED ON A RACK TO LET THE FAT DRAIN OUT. THE REASON THAT DUCK A L'ORANGE WORKS SO PERFECTLY AS A DISH IS THAT THE SWEET ACIDITY OF THE CITRUS FRUIT CUTS THROUGH THE RICH DUCK FAT.

5 oranges
1 x 4 lb. duck
2 cinnamon sticks
3/4 cup mint leaves
1/2 cup light brown sugar
1/2 cup cider vinegar
1/3 cup Grand Marnier
2 tablespoons butter

SERVES 4

PREHEAT the oven to 300°F. Halve two of the oranges and rub them all over the duck. Place them inside the duck cavity with the cinnamon sticks and mint. Tie the legs together and tie the wings together. Prick all over with a fork so that the fat can drain out as the duck cooks.

PUT the duck on a rack, breast side down, and put the rack in a shallow roasting pan. Roast for 45 minutes, turning the duck halfway through.

MEANWHILE, zest and juice the remaining oranges (if you don't have a zester, cut the orange peel into thin strips with a sharp knife). Heat the sugar in a saucepan over low heat until it melts and then caramelizes: swirl the saucepan gently to make sure it caramelizes evenly. When the sugar is a rich brown, add the vinegar (be careful as it will spatter) and boil for 3 minutes. Add the orange juice and Grand Marnier and simmer for 2 minutes.

BLANCH the orange zest in boiling water for 1 minute three times, changing the water each time. Refresh under cold water, drain and reserve.

REMOVE the excess fat from the roasting pan. Increase the oven temperature to 350°F. Spoon some of the orange sauce over the duck and roast for 45 minutes, spooning the remaining sauce over the duck every 5 to 10 minutes and turning the duck to baste all sides.

REMOVE the duck from the oven, cover with aluminum foil and strain the juices back into a saucepan. Skim off any excess fat and add the orange zest and butter to the saucepan. Stir to melt the butter. Reheat the sauce and serve over the duck.

A butcher's shop in Paris.

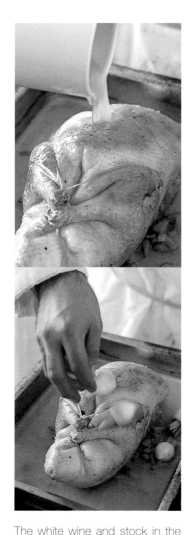

DUCKLING WITH TURNIPS

1 x 3³/₄ lb. duckling
bouquet garni
2 tablespoons clarified butter
1 carrot, chopped
1 celery stalk, chopped
¹/₂ large onion, chopped
2 teaspoons sugar
8 shallots
8 baby turnips
¹/₃ cup white wine
2 cups chicken stock
¹/₂ tablespoon softened butter
¹/₂ tablespoon all-purpose flour

SERVES 2

PREHEAT the oven to 400°F and put a roasting pan in the oven to heat up. Truss the duckling by tying the legs together and tying the wing tips together behind the body. Prick all over, put the bouquet garni in the cavity and season.

HEAT the clarified butter in a large frying pan and brown the duckling on both sides. Lift the duckling out of the pan and pour all but a tablespoon of the fat into a pitcher. Add the carrot, celery and onion to the pan and soften over the heat, then brown. Remove the vegetables.

ADD ANOTHER 2 tablespoons of duck fat to the frying pan. Add the sugar and let it dissolve over low heat. Turn up the heat and add the shallots and turnips. Caramelize over high heat, then remove from frying pan. Pour in the white wine and boil, stirring, for 30 seconds to deglaze the pan.

PUT the carrot, celery and onion in the middle of the hot roasting pan, place the duckling on top and pour in the white wine and stock. Add the turnips to the pan and roast for 45 minutes. Baste well, add the shallots and roast for another 20 minutes. Baste again and roast for another 25 minutes.

TAKE OUT the duck, turnips and shallots and keep warm. Strain the sauce, pressing the chopped vegetables in the sieve to extract all the juices, then throw away the chopped vegetables.

POUR the strained sauce into a saucepan and boil rapidly to reduce by half. Mix together the butter and flour to make a *beurre manié*. Whisk into the sauce and boil, stirring, for 2 minutes until thickened.

PUT the duckling, turnips and shallots on a serving plate and pour a little sauce over them. Serve the rest of the sauce in a gravy boat.

The white wine and stock in the roasting pan adds flavor and helps to keep the duckling moist.

DUCK CONFIT

A CONFIT IS THE TRADITIONAL METHOD OF PRESERVING MEAT FOR USE THROUGHOUT THE YEAR.
TODAY IT IS STILL A DELICIOUS WAY TO COOK AND EAT DUCK. THE THIGHS AND LEGS ARE USUALLY
PRESERVED, WITH THE BREAST BEING SERVED FRESH.

8 large duck legs
8 tablespoons coarse sea salt
12 bay leaves
8 thyme sprigs
16 juniper berries, lightly crushed
4 lb. duck or goose fat, cut into
  pieces

SERVES 8

PUT the duck legs in a bowl or dish in which they
fit snuggly. Scatter the salt over the top, season
with black pepper and tuck half the bay leaves,
thyme sprigs and juniper berries into the dish.
Cover and leave in the refrigerator overnight.

PREHEAT the oven to 350°F. Put the duck legs in
a large roasting pan, leaving behind the herbs and
any liquid that has formed in the bottom of the
bowl. Add the duck or goose fat to the pan and
roast for 1 hour. Reduce the oven to 300°F and
roast the duck for another 2 hours, basting
occasionally, until the duck is very well cooked.

WASH one large or two smaller canning jars and
dry in the hot oven for 5 minutes to sterilize them.
Use tongs to put the hot duck legs into the hot jar
and add the remaining bay leaves, thyme sprigs
and juniper berries. Strain the cooking fat through
a sieve and into a large pitcher. Now pour the fat
into the jar to cover the duck. Close the lid and
allow to cool. The fat will solidify when cooled.

Use tongs to push the duck legs
into the jars, then cover with the
strained hot fat to seal.

DUCK CONFIT will keep for several months in a
cool pantry or refrigerator. To use, remove as
much duck as you need from the jar, returning any
excess fat to cover the remaining duck. The meat
can then be roasted in a very hot oven until really
crisp and served with lentils, beans or salad. Or it
can be used to make cassoulet.

Confit de canard is used to add
richness to cassoulet.

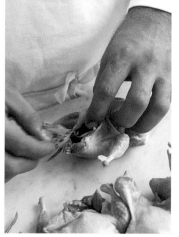

QUAILS WITH GRAPES AND TARRAGON

8 tarragon sprigs
8 x 5 oz. quails
2 tablespoons clarified butter
$1/2$ cup wine
$12/3$ cups chicken stock
5 oz. seedless green grapes

SERVES 4

PUT a sprig of tarragon into the cavity of each quail and season well. Heat the clarified butter in a sauté pan or deep frying pan and brown the quails on all sides. Add the wine and boil for 30 seconds, then add the stock and grapes.

COVER the pan and simmer for 8 minutes or until the quails are cooked through. Lift out the quails and grapes and keep warm. Boil the sauce until it has reduced by two thirds and become syrupy. Strain the sauce and pour over the quails and grapes to serve.

Push a fresh tarragon sprig into each quail before cooking, so that the flavor infuses the flesh.

PRUNE AND WALNUT-STUFFED POUSSINS

FRENCH AGEN PRUNES ARE SAID TO BE THE BEST IN THE WORLD AND THE COMBINATION OF PRUNES WITH WALNUTS IS A CLASSIC ONE, WITH BOTH THE FRUIT AND THE NUTS COMING FROM THE SAME AREA OF SOUTHWEST FRANCE.

STUFFING
1 tablespoon butter
4 shallots, finely chopped
1 large garlic clove, crushed
$21/4$ oz. shelled walnuts, chopped
14 prunes, pitted and chopped

4 poussins (very young chickens)
4 bay leaves
4 slices bacon
3 tablespoons butter
juice of 1 small lemon
2 tablespoons honey
$1/4$ cup heavy cream or crème
　fraîche

SERVES 4

TO MAKE the stuffing, heat the butter in a frying pan, add the shallots and cook for 10–15 minutes. Add the garlic and cook for 1 minute. Remove the frying pan from the heat and stir in the walnuts and prunes. Season and allow to cool. Preheat the oven to 350°F.

SPOON an equal amount of stuffing into each poussin, then add a bay leaf. Tie the legs together and tuck the wing tips under. Arrange the poussins in a roasting pan and wrap a slice of bacon around each poussin breast.

PLACE the butter in a small pan with the lemon juice and honey. Melt together, then pour over the poussins. Roast, basting often, for 45 minutes, or until a skewer pushed into the center of the stuffing comes out too hot to touch.

TAKE the poussins out of the pan, cover and keep warm. Put the roasting pan on the stove top, heat until the juices bubble and stir in the cream or crème fraîche. Season the sauce, pour a little over the poussins and serve the rest separately.

PRUNE AND
WALNUT-STUFFED POUSSINS

148

VENISON WITH BLACKBERRY SAUCE

4 tablespoons clarified butter

12 pickling or pearl onions

1/4 cup blackberries or
    black currants

3 tablespoons red currant jelly

16 x 2 oz. venison medallions

1/4 cup red wine

1 2/3 cups brown stock

1/2 tablespoon softened butter

1/2 tablespoon all-purpose flour

SERVES 4

HEAT half the clarified butter in a saucepan. Add the onions, cover with crumpled wet waxed paper and a lid. Cook gently for 20–25 minutes, stirring occasionally, until brown and cooked. Put the berries in a saucepan with the red currant jelly and 3 tablespoons water. Boil for 5 minutes until the fruit is softened and the liquid syrupy.

SEASON the venison, heat the remaining clarified butter in a frying pan and cook in batches over high heat for 1–2 minutes. Remove the venison and keep warm. Add the wine to the frying pan and boil for 30 seconds. Add the stock and boil until reduced by half.

MIX TOGETHER the butter and flour to make a *beurre manié* and whisk into the stock. Boil, stirring, for 2 minutes, then drain the syrup from the fruit into the stock to make a sauce. Stir well, season and serve with the venison and onions. Use the drained fruit as a garnish if you like.

Brown the venison in batches so that it fries without stewing. Drain the syrup from the fruit to add flavor to the sauce.

ROASTED PHEASANT WITH GARLIC AND SHALLOTS

1 x 2 lb. pheasant

1/2 teaspoon juniper or allspice
    berries, lightly crushed

a few parsley sprigs

2 tablespoons butter

6 slices bacon

6 shallots, unpeeled

6 garlic cloves, unpeeled

1 teaspoon all-purpose flour

1/2 cup chicken stock

SERVES 2

PREHEAT the oven to 400°F. Rub the pheasant with salt, pepper and the juniper berries. Fill the cavity with the parsley and butter, tie the legs together and tuck the wing tips under. Place in a small roasting pan and lay the bacon over the pheasant to prevent it from drying out. Scatter with the unpeeled shallots and garlic and roast for 20 minutes. Remove the bacon and roast for another 10 minutes.

REMOVE shallots, garlic and pheasant from the pan and cut off the pheasant legs. Put the legs back in the pan and cook for another 5 minutes, then remove and keep all the pheasant warm.

TO MAKE the gravy, transfer the roasting pan to the stove top. Stir in the flour and cook, stirring, for 2 minutes. Add the stock and bring to a boil, whisking constantly. Boil for 2 minutes to thicken slightly, then strain the gravy. Serve the pheasant, shallots and garlic with a little gravy poured over.

ROASTED PHEASANT WITH
GARLIC AND SHALLOTS

The easiest way to mix the venison with the marinade is to toss it together with your hands.

VENISON CASSEROLE

THIS WINTER CASSEROLE IS SERVED UP DURING THE HUNTING SEASON IN POPULAR GAME AREAS SUCH AS THE ARDENNES, AUVERGNE AND ALSACE. VENISON BENEFITS FROM BEING MARINATED BEFORE COOKING, OTHERWISE IT CAN BE A LITTLE TOUGH.

MARINADE
1/2 onion
4 cloves
8 juniper berries, crushed
8 black peppercorns, crushed
1 cup red wine
1 carrot, roughly chopped
1/2 celery stalk
2 bay leaves
2 garlic cloves
2 pieces lemon zest
5 rosemary sprigs

2 lb. venison, cubed
3 tablespoons all-purpose flour
1 tablespoon vegetable oil
1 tablespoon clarified butter
8 shallots
2 cups brown stock
2 tablespoons red currant jelly
rosemary sprigs

SERVES 4

TO MAKE the marinade, cut the half onion into four pieces and stud each piece with a clove. Mix together in a large bowl with the rest of the marinade ingredients. Add the venison, toss it well and put in the fridge overnight to marinate.

TAKE the venison out of the marinade (reserving the marinade), drain and pat dry with paper towels. Season the flour and use it to coat the venison (the cleanest way to do this is to put the flour and venison in a plastic bag and toss well).

PREHEAT the oven to 315°F. Heat the oil and clarified butter in a large casserole, brown the shallots and then remove from the casserole. Brown the venison in the oil and butter, then remove from the casserole.

STRAIN the marinade liquid through a sieve into the casserole and boil, stirring, for 30 seconds to deglaze. Pour in the stock and bring to a boil.

REMOVE the remaining marinade ingredients from the sieve onto a piece of cheesecloth and tie up in a package to make a bouquet garni. Add to the casserole with the venison. Bring the liquid to a simmer, then put the casserole in the oven. Cook for 45 minutes and then add the shallots. Cook for another 1 hour.

DISCARD the bouquet garni, remove the venison and shallots from the cooking liquid and keep warm. Add the red currant jelly to the liquid and boil on the stove top for 4–5 minutes to reduce by half. Strain the sauce and pour over the venison. Serve garnished with sprigs of rosemary.

RABBIT FRICASSÉE

THE NAME OF THE DISH COMES FROM AN OLD FRENCH WORD, *FRICASSER*, TO FRY. A FRICASSÉE IS A DISH OF WHITE MEAT, USUALLY CHICKEN, VEAL OR RABBIT, IN A VELOUTÉ SAUCE WITH EGG YOLKS AND CREAM. WILD RABBIT, IF YOU CAN GET IT, HAS A BETTER FLAVOR THAN FARMED.

4 tablespoons clarified butter
1 x 3 lb. rabbit, cut into 8 pieces
6 oz. button mushrooms
1/2 cup white wine
2/3 cup chicken stock
bouquet garni
1/3 cup oil
small bunch of sage
1/2 cup heavy cream
2 egg yolks

SERVES 4

HEAT HALF the clarified butter in a large saucepan, season the rabbit and brown in batches, turning once. Remove from the saucepan and set aside. Add the remaining butter to the saucepan and brown the mushrooms.

PUT the rabbit back into the saucepan with the mushrooms. Add the wine and boil for a couple of minutes before adding the stock and bouquet garni. Cover the saucepan tightly and simmer gently over very low heat for 40 minutes.

MEANWHILE, heat the oil in a small saucepan. Remove the leaves from the bunch of sage and drop them, a few at a time, into the hot oil. The leaves will immediately start to bubble around the edges. Cook them for 30 seconds, or until bright green and crispy. Make sure you don't overheat the oil or cook the leaves for too long or they will turn black and taste burnt. Drain the leaves on paper towels and sprinkle with salt.

TAKE the cooked rabbit and mushrooms out of the saucepan and keep warm. Discard the bouquet garni. Remove the saucepan from the heat, mix together the cream and egg yolks and stir quickly into the stock. Return to a very low heat and cook, stirring, for about 5 minutes to thicken slightly (don't let the sauce boil or the eggs will scramble). Season with salt and pepper.

TO SERVE, pour the sauce over the rabbit and mushrooms and garnish with crispy sage leaves.

While the rabbit is simmering, deep-fry the sage until crispy.

If you have time, allow the beef to marinate overnight to deepen the flavors of this dish.

BEEF BOURGUIGNON

ALMOST EVERY REGION OF FRANCE HAS ITS OWN STYLE OF BEEF STEW, BUT BURGUNDY'S VERSION IS THE MOST WELL KNOWN. IF YOU CAN, MAKE IT A DAY IN ADVANCE TO LET THE FLAVORS DEVELOP. SERVE WITH A SALAD OF CURLY ENDIVE, CHICORY AND WATERCRESS AND BREAD OR NEW POTATOES.

3 lb. beef blade or chuck steak
3 cups red wine (preferably Burgundy)
3 garlic cloves, crushed
bouquet garni
5 tablespoons butter
1 onion, chopped
1 carrot, chopped
2 tablespoons all-purpose flour
6 oz. bacon, cut into short strips
10 oz. shallots, peeled but left whole
6 oz. small button mushrooms

SERVES 6

CUT the meat into 1¹/₂-inch cubes and trim away any excess fat. Put the meat, wine, garlic and bouquet garni in a large bowl, cover with plastic wrap and put in the refrigerator for at least 3 hours and preferably overnight.

PREHEAT the oven to 315°F. Drain the meat, reserving the marinade and bouquet garni. Dry the meat on paper towels. Heat 2 tablespoons of the butter in a large casserole. Add the onion, carrot and bouquet garni and cook over low heat, stirring occasionally, for 10 minutes. Remove from the heat.

HEAT 1 tablespoon of the butter in a large frying pan over high heat. Fry the meat in batches for about 5 minutes or until well browned. Add to the casserole.

POUR the reserved marinade into the frying pan and boil, stirring, for 30 seconds to deglaze the pan. Remove from the heat. Return the casserole to a high heat and sprinkle the meat and vegetables with the flour. Cook, stirring constantly, until the meat is well coated with the flour. Pour in the marinade and stir well. Bring to a boil, stirring constantly, then cover and cook in the oven for 2 hours.

HEAT the remaining butter in the clean frying pan and cook the bacon and shallots, stirring, for 8–10 minutes or until the shallots are softened but not browned. Add the mushrooms and cook, stirring occasionally, for 2–3 minutes or until browned. Drain on paper towels. Add the shallots, bacon and mushrooms to the casserole.

COVER the casserole and return to the oven for 30 minutes, or until the meat is soft and tender. Discard the bouquet garni. Season and skim any fat from the surface before serving.

BEEF CARBONNADE

CARBONNADE A LA FLAMANDE IS, AS THE NAME IMPLIES, A FLEMISH RECIPE, BUT IT IS ALSO TRADITIONAL THROUGHOUT THE NORTH OF FRANCE. CARBONNADE MEANS "CHARCOAL COOKED" BUT THIS IS, IN FACT, A RICH OVEN-COOKED STEW OF BEEF IN BEER. DELICIOUS WITH BAKED POTATOES.

2 tablespoons butter
2–3 tablespoons oil
2 lb. lean beef rump or chuck
  steak, cubed
4 onions, chopped
1 garlic clove, crushed
1 teaspoon brown sugar
1 tablespoon all-purpose flour
2 cups beer (bitter or stout)
2 bay leaves
4 thyme sprigs

CROUTONS
6–8 slices baguette
Dijon mustard

SERVES 4

PREHEAT the oven to 300°F. Melt the butter in a large sauté pan with a tablespoon of oil. Brown the meat in batches over high heat and then remove to a plate.

ADD ANOTHER tablespoon oil to the pan and add the onions. Cook over moderate heat for 10 minutes, then add the garlic and sugar and cook for another 5 minutes, adding another tablespoon of oil if necessary. Remove the onion to a second plate.

REDUCE the heat to low and pour in any juices that have drained from the browned meat, then stir in the flour. Remove from the heat and stir in the beer, a little at a time (the beer will foam). Return to the heat and let the mixture gently simmer and thicken. Season with salt and pepper.

LAYER the meat and onion in a casserole, tucking the bay leaves and sprigs of thyme between the layers and seasoning with salt and black pepper as you go. Pour the liquid over the meat, cover with a lid and cook in the oven for $2^{1}/_{2}$–3 hours, or until the meat is tender.

TO MAKE the croutons, preheat the broiler. Lightly toast the baguette on both sides, then spread one side with mustard. Arrange on top of the carbonnade, mustard side up, and place the whole casserole under the broiler for a minute.

Layer the meat and onion in the casserole, adding the herbs and seasoning between the layers, then pour the liquid over the top.

BEEF EN DAUBE

DAUBES ARE TRADITIONALLY COOKED IN SQUAT EARTHENWARE DISHES CALLED "*DAUBIÈRES*," BUT A CAST-IRON CASSEROLE WITH A TIGHT-FITTING LID WILL WORK JUST AS WELL. DAUBES HAIL FROM PROVENCE AND ARE USUALLY SERVED WITH BUTTERED MACARONI OR NEW POTATOES.

The pig's trotter (foot) will give a gelatinous texture to the daube, as well as adding extra flavor.

MARINADE
2 cloves
1 onion, cut into quarters
2 cups red wine
2 strips of orange zest
2 garlic cloves
1/2 celery stalk
2 bay leaves
a few parsley stalks

3 lb. boneless beef stew meat, such as blade or rump, cut into large pieces
2 tablespoons oil
2 oz. pork fat
1 pig's trotter (foot) or 7 oz. piece bacon
2 1/2 cups beef stock

SERVES 6

TO MAKE the marinade, push the cloves into a piece of onion and mix together in a large bowl with the remaining marinade ingredients. Season the beef with salt and pepper, add to the marinade and allow to marinate overnight.

HEAT the oil in a saucepan. Take the beef out of the marinade and pat dry, then brown in batches in the oil and remove to a plate. You might need to use a little of the marinade liquid to deglaze the saucepan between batches to prevent bits from sticking to the bottom of it and burning.

STRAIN the marinade through a sieve into a bowl and tip the contents of the sieve into the pan to brown. Remove from the saucepan. Add the marinade liquid to the saucepan and boil, stirring, for 30 seconds to deglaze the saucepan.

PLACE the pork fat in a large casserole, then add the pig's trotter, beef and marinade ingredients. Pour in the marinade liquid and stock. Bring to a boil, then cover, reduce the heat and simmer gently for 2–2 1/2 hours or until the meat is tender.

REMOVE the meat from the casserole to a serving dish, cover and keep warm. Discard the garlic, onion, pork fat and pig's trotter. Pour the liquid through a fine sieve and skim off as much fat as possible, then return to the casserole. Bring to a boil and boil until reduced by half and syrupy. Pour the gravy over the meat to serve.

Specialty award-winning meats for sale at a Paris butcher's shop.

BEEF A LA FICELLE

THE NAME MEANS SIMPLY "BEEF ON A STRING," WHICH DESCRIBES THE DISH VERY WELL. THE STRING ALLOWS THE PIECES OF BEEF TO BE LOWERED INTO AND REMOVED FROM THE COOKING STOCK. YOU CAN USE THE SAME METHOD TO COOK ONE LARGE PIECE OF BEEF.

1 x 1 lb. 10 oz. center-cut beef fillet
3¹/₂ cups beef stock
1 rutabaga, cut into sticks
1 carrot, cut into sticks
1 celery stalk, cut into sticks
2 potatoes, cut into chunks
¹/₄ cabbage, chopped
4 scallions, trimmed into long
   lengths
1 bay leaf
2 thyme sprigs
a few parsley sprigs

SERVES 4

TRIM the beef of any fat and sinew and cut into four even pieces. Tie each piece of beef around its circumference with kitchen string so it keeps its compact shape. Leave a long length of string attached to lower the beef in and out of the stock.

PLACE the stock in a saucepan, bring to a boil and add the vegetables and herbs. Cook over moderate heat for about 8 minutes, or until the vegetables are tender. Remove the vegetables with a slotted spoon and keep warm. Discard the herbs and skim the stock of any fat or foam that floats to the surface.

SEASON the beef with salt, then lower into the simmering stock, keeping the strings tied around the saucepan handle or a wooden spoon balanced over the saucepan. Cook for about 6 minutes for rare, or 10 minutes for medium-rare, depending on your tastes.

PLACE each piece of beef in a large shallow bowl and loop the end of the string onto the rim of the bowl. Add the cooked vegetables and ladle some of the cooking broth over the top to serve.

Tie a length of string around the beef. Leave long tails to lower the meat into the stock (tie them around the saucepan handle while you are cooking).

A Paris butcher delivers fresh meat by scooter.

Press the peppercorns firmly into the steaks, so they don't come off while you are frying.

STEAK AU POIVRE

4 x 6 oz. beef steaks
2 tablespoons oil
6 tablespoons black peppercorns, crushed
3 tablespoons butter
3 tablespoons Cognac
1/4 cup white wine
1/2 cup heavy cream

SERVES 4

RUB the steaks on both sides with the oil and press the crushed peppercorns into the meat. Melt the butter in a large frying pan and cook the steaks for 2–4 minutes on each side, depending on how you like your steak.

ADD the Cognac and flambé by lighting the frying pan with your gas flame or a match (stand back when you do this and keep a pan lid handy for emergencies). Put the steaks on a warm plate. Add the wine to the pan and boil, stirring, for 1 minute to deglaze the pan. Add cream and stir for 1–2 minutes. Season and pour over the steaks.

STEAK BÉARNAISE

1 shallot, finely chopped
2 tablespoons white wine vinegar or tarragon vinegar
2 tablespoons white wine
3 tarragon sprigs
1 teaspoon dried tarragon
3 egg yolks
3/4 cup clarified butter, melted
1 tablespoon chopped tarragon leaves
4 x 6 oz. fillet steaks
1 tablespoon oil

SERVES 4

PUT the shallot, vinegar, wine, tarragon sprigs and dried tarragon in a saucepan. Bring to a boil and cook until reduced to 1 tablespoon. Remove from the heat and cool slightly.

WHISK the egg yolks with 1 1/2 tablespoons water, and add to the saucepan. Place the saucepan over very low heat or over a simmering bain-marie and continue to whisk until the sauce is thick. Do not boil or the eggs will scramble.

REMOVE the sauce from the heat, continue to whisk and slowly add the butter in a thin steady stream. Pass through a fine strainer, then stir in the chopped tarragon. Season with salt and pepper and keep warm while cooking the steaks.

RUB the steaks with the oil, season them with salt and pepper and cook for 2–4 minutes on each side, depending on how you like your steak. Serve with the sauce.

STEAK BÉARNAISE

ENTRECÔTE A LA BORDELAISE

SAUCE
3 tablespoons unsalted butter,
    chilled and diced
3 shallots, finely chopped
2 cups red wine (preferably
    Bordeaux)
1 cup brown stock
2³/₄ oz. bone marrow
1 tablespoon chopped parsley

4 x 6 oz. entrecôte or sirloin steaks
1¹/₂ tablespoons oil

SERVES 4

TO MAKE the sauce, melt 1 tablespoon of the butter in a saucepan, add the shallots and cook, stirring, for 7 minutes or until very soft. Pour in the wine and simmer until reduced by two-thirds. Add the stock and bone marrow and simmer until reduced by half, breaking up the marrow as it cooks.

WHISK IN the remaining pieces of butter. Season to taste with salt and pepper. Add the parsley.

TRIM and season the steaks and rub with some of the oil. Heat the remaining oil in a frying pan, and sauté the steaks for 2–4 minutes on each side, depending on how you like your steak. Pour the sauce over the top to serve.

BIFTECK HACHÉ

BIFTECK HACHÉ MEANS "CHOPPED" OR "GROUND STEAK," OTHERWISE KNOWN AS A HAMBURGER.

GOOD HAMBURGERS NEED TO BE MADE WITH A TENDER MEAT BECAUSE THEY ARE COOKED QUICKLY.

ADD THE SALT JUST BEFORE YOU COOK SO AS NOT TO DRAW THE MOISTURE OUT OF THE MEAT.

Biafteck haché has a better flavor and texture if you use ground steak rather than ground beef.

2 tablespoons butter
1 garlic clove, crushed
1 small onion, finely chopped
1 lb. ground lean beef steak
1 tablespoon finely chopped parsley
large pinch of grated nutmeg
1 large egg, lightly beaten
1 tablespoon oil

SERVES 4

MELT 1 tablespoon of the butter in a saucepan and gently cook the garlic and onion for 10–15 minutes, or until the onion s softened but not browned. Cool.

PUT the ground steak in a large bowl and add the onion mixture, parsley, nutmeg, beaten egg and plenty of ground black pepper. Mix together well, then divide the mixture into four and roll into four balls. Put the balls on a large plate and gently pat each one down into a burger shape. Cover and chill in the refrigerator for at least 1 hour.

MELT the remaining butter and the oil in a frying pan, slide in the burgers and season with salt. Cook for 10–12 minutes over moderate heat, turning them halfway through. The burgers should be crusty on the outside and slightly pink on the inside. Serve with salad and *frites*.

BIFTECK HACHÉ

Fold the beef tightly into the pastry package as the meat will shrink slightly when cooked.

Cattle farming is a major industry of the Alpine areas.

BEEF EN CROÛTE

FOR THIS DISH TO WORK REALLY WELL, YOU NEED TO ASK THE BUTCHER FOR A PIECE OF CENTER-CUT BEEF FILLET THAT IS AN EVEN THICKNESS ALL THE WAY ALONG. THE PASTRY CAN BE PUFF, FLAKY OR EVEN BRIOCHE DOUGH. IT IS ALSO KNOWN AS BEEF WELLINGTON.

PÂTÉ
3/4 cup butter
3 shallots, chopped
1 garlic clove, chopped
12 oz. chicken livers
1 tablespoon brandy or Cognac

1 x 2 lb. thick beef fillet
2 tablespoons drippings or butter
1 batch puff pastry (page 281)
1 egg, lightly beaten

SERVES 6

PREHEAT the oven to 425°F. To make the pâté, melt half the butter in a frying pan and add the shallots and garlic. Cook until they are softened but not browned.

REMOVE any discolored spots from the chicken livers, wash and pat dry. Add the chicken livers to the frying pan and sauté for 4–5 minutes, or until cooked but still a little pink in the middle. Let the livers cool completely and then process in a food processor with the rest of the butter and the brandy. Alternatively, push the chopped livers through a sieve and mix with the butter and brandy. Season.

TIE the beef four or five times along its length to keep its shape. Heat the drippings in a roasting pan and brown the beef on all sides, then put in the oven and roast for 20 minutes. Allow to cool and remove the string.

REDUCE the oven temperature to 400°F. Roll the pastry into a rectangle just big enough to cover the beef fillet completely. Trim the edges and keep them for decoration. Spread the pâté over the pastry, leaving a border around the edge. Brush the border with beaten egg.

LAY the fillet on the pastry and wrap it up tightly like a package, pressing the seams together firmly and tucking the ends under. Put the package, seam side down, on a baking sheet and brush all over with beaten egg. Cut pieces from the trimmings to decorate the pastry and brush with beaten egg. Bake for 25–30 minutes for rare and 35–40 minutes for medium. Allow the beef to rest for 5 minutes before carving.

PAVÉ meaning cobblestone, these are thick pieces of cured pork *saucisson sec*. The casing is made from pig's stomach and they are air-dried.

FAGOT thin, long air-dried pork *saucissons secs* that resemble the bundles of sticks they are named after. Single lengths of sausage are called batons.

CERVELAS a specialty of Lyon found on its *assiette lyonnaise*, this boiling sausage is cooked by poaching in water or red wine and is flavored with pistachio (*above*), truffle or mushroom.

BRIDE a rustic *saucisson sec* that is eaten thinly sliced. The white bloom is produced by yeast during the curing process. Eat thinly sliced with cornichons and butter.

BOUDIN BLANC an expensive northern specialty made from white pork meat or chicken, cream and seasoning. Precooked, they are heated up and often served with apples or in a cream sauce.

CONFIT DE CANARD pieces of duck that are salted, then cooked in their own fat until very tender. Used in dishes like cassoulet, goose is also traditionally prepared in this way.

JAMBON hams are produced all over France, with the most famous coming from Ardennes and Bayonne. This local ham from the South is salt-cured and sold on the bone. Eat thinly sliced.

CRÉPINE the white lacy caul-fat from pigs used to wrap packages of sausage meat such as crépinettes and caillettes. It helps keep the shape as well as baste it while it cooks.

SAUCISSE A CUIRE known as boiling sausages, these fatty sausages are usually poached. They are often served with a hot wine sauce.

JÉSUS an air-cured coarse pork and pork fat *saucisson sec* from Lyon. The name comes from the idea that the sausage looks like the swaddled baby Jesus. Eat thinly sliced.

JAMBON DE PARIS a cooked ham sold on or off the bone and unsmoked or lightly smoked. Produced all over France by artisans and commercially.

RILETTES a slow-cooked preserved meat traditionally shredded using two forks. They can be pork, goose, duck or rabbit depending on the region. Serve with bread or toast.

ARTISAN CHARCUTIERS are found selling their products in markets and charcuteries all over France, often made using traditional methods of drying, smoking and cooking. Each region has its own specialties, such as these myrtilles from Provence, many of which are not found outside the area, and are flavored with local vegetables, fruits, herbs and spices. Flavorings include garlic, though this is usually used in

CHARCUTERIE

IN FRANCE, ALMOST EVERY VILLAGE HAS A CHARCUTERIE SELLING FRESH AND AIR-DRIED SAUSAGES, HAMS AND PÂTÉS, AND THE ART OF THE ARTISAN CHARCUTIER LIVES ON IN A WEALTH OF SPECIAL LOCAL AND REGIONAL CHARCUTERIE.

Meaning literally "cured meat," the term charcuterie generally refers to cured or cooked pork products, though other meats can be used, from game and beef in sausages, to goose and duck in foie gras and pâtés. Traditionally horse and donkey meat were also used, but this is increasingly rare. Charcuterie is associated with pork more than any other meat as virtually any part of the pig can be transformed into something to eat. Pigs have traditionally been kept by rural families and slaughtered in the autumn, some meat eaten fresh and the rest made into items that could be preserved and eaten through the winter.

Charcuterie is made commercially and by artisan charcutiers all over France. In the Northeast, charcuterie from Alsace has been influenced by Germanic traditions, while the forests of the Ardennes have provided the game, such as wild boar, for hams and pâtés. The Northwest is famous for its rillettes from Tours and Vouvray, and the Southwest for its goose and duck foie gras and Bayonne ham. The East, specifically Lyon, is the acknowledged home of charcuterie and its andouillettes, Jésus, cervelas and rosettes are well known all over France. The South makes good *saucissons secs* and air-dried hams.

SAUCISSES

Saucisses, or fresh sausages, vary from the coarse pork saucisse de Toulouse to the hot dog-like saucisse de Strasbourg. Boudin noir, a kind of black pudding, and boudin

FOIE GRAS has been a great delicacy since ancient times, and in Castels in Périgord, Marc and Marcelle Boureau continue to produce it at their farm by traditional methods. Their geese are raised in warm barns where they listen to music to calm them (stressed birds do not eat or grow well), and they come outside during the day to feed and wander about. When they are from three to six months old, Marc begins the

fresh sausages rather than *saucissons secs* as it may turn rancid; caraway seeds (*carvi*), used in the charcuterie of Alsace; *quatre-épices* (cinnamon, pepper, nutmeg and cloves), added to sausages and pâtés; juniper berries (*baies de genièvre*), used to flavor game; sage (*sauge*), mixed with pork; and thyme (*thym*), added to sausages and pâtés, especially rabbit and chicken.

blanc are sausage-like charcuterie, while andouilles and andouillettes are sausages made from chitterlings or tripe. Fresh sausages are often poached rather than broiled and these *saucisses à cuire* (boiling sausages), like cervelas, are generally larger and fattier and used in dishes such as a potato salad, *choucroute garnie* or *cassoulet*.

SAUCISSONS SECS

Saucissons secs, or dried sausages, are like Italian salamis and are usually cured by air-drying. They need no cooking and are sliced and eaten cold. Most are made from pork, though some may include horse meat or beef. Spicing and flavoring vary by region and much of what is made is only sold locally. Lyon is a great center for this charcuterie, including rosettes and Jésus, and elsewhere other fine products include pork and beef saucisson d'Arles from Provence, French and German-influenced *saucissons* from Alsace, and rustic, coarse sausages, such as saucisson sec d'Auvergne, from Limousin and the Auvergne.

JAMBON

Hams have been made in France since before the Romans arrived. Jambon de Bayonne is one of the best-known *jambon cru* (raw ham), air-dried and sweet like Parma ham Alsace and the Ardennes are famous for *jambon cru fumé* (smoked raw hams). Cooked hams are called *jambon* or *jambon cuit*.

PÂTES AND TERRINES

Originally meaning more a "pie" (now called *pâté en croûte*), pâté now refers only to the filling and is similar to a terrine. Other prepared items sold by charcuteries include *galantines*, *rillettes* and *rillons* (fried pieces of pork belly).

FOIE GRAS AND CONFITS

Fattened duck and goose livers, a specialty of southwest France, are sold on their own or made into parfait (mixed with a little chicken liver) or pâté (made with half pork pâté). Confit is made from pork, duck or goose meat cooked in ts own fat and used in *cassoulet* and *garbure*, a hearty cabbage soup.

gavage, feeding them corn by hand through a funnel so that in a few weeks their liver becomes three or four times its normal size. The geese are killed on the farm and the foie gras prepared there, along with confit made from the meat by cooking it slowly in goose fat. Today, *foie gras d'oie* is increasingly rare as more farmers switch to ducks, which are less delicate to raise and take less time to fatten.

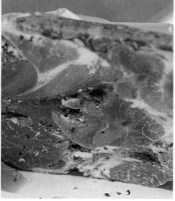

MEDALLION AUX AMANDES air-dried pork *saucisson sec* studded with almonds and pressed into a flattish shape. Eaten as part of an *assiette de charcuterie* (charcuterie plate).

TERRINE DE CAMPAGNE a cooked country terrine made from coarsely chopped pork, rabbit or game, flavored with garlic, herbs or spices. Generally made in an earthenware terrine.

SAUCISSE SÈCHE a coarse air-dried link of pork sausage set in a loop shape. A specialty of the South and usually smaller than *saucissons secs*, these garlic ones are from Provence.

JAMBON PERSILLÉ cured ham and pork shoulder set in aspic and flavored with wine, parsley and vegetables. This Burgundian specialty is thinly sliced to eat as hors d'oeuvres or on a picnic.

BOUDIN NOIR blood sausage made all over France, but a specialty of the Northwest. Often flavored with apples or chestnuts, this precooked sausage is fried or broiled before eating.

MYRTILLE coarse air-dried *saucisson sec*. It is named after bilberries (a relative of blueberries) that grow wild and are the same color as the sausage's skin.

ANDOUILLETTE made all over France, these vary regionally and can be made from calves' or pigs' intestines (chitterlings). Sold precooked, they are then fried or broiled and eaten hot.

SAUCISSE DE FRANCFORT a pork boiling sausage made in the style of hot dogs and poached before being eaten. Widely eaten all over France and used in casseroles and salads.

FROMAGE DE TÊTE "head cheese," or brawn, made from the meat of a pig's head, which is cooked and then set in a flavored aspic.

MERGUEZ a sausage originating in North Africa and made from beef, which has been adopted by the French. They are flavored with harissa and are often broiled and served with couscous.

SAUCSSON D'ARDÈCHE air-dried pork *saucisson sec* from the Ardèche flavored with garlic and wine. The wrapping implies this local sausage is an old family recipe. Eaten sliced.

ROSETTE one of France's, and especially Lyon's, great *saucissons secs*, it is made from seasoned pork and back fat in a natural case. Tied into long links, they are slightly fatter at one end.

PORK NOISETTES WITH PRUNES

PORK WITH PRUNES IS A TYPICAL DISH OF THE ORCHARD-RICH TOURAINE REGION. IT IS SOMETIMES SAID THAT THE FRENCH GENERALLY DO NOT COMBINE FRUIT WITH MEAT, SWEET FLAVORS WITH SAVORY, BUT PRUNES AND APPLES ARE BOTH ENTHUSIASTICALLY COMBINED WITH PORK.

8 pork noisettes (medallions)
  or 2 x 13 oz. pork fillets
16 prunes, pitted
1 tablespoon oil
3 tablespoons butter
1 onion, finely chopped
1/2 cup white wine
1 1/4 cups chicken or brown stock
1 bay leaf
2 thyme sprigs
1 cup heavy cream

SERVES 4

TRIM any excess fat from the pork, making sure you get rid of any membrane that will cause the pork to shrink. If you are using pork fillet, cut each fillet into four diagonal slices. Put the prunes in a small saucepan, cover with cold water and bring to a boil. Reduce the heat and simmer for 5 minutes. Drain well.

HEAT the oil in a large heavy-bottomed frying pan and add half the butter. When the butter starts foaming, add the pork, in batches if necessary, and sauté on both sides until cooked. Transfer the pork to a warm plate, cover and keep warm.

POUR OFF the excess fat from the frying pan. Melt the remaining butter, add the onion and cook over a low heat until softened but not browned. Add the wine, bring to a boil and simmer for 2 minutes. Add the stock, bay leaf and thyme and bring to a boil. Reduce the heat and simmer for 10 minutes or until reduced by half.

STRAIN the stock into a bowl and rinse the frying pan. Return the stock to the frying pan, add the cream and prunes and simmer for 8 minutes, or until the sauce thickens slightly. Put the pork back into the pan and simmer until heated through.

Sauté the pork on both sides, then keep it warm while you make the sauce.

Cervelas often contain pistachio nuts for extra flavor.

LYONNAIS SAUSAGES

3 tablespoons butter
1 lb. onions, chopped
large pinch of sugar
12 pork sausages with pistachio
　　nuts (*cervelas* or *saucisses*
　　à cuire)
2 tablespoons white wine vinegar
1/2 cup dry white wine
3 tablespoons finely chopped
　　parsley

SERVES 6

MELT the butter in a large saucepan and add the onions and sugar, stirring to coat the onions in the butter. Cover the saucepan and cook the onions over low heat for 40–45 minutes, or until caramelized. Preheat the broiler.

PRICK the sausages and poach gently in boiling water for 15 minutes until cooked through. Drain and then broil until golden brown.

MIX TOGETHER the vinegar and wine. Increase the heat under the caramelized onions and add the vinegar and wine. Allow to bubble for a few minutes until about half of the liquid has evaporated. Stir in the parsley and taste for seasoning. Serve with the sausages.

ANDOUILLETTES

THESE TRIPE SAUSAGES ARE OFTEN BOUGHT PRE-COOKED AND DO NOT NEED TO BE BOILED. THEY CAN BE FOUND THROUGHOUT FRANCE, ALTHOUGH TYPES DO VARY A LITTLE BETWEEN REGIONS. SOME ARE MADE FROM PIG'S INTESTINES, OTHERS CONTAIN VEAL.

8 andouillettes

SERVES 4

IF YOU have bought andouillettes that are loosely wrapped rather than cased in sausage skins, slash them a couple of times across the top.

PREHEAT the broiler to moderate heat. Prick the andouillettes all over with a small skewer and arrange them in one layer on a baking sheet. Broil the sausages gently, turning them frequently until they are browned and cooked through. Serve with mashed potatoes or potato gratin and plenty of French mustard.

ANDOUILLETTES

SALT PORK WITH LENTILS

IT IS THOUGHT THAT THE DRY CLIMATE AND VOLCANIC SOIL AROUND THE TOWN OF LE PUY-EN-VELAY
IN THE AUVERGNE IS THE LUCKY COMBINATION THAT PRODUCES THE REGION'S SUPERIOR GREEN
LENTILS. THEY ARE MORE EXPENSIVE THAN OTHER VARIETIES, BUT HAVE A SUPERB FLAVOR.

2 lb. salt pork belly, cut into thick
 strips
1 small salt pork knuckle
1 large carrot, cut into chunks
1/4 lb. rutabagas or turnips, peeled
 and cut into chunks
1 cup leeks, white part only, thickly
 sliced
1 parsnip, cut into chunks
1 onion, studded with 4 cloves
1 garlic clove
bouquet garni
2 bay leaves
6 juniper berries, slightly crushed
11 oz. Puy lentils
2 tablespoons chopped parsley

SERVES 6

DEPENDING ON the saltiness of the pork you are
using, you may need to soak it in cold water for
several hours or blanch it before using. Ask your
butcher whether to do this.

PUT the pork in a large saucepan with all the
ingredients except the lentils and parsley. Stir
thoroughly, then add just enough water to cover
the ingredients. Bring to a boil, then reduce the
heat, cover the saucepan and allow to simmer
gently for 1¼ hours.

PUT the lentils in a sieve and rinse under cold
running water. Add to the saucepan and stir,
then replace the lid and simmer for another
45–50 minutes, or until the pork and lentils
are tender.

DRAIN the saucepan into a colander, discarding
the liquid. Return the contents of the colander to
the saucepan, except for the whole onion which
can be thrown away. Season the pork and lentils
with plenty of black pepper, and taste to see if
you need any salt. Stir in the parsley.

Use a saucepan large enough to
fit all the ingredients comfortably.
Unlike other varieties, Puy lentils
keep their shape when cooked.

Braise the red cabbage slowly to bring out the sweetness.

PORK CHOPS WITH BRAISED RED CABBAGE

BRAISED RED CABBAGE
2 tablespoons clarified butter
1 onion, finely chopped
1 garlic clove, crushed
1 small red cabbage, shredded
1 eating apple, peeled, cored and
  finely sliced
$1/3$ cup red wine
1 tablespoon red wine vinegar
$1/4$ teaspoon ground cloves
1 tablespoon finely chopped sage

1 tablespoon clarified butter
4 x 6 oz. pork chops, trimmed
$1/3$ cup white wine
$12/3$ cups chicken stock
3 tablespoons heavy cream
$11/2$ tablespoons Dijon mustard
4 sage leaves

SERVES 4

TO BRAISE the cabbage, put the clarified butter in a large saucepan, add the onion and garlic and cook until softened but not browned. Add the cabbage, apple, wine, vinegar, cloves and sage and season with salt and pepper. Cover the saucepan and cook for 30 minutes over very low heat. Uncover the saucepan and cook, stirring, for another 5 minutes to evaporate any liquid.

MEANWHILE, heat the clarified butter in a frying pan, season the pork chops and brown well on both sides. Add the wine and stock, cover and simmer for 20 minutes, or until the pork is tender.

REMOVE the chops from the frying pan and strain the liquid. Return the liquid to the frying pan, bring to a boil and cook until reduced by two-thirds. Add the cream and mustard and stir over very low heat without allowing it to boil, until the sauce has thickened slightly. Pour over the pork chops and garnish with sage. Serve with the red cabbage.

PORK CHOPS WITH CALVADOS

2 tablespoons butter
2 eating apples, cored, each cut
  into 8 wedges
$1/2$ teaspoon sugar
$11/2$ tablespoons oil
4 x 6 oz. pork chops, trimmed
3 tablespoons Calvados
2 shallots, finely chopped
1 cup dry cider
$1/2$ cup chicken stock
$1/2$ cup heavy cream

SERVES 4

MELT half the butter in a frying pan, add the apples and sprinkle with the sugar. Cook over low heat, turning occasionally, until tender and glazed.

HEAT the oil in a frying pan and sauté the pork chops until cooked, turning once. Pour the excess fat from the pan, add the Calvados and flambé by lighting the pan with your gas flame or a match (stand back when you do this and keep a pan lid handy for emergencies). Transfer the pork to a plate and keep warm.

ADD the remaining butter to the pan and cook the shallots until soft but not brown. Add the cider, stock and cream and bring to a boil. Reduce the heat and simmer for 15 minutes, or until reduced enough to coat the back of a spoon.

SEASON the sauce, add the pork and simmer for 3 minutes to heat through. Serve with the apples.

BLANQUETTE DE VEAU

BLANQUETTES ARE USUALLY SERVED WITH PLAIN WHITE RICE OR BOILED NEW POTATOES. THEY CAN VARY FROM REGION TO REGION, BUT THIS ONE WITH MUSHROOMS AND ONIONS AND A SAUCE THICKENED WITH CREAM AND EGGS IS A CLASSIC RECIPE.

1 lb. 10 oz. boneless veal shoulder, cut into 1¼ inch cubes
4 cups brown stock
4 cloves
½ large onion
1 small carrot, roughly chopped
1 leek, white part only, roughly chopped
1 celery stalk, roughly chopped
1 bay leaf
2 tablespoons butter
4 tablespoons all-purpose flour
1 tablespoon lemon juice
1 egg yolk
¼ cup heavy cream

ONION GARNISH
½ lb. pickling or pearl onions
1 tablespoon butter
1 teaspoon superfine sugar

MUSHROOM GARNISH
1 tablespoon butter
2 teaspoons lemon juice
5 oz. button mushrooms, trimmed

SERVES 6

PUT the veal in a large saucepan, cover with cold water and bring to a boil. Drain, rinse well and drain again. Return to the saucepan and add the stock. Press the cloves into the onion and add to the saucepan with the remaining vegetables and bay leaf.

BRING to a boil, reduce the heat, cover and simmer for 40–60 minutes, or until the veal is tender. Skim the surface occasionally. Strain, reserving the cooking liquid and throwing away the vegetables. Keep the veal warm.

TO MAKE the onion garnish, put the onions in a small saucepan with enough water to half cover them. Add the butter and sugar. Place a crumpled piece of waxed paper directly over the onions. Bring to a simmer and cook over low heat for 20 minutes, or until the water has evaporated and the onions are tender.

TO MAKE the mushroom garnish, half-fill a small pan with water and bring to a boil. Add the butter, lemon juice and mushrooms and simmer for 3 minutes, or until the mushrooms are tender. Drain the mushrooms, discarding the liquid.

HEAT the butter in a large saucepan. Stir in the flour to make a roux and cook, stirring, for 3 minutes without allowing the roux to brown. Remove from the heat and gradually add the cooking liquid from the veal, stirring each time you add, until the mixture is smooth. Return to the heat and whisk until the sauce comes to a boil, then reduce the heat to low and simmer for 8 minutes, or until the sauce coats the back of the spoon.

ADD the lemon juice and season well. Quickly stir in the egg yolk and cream, then add the veal and the onion and mushroom garnishes. Reheat gently, without boiling, to serve.

Strain the cooking liquid from the veal and then use to give flavor to the velouté sauce.

Weekly markets offer commercial and homegrown produce.

Spread the spinach filling over the piece of veal, then roll up like a jelly roll. Tie with string to keep the bacon slices in place and prevent the veal from unrolling.

ROAST VEAL STUFFED WITH HAM AND SPINACH

1/2 lb. spinach leaves
2 garlic cloves, crushed
2 tablespoons finely chopped
    parsley
2 teaspoons Dijon mustard
3 1/2 oz. ham on the bone, diced
finely grated zest of 1 lemon
1 x 1 1/4 lb. piece boneless veal loin
    or fillet, beaten with a meat mallet
    to measure 12 x 6 inches (ask
    your butcher to do this)
4 slices bacon
2 tablespoons olive oil
3 tablespoons butter
16 baby carrots
8 small potatoes, unpeeled
8 shallots
3/4 cup dry (*Sercial*) Madeira

SERVES 4

PREHEAT the oven to 325°F. Wash the spinach and put in a large saucepan with just the water clinging to the leaves. Cover the saucepan and steam the spinach for 2 minutes or until just wilted. Drain, cool and squeeze dry with your hands. Chop and mix with the garlic, parsley, mustard, ham and lemon zest. Season well.

SPREAD the spinach filling over the center of the piece of veal. Starting from one of the shorter sides, roll up like a jelly roll. Wrap the slices of bacon over the meat and season well. Tie with string several times along the roll to secure the bacon and make sure the roll doesn't unravel.

HEAT the olive oil and half of the butter in a large frying pan and add the carrots, potatoes and shallots. Briefly brown the vegetables and then transfer to a roasting pan. Brown the veal package on all sides, then place on top of the vegetables. Add 4 tablespoons of the Madeira to the frying pan and boil, stirring, for 30 seconds to deglaze the pan. Pour over the veal.

ROAST the meat for 30 minutes, then cover the top with aluminum foil to prevent from over-browning. Roast for another 45–60 minutes or until the juices run clear when you pierce the thickest part of the meat with a skewer. Wrap the meat in aluminum foil and allow to rest. Test the vegetables and return to the oven for a while if they're not yet tender. Remove them from the pan.

PLACE the roasting pan over moderate heat and add the rest of the Madeira. Allow it to bubble, then add the rest of the butter and season the sauce to taste. Slice the veal thickly and arrange the slices of meat on top of the vegetables. Pour over some of the Madeira sauce and serve the rest separately in a gravy boat.

VEAL PAUPIETTES

PAUPIETTES ARE SLICES OF MEAT WRAPPED AROUND A SAVORY STUFFING AND ROLLED UP TO MAKE LITTLE BUNDLES. IN FRANCE, THEY ARE ALSO REFERRED TO AS "*OISEAUX SANS TÊTES*," WHICH MEANS LITERALLY "BIRDS WITHOUT HEADS."

STUFFING
2 tablespoons butter
2 shallots, finely chopped
1 garlic clove, crushed
6¹/₂ oz. ground pork
6¹/₂ oz. ground veal
1 egg
2 tablespoons dry white wine
3 tablespoons fresh white
   bread crumbs
2 tablespoons finely chopped
   parsley

4 x 5 oz. veal escalopes (scallopine
   slices), pounded flat

SAUCE
2 tablespoons clarified butter
1 onion, diced
1 carrot, diced
1 celery stalk, diced
¹/₃ cup white wine
2 teaspoons tomato paste
1 bay leaf
1¹/₃ cups brown stock

SERVES 4

TO MAKE the stuffing, melt the butter in a small saucepan and cook the shallots over gentle heat until softened but not browned. Add the garlic and cook for another 2 minutes, then set aside to cool. Mix with the other stuffing ingredients and season with salt and pepper.

LAY the veal escalopes flat and spread evenly with the stuffing, leaving a narrow border around the edge. Roll up the paupiettes, then tie up with string as you would a package.

TO MAKE the sauce, melt half the clarified butter in a large sauté pan or frying pan. Add the onion, carrot and celery and soften over low heat. Increase the heat to brown the vegetables, stirring occasionally. Remove from the pan.

HEAT the remaining clarified butter in the sauté pan and brown the paupiettes, turning once. Remove from the pan, pour in the white wine and boil, stirring, for 30 seconds to deglaze the pan. Add the tomato paste and bay leaf. Pour in the stock and bring to a simmer before adding the vegetables and paupiettes.

COVER the pan and cook for 12–15 minutes, or until a skewer poked into the center of a paupiette comes out too hot to touch. Remove the paupiettes from the pan and keep warm.

STRAIN the sauce, pressing down on the vegetables with a spoon to extract as much liquid as possible. Return the sauce to the pan and boil until reduced by half and syrupy. Slice each paupiette into five pieces and serve with a little sauce poured over the top.

Spread the filling over the veal escalopes, then roll up and tie into packages with string.

Sidewalk tables in Paris.

Season the lamb generously and roast with just the rosemary and garlic for 20 minutes. Add the vegetables in stages, depending on how long they take to cook.

ROAST LEG OF LAMB WITH SPRING VEGETABLES

A POPULAR MEAT IN FRANCE, LAMB COMES IN VARIOUS GUISES. IN SOME AREAS IT FEEDS ON LUSH GRASSLANDS AND, IN OTHERS, ON WILD HERBS. IN NORMANDY, PICARDIE AND BORDEAUX, FLAVORSOME PRE-SALÉ LAMBS FEED ON SALT MARSHES AND ARE OFTEN SERVED WITHOUT ADDED FLAVORINGS.

1 x 4 lb. leg of lamb
3 rosemary sprigs
6 garlic cloves, unpeeled
1 lb. small potatoes, halved
1/2 lb. baby carrots
6 small leeks
1/2 lb. small zucchini
1 1/2 tablespoons all-purpose flour
1/2 cup red wine
2/3 cup brown stock

SERVES 6

PREHEAT the oven to 400°F. Rub the lamb all over with salt and pepper. Put the lamb in a roasting pan, lay the rosemary sprigs on top and scatter the garlic around the lamb. Roast for 20 minutes, then turn the lamb over.

ADD the potatoes to the roasting pan and toss in the lamb fat, then return to the oven for another 15 minutes. Turn the lamb again and cook for another 15 minutes.

ADD the baby carrots and leeks to the pan, toss with the potatoes in the lamb fat and turn the lamb again. Roast for 15 more minutes, then add the zucchini. Toss all the vegetables in the lamb fat and turn the leg of lamb again.

ROAST for another 15 minutes, then take the lamb out of the roasting pan to rest. The lamb will be rare—if you prefer, cook it for another 5–10 minutes. Remove the vegetables and garlic from the pan and keep warm.

TO MAKE the gravy, spoon the fat from the surface of the meat juices. Place the roasting pan over moderate heat on the stove top and stir in the flour to make a roux. Cook, stirring, for 2 minutes, then gradually stir in the wine and stock. Boil the gravy for 2 minutes, then strain into a gravy boat.

CARVE the lamb and serve with the spring vegetables and garlic. Serve the gravy separately.

LAMB BRAISED WITH BEANS

2/3 cup dried haricot (white) beans
1 x 2 lb. boned shoulder of lamb,
   tied with string to keep its shape
2 tablespoons clarified butter
2 carrots, diced
2 large onions, chopped
4 garlic cloves, unpeeled
bouquet garni
1 cup dry red wine
1 cup brown stock

SERVES 4

PUT the beans in a large bowl and cover with plenty of water. Allow to soak for 8–12 hours, then drain. Bring a large saucepan of water to a boil, add the beans and return to a boil. Reduce the heat to moderate and cook the beans, partially covered, for 40 minutes. Drain well.

RUB the lamb all over with salt and pepper. Heat the butter over high heat in a large casserole with a tight-fitting lid. Add the lamb and cook for 8–10 minutes, turning every few minutes until well browned. Remove the lamb.

REHEAT the casserole over high heat and add the carrots, onions, garlic and bouquet garni. Reduce the heat and cook, stirring, for 8–10 minutes or until softened. Increase the heat to high and pour in the wine. Boil, stirring, for 30 seconds to deglaze the casserole, then return the lamb to the casserole. Add the stock.

BRING TO a boil, then cover and reduce the heat to low. Braise the meat for 1 1/2 hours, turning twice. If the lid is not tight fitting, cover the casserole with aluminum foil and then put the lid on top.

ADD the cooked beans to the lamb and return to a boil over high heat. Reduce the heat to low, cover the casserole again and cook for another 30 minutes.

TAKE the lamb out of the casserole, cover and allow to rest for 10 minutes before carving. Discard the bouquet garni. Skim the excess fat from the surface of the sauce and, if the sauce is too thin, boil over high heat for 5 minutes or until thickened slightly. Taste for seasoning. Carve the lamb and arrange on a platter. Spoon the beans around the lamb and drizzle with the gravy. Serve the rest of the gravy separately.

Use the same casserole to brown the lamb, to soften the vegetables and then braise the meat. This will help to strengthen the flavor of the dish.

Fruit delivery at Saint-Rèmy produce shop.

NAVARIN A LA PRINTANIÈRE

NAVARIN A LA PRINTANIÈRE IS TRADITIONALLY MADE TO WELCOME SPRING AND THE NEW CROP OF YOUNG VEGETABLES. NAVARINS, OR STEWS, CAN ALSO BE MADE ALL YEAR ROUND, USING OLDER WINTER ROOT VEGETABLES SUCH AS POTATOES, CARROTS AND TURNIPS.

2 lb. lean lamb shoulder
2 tablespoons butter
1 onion, chopped
1 garlic clove, crushed
1 tablespoon all-purpose flour
2 cups brown stock
bouquet garni
18 baby carrots
8 large-bulb scallions
6 oz. baby turnips
6 oz. small potatoes
1 cup peas, fresh or frozen

SERVES 6

TRIM the lamb of any fat and sinew and then cut it into bite-size pieces. Heat the butter over high heat in a large casserole. Brown the lamb in two or three batches, then remove from the casserole.

ADD the onion to the casserole and cook, stirring occasionally, over moderate heat for 3 minutes or until softened but not browned. Add the garlic and cook for another minute or until aromatic.

RETURN the meat and any juices to the casserole and sprinkle with the flour. Stir over high heat until the meat is well coated and the liquid is bubbling, then gradually stir in the stock. Add the bouquet garni and bring to a boil. Reduce the heat to low, cover the casserole and cook for 1 1/4 hours.

TRIM the carrots, leaving a little bit of green stalk, and do the same with the scallions and baby turnips. Cut the potatoes in half if they are large.

ADD the vegetables to the casserole, bring to a boil and simmer, covered, for 15 minutes or until the vegetables are tender. (If you are using frozen peas, add them right at the end so they just heat through.) Season with plenty of salt and pepper before serving.

Brown the lamb in a couple of batches so that you don't lower the temperature by overcrowding. Once all the meat is browned and coated with flour, slowly stir in the stock.

LAMB STUFFED WITH COUSCOUS AND ALMONDS

THE ALMONDS GIVE THIS STUFFING A LOVELY CRUNCHY TEXTURE. WHEN YOU BUY THE MEAT, BE SURE TO TELL THE BUTCHER YOU ARE INTENDING TO STUFF THE LAMB AND YOU WILL NEED THE HOLE IN THE MEAT TO BE FAIRLY LARGE. SERVE WITH BOULANGÈRE POTATOES.

1/3 cup olive oil
1 small red pepper
1 small yellow pepper
1/4 cup whole blanched almonds
1 small onion, chopped
4 garlic cloves
4 oz. eggplant, diced
14 1/2 oz. can diced tomatoes
pinch of sugar
1 tablespoon thyme leaves
2 teaspoons capers, rinsed and
   squeezed dry
8 black olives, pitted and finely
   chopped
1/4 cup couscous
1 x 3 lb. butterflied leg of lamb
1/2 small onion

GRAVY
1 tablespoon all-purpose flour
1 teaspoon tomato paste
1 1/4 cups brown stock
1/3 cup red wine

SERVES 6

PREHEAT the oven to 400°F. Rub 1 tablespoon of oil over the peppers and roast for 40–45 minutes, or until blackened. Cool, then peel the peppers and cut into long thin strips.

LIGHTLY TOAST the almonds in a dry frying pan, then chop. Heat 1 tablespoon of oil in the pan and cook the onion until softened. Crush 2 garlic cloves, add to the onion and cook for 5 minutes. Add 2 tablespoons of oil and the eggplant and cook for 10 minutes. Add the tomato and sugar and simmer until fairly dry. Remove from the heat and mix in the thyme, capers and olives. Cool.

POUR 1/3–1/2 cup boiling water onto the couscous. Let sit for 5 minutes, then fluff the grains with a fork. Add the couscous, peppers and almonds to the eggplant mixture and season well.

INCREASE the oven to 450°F. Push as much stuffing as you can into the cavity of the lamb. (Put any leftover stuffing in a flameproof dish.) Fold the meat over the stuffing at each end and secure with skewers. Put the remaining cloves of garlic and the half onion in a roasting pan and place the lamb on top. Roast for 30 minutes, then reduce the oven to 350°F and cook for 1 1/2 hours (cover with aluminum foil if lamb appears to be over-browning). Bake any extra stuffing for the last 20 minutes.

TO MAKE the gravy, remove the meat from the pan, cover and allow to rest. Strain off all but 2 tablespoons of the fat from the pan, then place over moderate heat. Stir in the flour and tomato paste and gradually add the stock, stirring. Add the wine slowly, stirring until the gravy reaches the consistency you like. Season well. Slice the meat and serve with the gravy and any extra stuffing.

The couscous and almond filling should be fairly dry. Pack as much as you can into the lamb and cook the rest separately.

CASSOULET

CASSOULET TAKES ITS NAME FROM THE TRADITIONAL CASSEROLE USED FOR COOKING THIS STEW. IT VARIES REGIONALLY IN THE SOUTH OF FRANCE, WITH THE BEST-KNOWN VERSIONS HAILING FROM CARCASSONNE, TOULOUSE AND CASTELNAUDARY.

Preparing a cassoulet can be time-consuming as the different ingredients are cooked separately and then layered in a deep casserole. Liquid is added to cover the beans.

2 cups dried haricot (white) beans
bouquet garni
1/2 large onion, cut into quarters
2 garlic cloves, crushed
7 oz. salt pork or unsmoked bacon, cut into cubes
1 tablespoon clarified butter
13 oz. lamb shoulder
11 oz. boiling sausages (*saucisses à cuire*)
1 celery stalk, sliced
4 pieces duck confit (page 147) or 4 pieces roasted duck
6 large tomatoes
6 oz. Toulouse sausage
4 slices baguette, made into crumbs

SERVES 6

PUT the beans in a bowl and cover with cold water. Soak overnight, then drain and rinse.

PUT the beans in a large saucepan with the bouquet garni, onion, garlic and salt pork. Add 8–12 cups of cold water, bring to a boil and then simmer for 1 hour.

HEAT the clarified butter in a frying pan. Cut the lamb into eight pieces and brown in the butter. Add the lamb, boiling sausages, celery and duck confit to the top of the beans and push into the liquid. Score a cross in the top of each tomato, plunge into boiling water for 20 seconds, then peel the skin away from the cross. Chop the tomatoes finely, discarding the cores, and add to the top of the cassoulet. Push into the liquid and cook for another hour.

BROWN the Toulouse sausage in the frying pan and add to the top of the cassoulet. Push into the liquid and cook for 30 minutes more. Preheat the oven to 315°F.

DISCARD the bouquet garni. Strain the liquid into a saucepan and boil over moderate heat until reduced by two-thirds. Remove all the meat from the saucepan and slice the sausages and pull the duck meat from the bones. Layer the meat and beans, alternately, in a deep casserole. Pour in the liquid to just cover the beans.

SPRINKLE the cassoulet with the bread crumbs and bake for 40 minutes. Every 10 minutes, break the bread crumb crust with the back of a spoon to let a little liquid come through. If the beans look a bit dry, add a little stock or water to the edge of the dish. Serve straight from the casserole.

POT AU FEU

THE SIMPLICITY OF THIS DISH OF BOILED MEAT AND VEGETABLES MEANS YOU NEED TO USE THE VERY BEST QUALITY INGREDIENTS. REGIONAL RECIPES VARY, BUT POT AU FEU IS USUALLY SERVED WITH THE MEATS SLICED AND THE BROTH IN A SEPARATE BOWL.

1 tablespoon oil
1 celery stalk, roughly chopped
2 carrots, roughly chopped
1/2 onion, roughly chopped
1³/₄ lb. beef shank with
   marrowbone
1³/₄ lb. piece beef chuck
2 bay leaves
4 thyme sprigs
a few parsley stalks
10 peppercorns
1³/₄ lb. beef short ribs

VEGETABLE GARNISH
1 large celery stalk
11 oz. small potatoes
10 oz. baby carrots, green tops
   trimmed
6 oz. baby turnips
11 oz. baby leeks

Dijon mustard and coarse sea salt,
   to serve

SERVES 4

HEAT the oil in a heavy-bottomed frying pan and cook the chopped celery, carrots and onion over moderately high heat for 10 minutes, or until they are browned.

REMOVE the meat from the beef shank and reserve the marrowbone. Tie the beef chuck with string so it looks like a package.

PUT 12 cups water in a large saucepan and bring to a boil. Add the browned vegetables, herbs, peppercorns, beef shank meat, ribs, and beef chuck to the saucepan. Return to a boil and skim off any fat that floats to the surface. Reduce the heat, and simmer for 2–2¹/₂ hours, or until the meat is very tender.

GENTLY REMOVE the meat to a clean saucepan and strain the cooking liquid over it. Throw away the vegetables. Season the meat with salt and pepper, add the marrowbone and simmer over moderate heat for about 10 minutes. Remove the marrowbone, gently push the marrow out of the bone and slice into six pieces.

MEANWHILE, to make the vegetable garnish, cut the celery into 2 inch lengths, then cut each piece in half lengthwise. Cook the potatoes in salted boiling water for 10 minutes, or until tender to the point of a knife, then drain. Add the celery, carrots, turnips and leeks to the meat and cook for 7 minutes. Add the potatoes and cook for another 3 minutes to heat through.

SLICE the meats and serve with the marrow and vegetables. Serve the broth separately in bowls, accompanied by plenty of mustard and sea salt.

While the pot au feu simmers, skim away the fat and foam that float to the surface.

CHOUCROUTE GARNIE

SAUERKRAUT (CHOUCROUTE), OR PICKLED CABBAGE, IS AN IMPORTANT INGREDIENT IN ALSACE CUISINE. THIS DISH CAN VARY ACCORDING TO THE NUMBER OF PEOPLE YOU WANT TO FEED—TRADITIONALLY, THE MORE PEOPLE THERE ARE, THE WIDER THE VARIETY OF MEAT USED.

Place the ham knuckle on top of the sauerkraut and add the other flavorings, then layer with the rest of the onion, sauerkraut and pork shoulder and belly.

2¹/₂ lb. fresh or canned sauerkraut
4 tablespoons bacon fat or lard
1 onion, chopped
1 large garlic clove, crushed
1 onion, studded with 4 cloves
1 ham knuckle or hock
2 bay leaves
2 carrots, diced
8 juniper berries, lightly crushed
1 x 14 oz. piece pork shoulder
14 oz. salt pork belly, cut into thick strips
²/₃ cup dry wine, preferably Riesling
12 small potatoes, unpeeled
3 boiling sausages (*saucisses à cuire*)
6 hot dogs

SERVES 8

PREHEAT the oven to 375°F. If you are using fresh sauerkraut, wash it under cold running water, then squeeze dry. If you are using a can or jar of sauerkraut, simply drain it well.

MELT the fat or lard in a large casserole, add the chopped onion and garlic and cook for 10 minutes, or until softened but not browned. Remove half the onion from the casserole and keep on one side. Add half the sauerkraut to the casserole, then place the whole onion and the ham knuckle or hock on the sauerkraut. Scatter the bay leaves, carrots and juniper berries over the top. Season.

NOW ADD the rest of the onion and the remaining sauerkraut and season again. Place the pork shoulder and strips of pork belly on top and pour in the wine and ¹/₂ cup water. Cook, covered, in the oven for 2¹/₂ hours (check after an hour and add a little more water if necessary). Add the whole potatoes and cook for another 30–40 minutes, or until the potatoes are tender.

POACH the boiling sausages in simmering water for 20 minutes, then add the hot dogs and poach for 10 minutes longer. Drain and keep warm. Discard the studded onion from the casserole. Cut any meat from the ham knuckle and slice the pork shoulder and sausages.

TO SERVE, arrange the piping hot sauerkraut on a large dish with the potatoes, sausages and pieces of meat.

SAUTÉED CALVES' LIVER

4 bacon slices, cut in half
4 x 5 oz. slices calves' liver
¾ cup all-purpose flour
1¹/₃ tablespoons butter

SERVES 4

HEAT a frying pan and cook the bacon until browned and crisp all over. Remove bacon with a slotted spoon and keep warm. Don't clean the pan.

PEEL OFF any membrane from the liver and cut out any veins with a sharp knife. Season the flour with salt and black pepper, then spread out on a baking sheet or board. Coat the liver with the flour and shake off the excess.

HEAT the butter in the frying pan with the bacon fat. When the butter is foaming, add the liver and cook for 90 seconds on each side (the liver should still be pink in the middle). Serve the liver and bacon with mashed potatoes.

BOUDIN NOIR WITH APPLES

THERE ARE SEVERAL VARIETIES OF BOUDIN NOIR AVAILABLE IN FRANCE. RECIPES VARY REGIONALLY AND CAN INCLUDE INGREDIENTS SUCH AS APPLES, CREAM AND CHESTNUTS. ENGLISH BLACK PUDDING CAN ALSO BE USED FOR THIS RECIPE.

Fry the boudin noir, then keep warm while you caramelize the apples in the same pan.

2 boudin noir or black puddings
2 eating apples
2 tablespoons butter
1 teaspoon brown sugar

SERVES 4

CUT the boudin noir into ¹/₂-inch slices. Peel and core the apples, cut them into quarters and then into thick slices. Heat the butter in a frying pan and fry the boudin noir on both sides until browned and warmed through. Remove from the pan and keep warm.

FRY the apple in the same pan over high heat, sprinkling it with the brown sugar to help it caramelize. When it is browned on both sides, place on a serving plate and arrange the boudin noir on top. Serve with pan-fried potatoes.

BOUDIN NOIR WITH APPLES

Use the same frying pan for browning all the ingredients separately. Once the sauce is made, return the kidneys and cocktail sausages to the pan.

KIDNEYS TURBIGO

THIS STEW OF KIDNEYS, SAUSAGES AND ONIONS IS NAMED AFTER THE TOWN OF TURBIGO IN LOMBARDY, THE SITE OF TWO FAMOUS FRENCH MILITARY VICTORIES OVER THE AUSTRIAN ARMY IN THE NINETEENTH CENTURY.

8 lamb kidneys
4 tablespoons butter
8 cocktail sausages
12 small pickling or pearl onions or
   shallots
1$^1/_3$ cups button mushrooms,
   sliced
1 tablespoon all-purpose flour
2 tablespoons dry sherry
2 teaspoons tomato paste
1 cup beef stock
2 tablespoons finely chopped
   parsley

CROUTES
oil, for brushing
2 garlic cloves, crushed
12 slices baguette, cut on an angle

SERVES 4

TRIM, HALVE and cut the white membrane from the kidneys with scissors. Heat half the butter in a large frying pan and cook the kidneys for 2 minutes to brown all over. Remove to a plate. Add the cocktail sausages to the frying pan and cook for 2 minutes until browned all over. Remove to a plate. Cut in half on the diagonal.

LOWER the heat and add the remaining butter to the frying pan. Cook the onions and mushrooms, stirring, for 5 minutes until soft and golden brown.

MIX TOGETHER the flour and sherry to make a smooth paste. Add the tomato paste and stock and mix until smooth.

REMOVE the frying pan from the heat and stir in the stock mixture. Return to the heat and stir until boiling and slightly thickened. Season well with salt and pepper. Return the kidneys and cocktail sausages to the sauce. Lower the heat, cover the pan and simmer for 25 minutes, or until the kidneys are cooked. Stir occasionally.

MEANWHILE, to make the croutes, preheat the oven to 350°F. Mix together the oil and garlic and brush over the bread slices. Place on a baking sheet and bake for 3–4 minutes. Turn over and bake for another 3 minutes until golden brown. Sprinkle the kidneys with parsley and serve with the croutes on the side.

VEGETABLES

A vegetable stall in Lyon's market.

Crème fraîche is regularly used in place of cream in French kitchens.

PURÉE OF RUTABAGAS

IT IS EASIEST TO MAKE VEGETABLE PURÉES IN A FOOD PROCESSOR OR BLENDER BUT, IF YOU DON'T HAVE ONE, MASH THEM WITH A POTATO MASHER OR USE A FOOD MILL. NEVER PURÉE POTATOES IN A PROCESSOR OR BLENDER—THEY BECOME GLUEY.

2 lb. rutabagas, peeled and chopped
3 tablespoons butter
1 tablespoon crème fraîche

SERVES 4

PUT the rutabagas in a saucepan, half-cover with water and add 1 teaspoon salt and 2 tablespoons of the butter. Bring to a boil and then reduce the heat, cover, and simmer for 30 minutes or until tender. Drain, reserving the cooking liquid.

PROCESS the rutabagas in a food processor or blender with enough of the cooking liquid to make a purée. Spoon into a saucepan and stir in the remaining butter and the crème fraîche. Reheat gently for a couple of minutes, stirring all the time.

PURÉE OF JERUSALEM ARTICHOKES

1 1/2 lb. Jerusalem artichokes, peeled
1/2 lb. potatoes, halved
1 tablespoon butter
2 tablespoons crème fraîche

SERVES 4

COOK the artichokes in boiling salted water for 20 minutes or until tender. Drain and then mix in a food processor or blender to purée.

COOK the potatoes in boiling salted water for 20 minutes, then drain and mash. Add to the artichoke with the butter and crème fraîche. Season, beat well and serve at once.

PURÉE OF SPINACH

2 lb. spinach leaves
3 tablespoons butter
4 tablespoons crème fraîche
1/2 teaspoon nutmeg

SERVES 4

WASH the spinach and put in a large saucepan with just the water clinging to the leaves. Cover the saucepan and steam the spinach for 2 minutes, or until just wilted. Drain, cool and squeeze dry with your hands. Finely chop.

PUT the spinach in a small saucepan and gently heat through. Increase the heat and add the butter, a little at a time, stirring continuously. Add the crème fraîche and stir into the spinach until it is glossy. Season well and stir in the nutmeg.

PURÉE OF SPINACH

STUFFED GREEN CABBAGE

CHOU FARCI IS A TRADITIONAL DISH FROM THE COOLER REGIONS OF FRANCE—THE CABBAGE CAN COPE WITH A HARSHER CLIMATE THAN MANY OTHER VEGETABLES AND IN THIS DISH IT IS PADDED OUT WITH MEAT TO MAKE A FILLING MAIN COURSE.

STUFFING
4 ripe tomatoes
1/3 cup pine nuts
1 lb. pork sausage meat
5 oz. bacon, finely chopped
1 onion, finely chopped
2 garlic cloves, crushed
5 oz. fresh bread crumbs
2 eggs
1 tablespoon mixed herbs

1 Savoy cabbage, or other loose-
  leafed cabbage
lemon juice

BRAISING LIQUID
2 tablespoons butter
2 shallots, chopped
1 large carrot, chopped
1 celery stalk, chopped
1 potato, diced
1/4 cup medium-dry white wine
1 cup chicken stock

SERVES 6

TO MAKE the stuffing, score a cross in the top of each tomato, plunge into boiling water for 20 seconds and then peel the skin away from the cross. Chop finely, discarding the cores. Toast the pine nuts under a hot broiler for 2–3 minutes until lightly browned. Mix together all the stuffing ingredients and season with salt and pepper.

CAREFULLY separate the cabbage leaves, trying not to tear them. Save the cabbage heart for later use. Bring a large saucepan of water to a boil, add a little lemon juice and blanch the cabbage leaves a few at a time. Refresh in cold water, then drain.

SPREAD a damp kitchen towel out on the work surface. Place the four largest leaves in a circle on the cloth with the stems meeting in the middle and the leaves overlapping each other slightly. Spread some of the stuffing over the leaves as evenly as you can.

ARRANGE ANOTHER four cabbage leaves on top and spread with more stuffing. Continue with the rest of the leaves and stuffing, finishing with the smallest leaves. Bring the sides of the kitchen towel up to meet each other, wrapping the cabbage in its original shape. Tie into a ball with string.

TO MAKE the braising liquid, melt the butter in a large casserole or saucepan and sauté the chopped vegetables for a couple of minutes. Add the wine and boil for 2 minutes, then add the stock. Lower the cabbage into the liquid and cover tightly. Simmer for 1 1/4 hours, or until a metal skewer comes out too hot to touch when poked into the center of the cabbage. Take out, unwrap and drain on a wire rack for 5 minutes.

TO SERVE, place some of the braising vegetables and liquid into shallow serving bowls and top with a wedge of stuffed cabbage.

The neater that you are able to fill and layer the cabbage leaves, the more regular the shape of the finished dish will be.

Mealy potatoes will soak up the liquid in the gratin dauphinois and give a softer, fluffy texture.

GRATIN DAUPHINOIS

POMMES ANNA

1³/4 lb. waxy potatoes
¹/2 cup clarified butter, melted

SERVES 4

PREHEAT the oven to 415°F. Grease a deep 8-inch round cake pan or flameproof dish with melted butter.

PEEL the potatoes and cut into very thin slices with a mandolin or sharp knife. Lay the potato slices on paper towels and pat dry. Starting from the center of the dish, overlap one-fifth of the potato slices over the bottom. Drizzle one-fifth of the butter over the top. Season well.

REPEAT the layers four more times, drizzling the last bit of butter over the top. Cut a circle of waxed paper to fit over the top of the potato. Bake for about 1 hour, or until cooked and golden and a knife blade slides easily into the center. Remove from the oven and leave for 5 minutes, then pour off any excess butter. Run a knife around the edge to loosen, then turn out onto a serving plate.

GRATIN DAUPHINOIS

THERE ARE A NUMBER OF VERSIONS OF THIS REGIONAL DISH FROM DAUPHINÉ, SOME WITHOUT THE TOPPING OF BROWNED CHEESE. IN FACT, THE WORD "GRATIN" ORIGINALLY REFERRED NOT TO THE TOPPING, BUT TO THE CRISPY BITS AT THE BOTTOM OF THE PAN.

2 lb. mealy (baking) potatoes
2 garlic cloves, crushed
¹/2 cup Gruyère, grated
pinch of nutmeg
1 cup heavy cream
¹/2 cup milk

SERVES 6

PREHEAT the oven to 325°F. Thinly slice the potatoes with a mandolin or sharp knife. Butter a 9 x 6¹/2 inch flameproof dish and layer the potatoes, sprinkling the garlic, grated cheese, nutmeg and seasoning between the layers and reserving some of the cheese for the top. Pour the cream and milk over the top and sprinkle with the reserved cheese.

BAKE FOR 50–60 minutes or until the potatoes are completely cooked and the liquid has been absorbed. If the top browns too much, cover loosely with aluminum foil. Allow to rest for 10 minutes before serving.

BOULANGÈRE POTATOES

2 lb. potatoes
1 large onion
2 tablespoons finely chopped
  parsley
2 cups hot chicken or vegetable
  stock
2 tablespoons butter

SERVES 6

PREHEAT the oven to 350°F.

THINLY SLICE the potatoes and onion with a mandolin or sharp knife. Build up alternate layers of potato and onion in an 8 x 4 inch deep dish, sprinkling parsley, salt and plenty of black pepper between each layer. Finish with a layer of potato. Pour the stock over the top and dot with butter.

BAKE, covered with aluminum foil, on the middle shelf of the oven for 30 minutes, then remove the foil and lightly press down on the potatoes to keep them submerged in the stock. Bake for another 30 minutes, or until the potatoes are tender and the top golden brown. Serve piping hot.

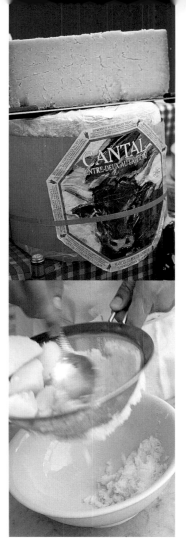

ALIGOT

THIS SPECIALTY OF THE AUVERGNE REGION IS A POTATO PURÉE BEATEN TOGETHER WITH CANTAL CHEESE TO MAKE A STRETCHY ELASTIC MIXTURE. CANTAL IS A SEMI-HARD SMOOTH CHEESE—USE MILD CHEDDAR IF YOU CAN'T FIND IT.

Pushing the mashed potato through a sieve will ensure that the aligot is smooth.

1 lb. 10 oz. mealy (baking) potatoes,
  cut into even-size pieces
1/3 cup butter
2 garlic cloves, crushed
3 tablespoons milk
2 1/2 cups Cantal (or mild Cheddar),
  grated

SERVES 4

COOK the potatoes in boiling salted water for 20–30 minutes, or until tender. Meanwhile, melt the butter in a small saucepan over low heat and add the garlic. Mash the potatoes and then put through a sieve to give a really smooth purée (don't use a food processor or they will become gluey).

RETURN the potato purée to the saucepan over gentle heat and add the garlic butter and milk. Mix together well and then add the cheese, handful by handful. Beat in the cheese—once it has melted the mixture will be stretchy. Season with salt and pepper before serving.

ALIGOT

Saint Cyprien in the Dordogne.

PEAS WITH ONIONS AND LETTUCE

LETTUCE IS OFTEN THOUGHT OF AS PURELY A SALAD GREEN, BUT UNTIL THE EIGHTEENTH CENTURY IT WAS MORE OFTEN SERVED COOKED THAN RAW, AND IN FRANCE IT IS STILL OFTEN EATEN THIS WAY, PARTICULARLY IN THIS DISH.

3 tablespoons butter
16 small pickling onions or shallots
1 lb. shelled fresh peas
1/2 lb. iceberg lettuce heart, finely shredded
2 parsley sprigs
1 teaspoon superfine sugar
1/2 cup chicken stock
1 tablespoon all-purpose flour

SERVES 6

MELT 2 tablespoons of the butter in a large saucepan. Add the onions and cook, stirring, for 1 minute. Add the peas, lettuce, parsley sprigs and sugar.

POUR IN the stock and stir well. Cover the saucepan and cook over moderately low heat for 15 minutes, stirring a couple of times, until the onions are cooked through. Remove the parsley.

MIX the remaining butter with the flour to make a beurre manié. Add small amounts to the vegetables, stirring until the juices thicken a little. Season well with salt and black pepper.

VICHY CARROTS

1 lb. carrots
1/2 teaspoon salt
11/2 teaspoons sugar
3 tablespoons butter
11/2 tablespoons chopped parsley

SERVES 6

SLICE the carrots quite thinly, then put in a deep frying pan. Cover with cold water and add the salt, sugar and butter. Simmer until the water has evaporated. Shake the pan to glaze the carrots, then add the parsley, toss together and serve.

VICHY CARROTS

VEGETABLE TIMBALES

1³/₄ cups carrots, chopped
9 cups watercress, trimmed
9 oz. red peppers
³/₄ cup heavy cream
7 egg yolks
pinch of nutmeg

SERVES 4

PREHEAT the oven to 315°F. Steam the carrots until they are soft. Wash the watercress and put in a saucepan with just the water clinging to the leaves. Cover the saucepan and steam the watercress for 2 minutes, or until just wilted. Drain, cool and squeeze dry with your hands.

PREHEAT the broiler. Cut the peppers in half, remove the seeds and membrane and place, skin side up, under the hot broiler until the skin blackens and blisters. Allow to cool before peeling away the skin.

PURÉE EACH vegetable individually in a food processor, adding a third of the cream to the carrots to make a smooth purée. Pour the pepper purée into a saucepan and stir over moderate heat until thickened. Put each purée in its own bowl to cool, then divide the remaining cream between the pepper and watercress purées.

STIR 2 egg yolks into each purée. Divide the last yolk between the pepper and watercress purées. Season with salt, pepper and nutmeg.

GREASE FOUR timbale molds and divide the carrot purée equally among them. Smooth the surface. Spoon the watercress purée on top and smooth the surface. Top with the pepper purée. Put the molds in a roasting pan and pour in hot water to come halfway up the sides of the timbales. Cook in this bain-marie for 1¹/₄ hours.

TO SERVE, hold a plate on top of each timbale and then turn it upside down. Give the plate and timbale one sharp shake and the timbale will release itself. Serve with a salad and baguette.

Smooth each layer as you put it in the mold, so the timbale is neat and even when turned out.

FENNEL, TOMATO AND GARLIC GRATIN

2 lb. fennel bulbs
1/3 cup olive oil
1 large red onion, halved and thinly
  sliced
2 garlic cloves, crushed
1 lb. tomatoes

GRATIN TOPPING
3/4 cup white bread, broken into
  coarse crumbs
2/3 cup Parmesan, grated
2 teaspoons grated lemon zest
1 garlic clove, crushed

SERVES 4

PREHEAT the oven to 400°F. Grease an 8¹/₂-inch square gratin dish with melted butter or oil. Cut the fennel in half lengthwise, then slice thinly.

HEAT the oil in a large frying pan. Cook the onion for 3–4 minutes until softened but not browned. Add the garlic and cook for 2 minutes. Add the fennel and cook, stirring frequently, for 7 minutes until softened and lightly golden brown.

SCORE a cross in the top of each tomato, plunge into boiling water for 20 seconds and then peel the skin away from the cross. Chop roughly and add to the fennel. Cook, stirring frequently, for 5 minutes until the tomatoes are softened. Season well and pour into the dish.

TO MAKE the gratin topping, mix all the ingredients together, sprinkle over the vegetables and bake for 15 minutes, or until golden brown and crisp. Serve immediately.

To make the vegetable tian, arrange a layer of zucchini in the dish, then top with cheese, the tomato mixture and thyme.

VEGETABLE TIAN

1/4 cup olive oil
1 lb. zucchini, thickly sliced on the
  diagonal
4 garlic cloves, crushed
pinch of nutmeg
1¹/₄ lb. tomatoes
2 red onions, chopped
1/4 cup white wine
2/3 cup chopped flat-leaf parsley
1 cup Gruyère, grated
a few small thyme sprigs

SERVES 4

PREHEAT the oven to 350°F. Grease a 6 x 10 inch flameproof dish with melted butter or oil. Heat half the oil in a large frying pan and add the zucchini and half the garlic. Cook, stirring, over low heat for 8 minutes, or until just beginning to soften. Season well with salt, pepper and nutmeg. Spread evenly into the dish.

SCORE a cross in the top of each tomato, plunge into boiling water for 20 seconds and then peel the skin away from the cross. Chop roughly. Cook the onion in the remaining oil over low heat for 5 minutes, stirring often. Add the remaining garlic, tomatoes, wine and parsley. Cook, stirring often, for 10 minutes until all the liquid has evaporated.

SPRINKLE the cheese over the zucchini and spread the tomato mixture over the top. Scatter thyme sprigs over the tomato and bake for 20 minutes, or until heated through.

VEGETABLE TIAN

RATATOUILLE

THE NAME RATATOUILLE COMES FROM THE FRENCH WORD FOR "MIX" AND WAS PREVIOUSLY USED AS A FAMILIAR TERM FOR ANY STEW. THIS RECIPE FOLLOWS THE TRADITIONAL VERSION, WITH EACH INGREDIENT BEING FRIED SEPARATELY BEFORE THE FINAL SIMMERING.

4 tomatoes
2 tablespoons olive oil
1 large onion, diced
1 red pepper, diced
1 yellow pepper, diced
1 eggplant, diced
2 zucchini, diced
1 teaspoon tomato paste
1/2 teaspoon sugar
1 bay leaf
3 thyme sprigs
2 basil sprigs
1 garlic clove, crushed
1 tablespoon chopped parsley

SERVES 4

SCORE a cross in the top of each tomato, plunge into boiling water for 20 seconds and then peel the skin away from the cross. Chop roughly.

HEAT the oil in a frying pan. Add the onion and cook over low heat for 5 minutes. Add the red and yellow peppers and cook, stirring, for 4 minutes. Remove from the pan and set aside.

FRY the eggplant until lightly browned all over and then remove from the frying pan. Fry the zucchini until browned and then return the onion, peppers and eggplant to the pan. Add the tomato paste, stir well and cook for 2 minutes. Add the tomatoes, sugar, bay leaf, thyme and basil, stir well, cover and cook for 15 minutes. Remove the bay leaf, thyme and basil.

MIX TOGETHER the garlic and parsley and add to the ratatouille at the last minute. Stir and serve.

You can braise white chicory or the purple-tipped variety. Both should be pale yellow, rather than green and bitter.

BRAISED CHICORY

8 chicory heads
1 tablespoon butter
1 teaspoon brown sugar
2 teaspoons tarragon vinegar
1/3 cup chicken stock
2 tablespoons heavy cream

SERVES 4

TRIM the ends from the chicory. Melt the butter in a deep frying pan and fry the chicory briefly on all sides. Add the sugar, vinegar and chicken stock and bring to a boil. Reduce the heat to a simmer and cover the pan.

SIMMER GENTLY for 30 minutes, or until tender, turning halfway through. Take the lid off the frying pan and simmer until nearly all the liquid has evaporated. Stir in the cream and serve.

BRAISED CHICORY

Olives growing in Provence.

Frying the scallions and bacon slices for the dressing of the salade lyonnaise.

SALADE NIÇOISE

THE TERM "A LA NIÇOISE" REFERS TO DISHES, TYPICAL OF NICE AND ITS SURROUNDING AREA, THAT CONTAIN TOMATOES, OLIVES, ANCHOVIES AND GARLIC. A DEBATE RAGES OVER WHAT A SALADE NIÇOISE SHOULD CONTAIN—APART FROM THE EGG, PURISTS PREFER TO USE ONLY RAW INGREDIENTS.

4 waxy potatoes
1 tablespoon olive oil
1³/4 cups small green beans, halved
10 oz. canned tuna in oil, drained
6 oz. green lettuce leaves
³/4 cup cherry tomatoes, halved
20 black olives, pitted
2 tablespoons capers
3 hard-boiled eggs, cut into wedges
8 anchovies

VINAIGRETTE
1 garlic clove, crushed
1 teaspoon Dijon mustard
2 tablespoons white wine vinegar
1 teaspoon lemon juice
1/2 cup olive oil

SERVES 4 AS A STARTER

COOK the potatoes in boiling salted water for 15 minutes or until just tender. Drain, cut into small cubes and place in a bowl. Drizzle with the olive oil and toss well. Cook the green beans in boiling salted water for 3 minutes, then drain and refresh under cold water. Keep on one side.

TO MAKE the vinaigrette, whisk together the garlic, mustard, vinegar and lemon juice. Add the oil in a thin steady stream, whisking until smooth.

PUT the tuna in a bowl and separate into large chunks with a fork. Cover the bottom of a serving dish with the lettuce leaves. Scatter the potatoes, beans, tuna, tomatoes, olives and capers over the leaves, pour the vinaigrette over the top and decorate with the eggs and anchovies.

SALADE LYONNAISE

1 garlic clove, cut in half
oil, for shallow-frying
4 slices white bread, crusts
    removed, cut into 1/2-inch cubes
1/4 cup olive oil
2 scallions, chopped
3 bacon slices, cut into short strips
1/3 cup red wine vinegar
3 teaspoons whole grain mustard
7 oz. frisée, mâche and dandelion
    leaves
4 eggs

SERVES 4 AS A STARTER

RUB the cut garlic over the bottom of a frying pan. Pour oil into the pan to a depth of 1/2 inch and fry the bread for 1–2 minutes, or until golden brown. Drain on paper towels. Wipe out the pan.

HEAT the olive oil in the frying pan and cook the scallions and bacon for 2 minutes. Add the vinegar and mustard and boil for 2 minutes to reduce by a third. Pour over the salad leaves and toss to wilt a little. Arrange on serving plates.

TO POACH the eggs, bring a saucepan of water to a boil. Crack each egg into a ramekin, reduce the heat and slide the egg into the simmering water. Poach for 3 minutes, take out with a slotted spoon and drain on paper towels. Place on the leaves and sprinkle with the croutons. Serve immediately.

SALADE LYONNAISE

SALADE AUX NOIX

4 thin slices baguette
1 garlic clove, cut in half
¹/₄ cup olive oil
1 large crisp green lettuce or a
  selection of mixed lettuce leaves
1¹/₂ tablespoons walnut oil
¹/₂ cup red wine vinegar
1 teaspoon Dijon mustard
¹/₂ cup walnuts, broken into pieces
5 oz. streaky bacon, cut into small
  pieces

SERVES 4 AS A STARTER

PREHEAT the broiler and rub the bread with the cut garlic to give it flavor. Drizzle a little of the olive oil on each side of the bread and then broil until golden brown. Allow to cool.

TEAR the lettuce leaves into pieces and arrange on a large platter. Mix together the remaining olive oil, walnut oil, vinegar and mustard and season to make a dressing.

PUT the walnuts in a bowl and cover with boiling water. Let sit for 1 minute, drain and shake dry.

COOK the bacon in a frying pan until crisp, then remove from the pan with a slotted spoon and sprinkle over the lettuce. Add the walnuts to the pan and cook for a couple of minutes until browned, then add to the salad. Pour the dressing into the pan and heat through.

POUR the dressing over the salad and toss well. Add the garlic croutons to serve.

Frying the sweetbreads before adding the creamy dressing gives them a crisp outer layer while the center stays soft.

SWEETBREADS SALAD

7 oz. sweetbreads (lamb or calves')
1 batavia lettuce or a selection of
  mixed lettuce leaves
1 tablespoon butter
1 shallot, finely chopped
2 tablespoons red wine vinegar
1 tablespoon Dijon mustard
¹/₃ cup olive oil
2 tablespoons whipping cream

SERVES 4 AS A STARTER

SOAK the sweetbreads in cold water for 2 hours, changing the water every 30 minutes, or whenever it turns pink. Put the sweetbreads in a saucepan of cold water and bring them to a boil. Simmer for 2 minutes, then drain and refresh under cold water. Pull off any skin and membrane and divide into bite-size pieces.

TEAR the lettuce leaves into pieces and arrange on a plate. Melt the butter in a frying pan and fry the shallot until tender. Add the sweetbreads and fry until browned and cooked through. Add the vinegar, mustard, oil and cream to the pan and stir well. Spoon over the salad leaves and serve.

SWEETBREADS SALAD

SALADE AU CHÈVRE

1/3 cup walnuts, broken into pieces
1 teaspoon sea salt
8 slices baguette
1 large garlic clove, cut in half
4 oz. chèvre, cut into 8 slices
2 oz. mesclun (mixed salad leaves
    and herbs)
1 small red onion, thinly sliced

DRESSING
2 tablespoons olive oil
1 tablespoon walnut oil
1 1/2 tablespoons tarragon vinegar
1 garlic clove, crushed

SERVES 4 AS A STARTER

PREHEAT the broiler to hot. Put the walnuts in a bowl and cover with boiling water. Let stand for 1 minute, then drain and shake dry. Toast under the broiler for 3–4 minutes until golden. Sprinkle sea salt over the top, toss lightly and allow to cool.

PUT the baguette under the broiler and toast one side until lightly golden. Remove from the heat and rub the toasted side with the cut garlic. Allow to rest for a few minutes to cool and crisp, then turn over and place a slice of chèvre on each one. Broil for 2–3 minutes, or until the cheese browns.

TO MAKE the dressing, mix together the olive oil, walnut oil, vinegar and garlic and season well.

TOSS the mesclun, onion and toasted walnuts together on a large platter. Arrange the chèvre croutons on top and drizzle with the dressing. Serve while the croutons are still warm.

For the salade au foie gras, cut the foie gras terrine into eight slices. Slice the truffle as finely as you can and place a slice on top of each piece of foie gras.

SALADE AU FOIE GRAS

1/4 lb. waxy potatoes such as Red
    Bliss or Yellow Finn, thickly sliced
12 asparagus spears, cut into short
    lengths
1 small black truffle, very thinly
    sliced into at least 8 pieces
1/4 lb. foie gras terrine, sliced into
    8 pieces
1 tablespoon butter
2 oz. mesclun (mixed salad leaves
    and herbs)

DRESSING
2 tablespoons olive oil
1 tablespoon walnut oil
1 tablespoon Armagnac
1 1/2 tablespoons red wine vinegar

SERVES 4 AS A STARTER

COOK the potatoes in salted water at a simmer for 15 minutes until tender. Remove with a slotted spoon, rinse in cold water and cool. Cook the asparagus at a simmer in the same water for 3–4 minutes until tender. Drain, rinse under cold water and chill.

TO MAKE the dressing, mix together the olive oil, walnut oil, Armagnac and vinegar. Season well.

PLACE a slice of truffle on the center of each slice of foie gras and press it in gently. Melt the butter in a frying pan, add the foie gras to the pan and brown lightly, turning after 30 seconds. The foie gras becomes quite soft as it heats, so use a spatula to turn it over and take it out. Drain on paper towels and keep warm.

PUT the potatoes, asparagus and mesclun in a bowl. Add the dressing and toss lightly. Top with the foie gras, truffle side up, and sprinkle with any leftover truffle slices. Serve at once.

SALADE AU FOIE GRAS

DESSERTS & PASTRIES

COFFEE CRÉMETS WITH CHOCOLATE SAUCE

DARK CHOCOLATE (INCLUDES SEMISWEET AND BITTERSWEET) IS AVAILABLE IN A VARIETY OF DIFFERENT QUALITIES. FOR A REALLY GOOD CHOCOLATE SAUCE, YOU WANT TO USE THE RICH, ALMOST-BLACK, IMPORTED CHOCOLATE THAT IS LABELED "WITH 70% COCOA SOLIDS." YOU CAN FIND IT IN GOURMET AND SPECIALTY FOOD STORES.

1 cup cream cheese
1 cup heavy cream
4 tablespoons very strong coffee
$^1/_3$ cup superfine sugar

CHOCOLATE SAUCE
$3^1/_2$ oz. dark chocolate
3 tablespoons unsalted butter

SERVES 4

LINE FOUR $^1/_2$-cup ramekins or heart-shaped molds with cheesecloth, leaving some cheesecloth hanging over the side to wrap over the crémet.

BEAT the cream cheese a little until smooth, then whisk in the cream. Add the coffee and sugar and mix together. Spoon into the ramekins and fold the cheesecloth over the top. Refrigerate for at least $1^1/_2$ hours, then unwrap the cheesecloth and turn the crémets out onto individual plates, carefully peeling the cheesecloth off each one.

TO MAKE the chocolate sauce, gently melt the chocolate in a saucepan with the butter and 4 tablespoons water. Stir well to make a shiny sauce, then let the sauce cool a little. Pour a little chocolate sauce over each crémet.

The crémets are spooned into cheesecloth-lined ramekins to make them easier to turn out.

PEARS IN RED WINE

1 tablespoon arrowroot
1 bottle red wine
$^1/_3$ cup sugar
1 cinnamon stick
6 cloves
zest of 1 small orange
zest of 1 small lemon
6 large pears (ripe but still firm)

SERVES 6

MIX the arrowroot with 2 tablespoons of the wine and set aside. Heat the remaining wine in a saucepan with the sugar, cinnamon stick, cloves and orange and lemon zest. Simmer gently for a couple of minutes, until the sugar has dissolved.

PEEL the pears, but don't remove the stems. Put the whole pears in the saucepan of wine, cover and poach gently for 25 minutes or until they are very tender, turning occasionally. Take out with a slotted spoon and place in a deep serving dish.

STRAIN the wine to remove the cinnamon stick, cloves and rind, then pour the wine back into the saucepan. Stir the arrowroot and add to the hot wine. Simmer gently, stirring now and then, until thickened. Pour over the pears and allow them to soak until they are cold. Serve with cream or crème fraîche.

PEARS IN RED WINE

CINNAMON BAVAROIS

THE NAME OF THIS CREAMY DESSERT IS A PECULIARITY OF THE FRENCH LANGUAGE IN THAT IT CAN BE

SPELLED IN BOTH THE MASCULINE FORM, "BAVAROIS" (FROM *FROMAGE BAVAROIS*) AND THE FEMININE,

"BAVAROISE" (FROM *CRÈME BAVAROISE*). HOWEVER, ITS CONNECTION TO BAVARIA HAS BEEN LOST.

1¼ cups milk
1 teaspoon ground cinnamon
¼ cup sugar
3 egg yolks
3 gelatin leaves or 1½ teaspoons
   powdered gelatin
½ teaspoon vanilla extract
¾ cup whipping cream
cinnamon, for dusting

SERVES 6

PUT the milk, cinnamon and half the sugar in a saucepan and bring to a boil. Whisk the egg yolks and remaining sugar until light and fluffy. Whisk the boiling milk into the yolks, then pour back into the saucepan and cook, stirring, until it is thick enough to coat the back of a wooden spoon. Do not let it boil or the custard will split.

SOAK the gelatin leaves in cold water until soft, drain and add to the hot custard with the vanilla extract. If using powdered gelatin, sprinkle it on to the hot custard, leave it to sponge for a minute, then stir it in. Strain the custard into a clean bowl and allow to cool. Whip the cream, fold into the custard and pour into six ½-cup greased bavarois molds. Set in the refrigerator.

UNMOLD by holding the mold in a hot cloth and inverting it onto a plate with a quick shake. Dust with the extra cinnamon.

Drape the warm tuiles over a rolling pin so that they set in a curved shape.

TUILES

2 egg whites
¼ cup superfine sugar
2 tablespoons all-purpose flour
⅓ cup ground almonds
2 teaspoons peanut oil

MAKES 12

BEAT the egg whites in a clean dry bowl until slightly frothy. Mix in the sugar, then the flour, ground almonds and oil. Preheat the oven to 400°F.

LINE a baking sheet with waxed paper. Place one heaping teaspoon of tuile mixture on the baking sheet and use the back of the spoon to spread it into a thin circle. Cover the baking sheet with tuiles, leaving ¾ inch between them for spreading during cooking.

BAKE for 5–6 minutes or until lightly golden. Take the tuiles off the baking sheet with a metal spatula and drape over a rolling pin while warm to make them curl (or use a bottle or a glass). Allow to cool while you cook the rest of the tuiles. Serve with ice cream and other creamy desserts.

TUILES

CHOCOLATE MOUSSES

2 cups dark chocolate, chopped
2 tablespoons unsalted butter
2 eggs, lightly beaten
3 tablespoons Cognac
4 egg whites
5 tablespoons superfine sugar
2 cups whipping cream

SERVES 8

PUT the chocolate in a heatproof bow over a saucepan of simmering water, making sure the bottom of the bowl isn't touching the water. Allow the chocolate to become soft and then stir until melted. Add the butter and stir until melted. Remove the bowl from the saucepan and cool for a few minutes. Add the eggs and Cognac and stir.

USING an electric mixer or wire whisk, beat the egg whites in a clean dry bowl until soft peaks form, adding the sugar gradually. Whisk one third of the egg white into the chocolate mixture to loosen it and then fold in the remainder with a large metal spoon or spatula.

WHIP the cream and fold into the mousse. Pour into glasses or a large bowl, cover and refrigerate for at least 4 hours.

PETITS POTS DE CRÈME

THE FLAVOR OF THESE PETITS POTS COMES FROM THE VANILLA BEAN USED TO INFUSE THE MILK. FOR CHOCOLATE POTS, ADD A TABLESPOON OF COCOA AND 1/3 CUP MELTED DARK CHOCOLATE INSTEAD OF THE VANILLA TO THE MILK. FOR COFFEE POTS, ADD A TABLESPOON OF INSTANT COFFEE.

1²/₃ cups milk
1 vanilla bean
3 egg yolks
1 egg
¹/₃ cup superfine sugar

SERVES 4

PREHEAT the oven to 275°F. Put the milk in a saucepan. Split the vanilla bean in two, scrape out the seeds and add the bean and seeds to the milk. Bring the milk just to a boil.

MEANWHILE, mix together the egg yolks, egg and sugar. Strain the boiling milk over the egg mixture and stir well. Skim off the surface to remove any foam.

LADLE the mixture into four 1 oz. ramekins and place in a roasting pan. Pour enough hot water into the pan to come halfway up the sides of the ramekins. Bake for 30 minutes, or until the custards are firm to the touch. Allow the ramekins to cool on a wire rack, then refrigerate until ready to serve.

PETITS POTS DE CRÈME

CHOCOLATE SOUFFLÉS

SOUFFLÉS ARE RENOWNED FOR BEING DIFFICULT TO MAKE, BUT CAN IN FACT BE VERY EASY. IF YOU ARE FEELING PARTICULARLY DECADENT WHEN YOU SERVE THESE CHOCOLATE SOUFFLÉS, MAKE A HOLE IN THE TOP OF EACH ONE AND POUR IN A LITTLE CREAM.

3 tablespoons unsalted butter, softened
3/4 cup superfine caster sugar

SOUFFLÉS
1 batch crème pâtissière (page 285)
3/4 cup unsweetened cocoa powder
3 tablespoons chocolate or coffee liqueur
1/2 cup dark chocolate, chopped
12 egg whites
3 tablespoons superfine sugar confectioners' sugar

SERVES 8

Beat egg whites in a clean dry bowl—any hint of grease will prevent them from aerating.

TO PREPARE the dishes, brush the insides of eight 1 1/3-cup soufflé dishes with the softened butter. Pour a little superfine sugar into each one, turn the dishes around to coat thoroughly and then pour out any excess sugar. Preheat the oven to 375°F and put a large baking sheet in the oven to heat up.

WARM the crème pâtissière in a bowl over a saucepan of simmering water, then remove from the heat. Whisk the cocoa powder, chocolate liqueur and chocolate into the crème pâtissière.

BEAT the egg whites in a clean dry bowl until firm peaks form. Whisk in the sugar gradually to make a stiff glossy mixture. Whisk half the egg white into the crème pâtissière to loosen it, and then fold in the remainder with a large metal spoon or spatula. Pour into the soufflé dishes and run your thumb around the inside rim of each dish, about 3/4 inch into the soufflé mixture to help the soufflés rise without sticking.

PUT the dishes on the hot baking sheet and bake for 15–18 minutes, or until the soufflés have risen and wobble slightly when tapped. Test with a skewer through a crack in the side of a soufflé—the skewer should come out clean or slightly moist. If it is slightly moist, by the time you get the soufflés to the table, they will be cooked in the center. Serve immediately, dusted with a little confectioners' sugar.

RASPBERRY SOUFFLÉ

THERE IS SOMETIMES CONFUSION ABOUT THE DIFFERENCE BETWEEN A SOUFFLÉ AND A MOUSSE. TECHNICALLY, A SOUFFLÉ IS HOT AND A MOUSSE IS COLD. A MOUSSE IS HELD UP BY GELATIN AND EGG WHITE AND WON'T COLLAPSE LIKE A HOT SOUFFLÉ, WHICH IS HELD UP BY HOT AIR.

3 tablespoons unsalted butter,
  softened
3/4 cup superfine sugar

SOUFFLÉ
1/2 batch crème pâtissière
  (page 285)
3 1/4 cups raspberries
3 tablespoons superfine sugar
8 egg whites
confectioners' sugar

SERVES 6

TO PREPARE the soufflé dish, brush the inside of a 6-cup soufflé dish with the softened butter. Pour in the superfine sugar, turn the dish around to coat thoroughly and then pour out any excess sugar. Preheat the oven to 375ºF and put a baking sheet in the oven to heat up.

WARM the crème pâtissière in a bowl over a saucepan of simmering water, then remove from the heat. Put the raspberries and half the sugar in a blender or food processor and mix until puréed (or mix by hand). Pass through a fine nylon sieve to get rid of the seeds. Add the crème pâtissière to the raspberries and whisk together.

BEAT the egg whites in a clean dry bowl until firm peaks form. Whisk in the remaining sugar gradually to make a stiff glossy mixture. Whisk half the egg white into the raspberry mixture to loosen it and then fold in the remainder with a large metal spoon or spatula. Pour into the soufflé dish and run your thumb around the inside rim of the dish, about 3/4 inch into the soufflé mixture, to help the soufflé rise without sticking.

PUT the dish on the hot baking sheet and bake for 10–12 minutes, or until the soufflé has risen and wobbles slightly when tapped. Test with a skewer through a crack in the side of the soufflé—the skewer should come out clean or slightly moist. If it is slightly moist, by the time you get the soufflé to the table, it will be cooked in the center. Serve immediately, dusted with a little confectioners' sugar.

When adding beaten egg white to a mixture, whisk in a small amount first to loosen it. This allows you to fold in the rest without losing the volume.

CHERRY CLAFOUTIS

IT IS TRADITIONAL TO LEAVE THE PITS IN THE CHERRIES WHEN YOU MAKE A CLAFOUTIS (THEY ADD A BITTER ALMOST-ALMOND FLAVOR DURING THE COOKING), BUT YOU'D BETTER POINT THIS OUT WHEN YOU'RE SERVING THE DESSERT.

3/4 cup heavy cream
1 vanilla bean
1/2 cup milk
3 eggs
1/4 cup superfine sugar
1/2 cup all-purpose flour
1 tablespoon kirsch
14 oz. black cherries, unpitted
confectioners' sugar

SERVES 6

PREHEAT the oven to 350°F. Put the cream in a small saucepan. Split the vanilla bean in two, scrape out the seeds and add the bean and seeds to the cream. Heat gently for a couple of minutes, then remove from the heat, add the milk and cool. Strain to remove the vanilla bean.

WHISK the eggs with the sugar and flour, then stir into the cream. Add the kirsch and cherries and stir well. Pour into a 9-inch round baking dish and bake for 30–35 minutes, or until golden on top. Dust with confectioners' sugar and serve.

Adding the unpitted cherries to the clafoutis batter.

PEACHES CARDINAL

4 large ripe peaches
3 1/2 cups raspberries
4 teaspoons confectioners' sugar,
  plus extra for dusting

SERVES 4

IF the peaches are very ripe, put them in a bowl and pour boiling water over them. Allow to rest for a minute, then drain and carefully peel away the skin. If the fruit you have is not ripe enough, dissolve 2 tablespoons sugar in a saucepan of water, add the peaches and cover the saucepan. Gently poach the peaches for 5–10 minutes, or until they are tender. Drain and peel.

LET the peaches cool and then halve each one and remove the pit. Put two halves in each serving glass. Put the raspberries in a food processor or blender and mix until puréed (or mix by hand). Pass through a fine nylon sieve to remove the seeds.

SIFT the confectioners' sugar over the raspberry purée and stir in. Drizzle the purée over the peaches, cover and chill thoroughly. Dust a little confectioners' sugar over the top to serve.

PEACHES CARDINAL

Dairy cows in Normandy.

Ladling the crème brûlée custard into the ramekins.

CRÈME BRÛLÉE

CRÈME CARAMEL

CARAMEL
1/2 cup superfine sugar

2 1/2 cups milk
1 vanilla bean
1/2 cup superfine sugar
3 eggs, beaten
3 egg yolks

SERVES 6

TO MAKE the caramel, put the sugar in a heavy-bottomed saucepan and heat the sugar until it dissolves and starts to caramelize—swirl the sugar in the saucepan to keep the coloring even. Remove from the heat and carefully add 2 tablespoons water to stop the cooking process. Pour into six 1/2-cup ramekins and allow to cool.

PREHEAT the oven to 350°F. Put the milk and vanilla bean in a saucepan and bring just to a boil. Mix together the sugar, eggs and egg yolks. Strain the boiling milk over the egg mixture and stir well. Ladle into the ramekins and place in a roasting pan. Pour enough hot water into the pan to come halfway up the sides of the ramekins. Cook for 35–40 minutes, or until firm to the touch. Remove from the pan and allow to stand for 15 minutes. Unmold onto plates and pour on any leftover caramel.

CRÈME BRÛLÉE

CRÈME BRÛLÉE HAS BEEN KNOWN IN ENGLAND SINCE THE SEVENTEENTH CENTURY BY THE NAME "BURNT CREAM." THE CREAMY CUSTARD IS SIMILAR TO THAT OF THE CRÈME CARAMEL, BUT THE TOPPING IS CARAMELIZED TO A HARD CRUST.

2 cups cream
3/4 cup milk
1/2 cup superfine sugar
1 vanilla bean
5 egg yolks
1 egg white
1 tablespoon orange blossom water
1/2 cup Demerara or turbinado sugar

SERVES 8

PREHEAT the oven to 250°F. Put the cream, milk and half the sugar in a saucepan with the vanilla bean. Bring just to a boil.

MEANWHILE, mix together the remaining sugar, egg yolks and white. Strain the boiling milk over the egg mixture, whisking well. Stir in the orange blossom water.

LADLE INTO eight 1/2-cup ramekins and place in a roasting pan. Pour enough hot water into the pan to come halfway up the sides of the ramekins. Cook for 1 1/2 hours, or until set in the center. Cool and refrigerate until ready to serve. Just before serving, sprinkle the tops with Demerara sugar and caramelize under a very hot broiler or with a kitchen torch. Serve immediately.

ÎLE FLOTTANTE

THIS ROUND ISLAND OF MERINGUE FLOATING ON A SEA OF CUSTARD IS OFTEN CONFUSED WITH ANOTHER FRENCH MERINGUE DESSERT, *OEUFS A LA NEIGE*. "FLOATING ISLAND" IS ONE LARGE BAKED MERINGUE, WHILE "EGGS IN THE SNOW" ARE SMALL POACHED MERINGUES ON CUSTARD.

MERINGUE
4 egg whites
1/3 cup superfine sugar
1/4 teaspoon vanilla extract

PRALINE
1/4 cup sugar
2/3 cup sliced almonds

2 batches crème anglaise
(page 285)

SERVES 6

PREHEAT the oven to 275°F and put a roasting pan in the oven to heat up. Grease and line the bottom of a 6-cup charlotte mold with a circle of waxed paper and lightly grease the bottom and side.

TO MAKE the meringue, beat the egg whites in a clean dry bowl until very stiff peaks form. Whisk in the sugar gradually to make a very stiff glossy meringue. Whisk in the vanilla extract.

SPOON the meringue into the charlotte mold, smooth the surface and place a greased circle of waxed paper on top. Put the mold into the hot roasting pan and pour boiling water into the pan until it comes halfway up the side of the mold.

BAKE for 50–60 minutes, or until a knife poked into the center of the meringue comes out clean. Remove the circle of paper, put a plate over the meringue and turn it over. Lift off the mold and the other circle of paper and allow to cool.

TO MAKE the praline, grease a sheet of aluminum foil and lay it out flat on the work surface. Put the sugar in a small saucepan with 3 tablespoons water and heat gently until completely dissolved. Bring to a boil and cook until a deep golden, then quickly pour in the sliced almonds and pour onto the greased aluminum foil. Spread a little and allow to cool. When the praline has hardened, grind it to a fine powder in a food processor or with a mortar and pestle.

SPRINKLE the praline over the meringue and pour a sea of warmed crème anglaise around its base. Serve in wedges with the remaining crème anglaise.

Grease and line the charlotte mold and place greased waxed paper over the top after filling so that the meringue will not stick.

Once the crêpe starts to come away from the side of the pan, it is cooked enough to turn over.

CRÊPES SUZETTE

THE ORIGIN OF THE NAME CRÊPES SUZETTE HAS BECOME A MYSTERY, BUT THEY SEEM TO HAVE APPEARED SOMETIME AT THE END OF THE NINETEENTH CENTURY. TRADITIONALLY FLAMBÉED AT THE TABLE IN RESTAURANTS, IN THIS RECIPE THE CRÊPES ARE QUICKLY SET ALIGHT ON THE STOVE TOP.

CRÊPES
2 tablespoons grated orange zest
1 tablespoon grated lemon zest
1 batch crêpe batter (page 282)

1/2 cup superfine sugar
1 cup orange juice
1 tablespoon grated orange zest
2 tablespoons brandy or Cognac
2 tablespoons Grand Marnier
3 1/2 tablespoons unsalted butter, diced

SERVES 6

TO MAKE the crêpes, stir the orange and lemon zest into the crêpe batter. Heat and grease a crêpe pan. Pour in enough batter to coat the bottom of the pan in a thin even layer and pour out any excess. Cook over moderate heat for about a minute, or until the crêpe starts to come away from the side of the pan. Turn the crêpe and cook on the other side for 1 minute or until lightly golden. Repeat with the remaining batter. Fold the crêpes into quarters.

MELT the sugar in a large frying pan over low heat and cook to a rich caramel, swirling the pan so the caramel browns evenly. Pour in the orange juice and zest and boil for 2 minutes. Put the crêpes in the pan and spoon the sauce over them.

ADD the brandy and Grand Marnier and flambé by lighting the pan with your gas flame or a match (stand back when you do this and keep a pan lid handy for emergencies). Add the butter and shake the pan until the butter melts. Serve immediately.

CRÊPES SOUFFLÉS

CRÊPES SOUFFLÉS

1 batch crème pâtissière
  (page 285)
1/2 cup orange juice
grated zest of 1 orange
2 tablespoons Grand Marnier
8 egg whites
2 tablespoons superfine sugar
1/2 batch cooked crêpes
  (page 282)
confectioners' sugar

SERVES 6

PREHEAT the oven to 400°F. Warm the crème pâtissière in a bowl over a saucepan of simmering water and whisk in the orange juice, orange zest and Grand Marnier.

BEAT the egg whites in a clean dry bowl until firm peaks form. Whisk in the sugar gradually to make a stiff glossy meringue. Whisk half into the crème pâtissière to loosen the mixture, then fold in the rest with a large metal spoon or spatula. Place two big spoonfuls of soufflé on the center of each crêpe. Fold in half with a spatula, without pressing. Bake on a buttered baking sheet for 5 minutes. Dust with confectioners' sugar and serve immediately.

Saint Cyprien in the Dordogne.

CARAMEL ICE CREAM

ALTHOUGH WE ALL THINK OF ICE CREAM AS A FROZEN DESSERT, IT SHOULD IDEALLY BE SERVED WHEN IT IS JUST ON THE VERGE OF MELTING. IF YOU SERVE IT TOO COLD THE FLAVOR WILL BE MASKED, SO TAKE IT OUT OF THE FREEZER HALF AN HOUR BEFORE SERVING TO LET IT SOFTEN.

1/4 cup sugar
1/3 cup whipping cream
3 egg yolks
1 1/2 cups milk
1 vanilla bean

SERVES 4

TO MAKE the caramel, put 3 tablespoons of the sugar in a heavy-bottomed saucepan and heat until it dissolves and starts to caramelize—swirl the sugar in the saucepan as it cooks to keep the coloring even. Remove from the heat and carefully add the cream (it will spatter). Stir over low heat until the caramel remelts.

WHISK the egg yolks and remaining sugar until light and fluffy. Put the milk and vanilla bean in a saucepan and bring just to a boil, then strain over the caramel. Bring back to a boil and pour over the egg yolk mixture, whisking continuously.

POUR the custard back into the saucepan and cook, stirring, until it is thick enough to coat the back of a wooden spoon. Do not let it boil or the custard will split. Pass through a sieve into a bowl and place over ice to cool quickly.

CHURN in an ice-cream maker, following the manufacturer's instructions. Alternatively, pour into a plastic freezer container, cover, freeze and stir every 30 minutes with a whisk during freezing to break up the ice crystals for a better texture. Freeze overnight with a layer of plastic wrap over the surface and the lid on the container. Keep in the freezer until half an hour before serving.

Add the hot milk to the caramel, then pour over the egg yolk mixture to make a custard.

BLACK CURRANT SORBET

WE'VE USED GLUCOSE FOR THIS SORBET BECAUSE IT STOPS THE SUGAR FROM CRYSTALLIZING FOR A GOOD TEXTURE. TO WEIGH GLUCOSE WITHOUT IT RUNNING EVERYWHERE, MEASURE THE SUGAR INTO THE PAN OF THE SCALE, THEN MAKE A WELL IN THE MIDDLE AND POUR IN THE GLUCOSE.

$1/2$ + $1/3$ cup superfine sugar
1 tablespoon liquid glucose
$2 1/4$ cups black currants, stalks
    removed
1 tablespoon lemon juice
2 tablespoons crème de cassis

SERVES 4

PUT the sugar and glucose in a saucepan with 1 cup water. Heat gently to dissolve the sugar and then boil for 2–3 minutes. Cool completely.

PUT the black currants and lemon juice in a blender with half of the cooled syrup and mix to a thick purée. (Alternatively, push the fruit through a sieve to purée and then mix with the lemon juice and syrup.) Add the remaining syrup and the crème de cassis and mix well.

CHURN in an ice-cream maker following the manufacturer's instructions. Alternatively, pour into a plastic freezer container, cover and freeze, stirring every 30 minutes with a whisk during freezing to break up the ice crystals for a better texture. Freeze overnight with a layer of plastic wrap over the surface and the lid on the container. Keep in the freezer until ready to serve.

RED WINE SORBET

1 cup superfine sugar
$1/3$ cup orange juice
1 cup light red wine

SERVES 4

DISSOLVE the superfine sugar in 1 cup boiling water, stirring until it has completely dissolved. Add the orange juice and red wine and stir well.

CHURN in an ice-cream maker following the manufacturer's instructions. Alternatively, pour into a plastic freezer container, cover and freeze. Stir every 30 minutes with a whisk during freezing to break up the ice crystals for a better texture. Freeze overnight with a layer of plastic wrap over the surface and the top on the container. Keep in the freezer until ready to serve.

Stir the sugar until it is completely dissolved before adding the orange juice and wine.

PÂTISSERIE is one of France's most respected culinary arts, one that is even protected by its own patron saint, Saint Honoré. Pâtissiers can become members of several professional organizations, such as The National Confederation of Pastry Chefs and Relais Desserts International Professional Organization of Master Pastry Makers. One of these signs hanging above a pâtisserie shows a real commitment to the trade.

PÂTISSERIE

PÂTISSERIE, THE ART OF CAKE AND PASTRY MAKING, IS THE MOST DELIGHTFUL AND ELABORATE OF CULINARY ARTS—THE ONLY ONE WHERE BEAUTIFUL DECORATION CARRIES EQUAL WEIGHT TO THE FLAVOR OF THE FOOD.

Pâtisserie can be traced back to the simple cakes of the ancient world and the pastry-making of the Middle East, with its use of spices, nuts and sugar. From the Crusades onwards, these techniques and ingredients filtered into Europe, particularly Italy, and when Catherine de Medici arrived at the French court in the sixteenth century with her retinue of Italian chefs, they revolutionized French pâtisserie with their skills, such as the invention of choux pastry. In the early nineteenth century, Antonin Carême became the first of a line of great Parisian *pâtissiers* (pastry chefs). He was famous for his fantastical architectural creations, including croquembouches shaped as famous buildings.

BUYING PÂTISSERIE

Pâtisserie refers not only to the pastries, but also to the place where they are made and sold. Pâtisseries are sometimes solely shops, but often have a *salon de thé* attached where patrons can enjoy a pâtisserie in the mid-morning or afternoon, the favored times for indulging in such a treat. Pâtisseries also sell candied fruits, chocolates, beautiful items to finish a meal or present as a gift. They display their pâtisserie elegantly, and after carefully choosing, customers are presented with their purchases beautifully wrapped.

MACARON a crisp, melt-in-the-mouth macaroon that comes in bright colors, including brown (chocolate) and green (pistachio), sandwiched with cream. Made of almonds, sugar and egg whites.

BABA AU RHUM a yeast sponge cake soaked in rum-flavored syrup and decorated with crème chantilly and fruit. Can be baba-shaped or made in a round savarin mold (pictured).

MIRLITON a puff-pastry shell filled with preserves and an almond cake mixture, decorated with almonds and an icing glaze. Mirlitons are a specialty of Normandy, especially Rouen.

ÉCLAIR a classic of French pâtisserie, this finger of choux pastry is filled with cream or a plain, coffee or chocolate pastry cream and dipped in chocolate or coffee fondant or caramel.

MERINGUE AUX NOISETTES a basic ingredient of pâtisserie, meringue is mixed here with hazelnuts to form a crisp but chewy ball of hazelnut meringue.

TARTE AUX PÊCHES fruit tarts are one of the most popular and varied pâtisserie items. Here a rectangular pastry shell is filled with pastry cream and peach halves, baked and glazed.

MILLEFEUILLE meaning a thousand leaves, this is made of layered puff pastry, pastry cream and preserves or another filling. The *quadrillage* pattern on top is made with piped icing.

MOUSSE AUX FRAMBOISES a raspberry mousse set on a sponge base and decorated with white chocolate. The piece of clear plastic holds the shape of the mousse until it is served.

GÂTEAU AUX PRUNES a cross between a cake and a tart, the plums are cooked in a brioche-type pastry and then glazed.

TARTE TATIN made famous by the Tatin sisters, this tart is cooked upside down in a special pan, then turned over to reveal a pastry base topped with halved or quartered caramelized apples.

TARTE AUX FRUITS a beautiful mixture of sliced fruit arranged on a pastry and pastry cream base and glazed. This is a creation from Gérard Mulot's pâtisserie in Paris.

PITHIVIERS a puff-pastry shell filled with a frangipane mixture. A version is made for Twelfth Night, when a token is hidden inside and it is decorated with a crown of gold posterboard.

FRAISIER fresh strawberries in a crème mousseline (a rich butter cream) and sandwiched between two layers of almond genoise sponge.

DACQUOISE in this version of a southwestern specialty, two or three layers of nut meringues are sandwiched with strawberries and crème chantilly.

JALOUSIE a puff-pastry slice with a sweet topping and a lattice or slatted pastry top. *Jalousie* is French for a slatted window blind, though today the pastry tends to have a lattice top.

CANNELÉ a specialty of the Bordeaux region, these tall little rum-flavored cakes are baked in ridged molds, which gives them their fluted sides.

MAGIE NOIR a rich chocolate cake meaning "black magic" and decorated with pieces of praline. A specialty of Gérard Mulot's pâtisserie in Paris to be served on a special occasion.

PÊCHES two hollowed out brioche filled with pastry cream, sandwiched together and decorated with red currant jelly to look like little peaches.

PETITS FOURS here a selection of tiny pastries, each a miniature version of its larger namesake and bought by weight. Petits fours can also refer to cookies, such as tuiles and macaroons.

TRIANGLES a specialty of Le Petit Duc pâtisserie in Saint Rémy in Provence, these triangles have a pastry base with a topping of Provençal almonds and honey.

LE SUCCÈS two layers of an almond meringue cake filled and topped with praline or chocolate butter cream and decorated with sliced nuts. Each pâtisserie has its own version of this cake.

CALISSONS from Aix-en-Provence, these square- or diamond-shaped candies are made from almonds and candied fruit and are topped with a sugar icing.

GÂTEAU SAINT HONORÉ this ring of choux and buttery pastry is filled with pastry cream and topped with balls of choux and caramel. It is named after the patron saint of pastry chefs.

TARTE AUX FRAISES a tart of strawberries sitting on a *pâte brisée* (a classic French pastry) and crème pâtissière base. The strawberries are heavily glazed to give them a glowing shine.

JOËL DURAND'S chocolates in his Saint Rémy shop are each numbered and described on a "menu." He flavors chocolate with Provençal lavender and herbs, green tea, Sichuan pepper and jasmine. The flavors change with the season—number 28 is perfumed with rose petals in summer and Carmargue saffron the rest of the year. Number 30, known as "Provence," is a mix of olives from Les Baux and praine.

REGIONAL PÂTISSERIE

Each area of France has its own pâtisserie specialties. In Alsace-Lorraine in the Northeast, there are Austrian-inspired Kugelhopf and strudels and wonderful fruit tarts, especially those using mirabelle plums. Paris is famed for its pâtisserie shops and dark, bitter chocolate is a northern specialty, especially in the cork-shaped *bouchons* from Champagne. In the Northwest, Brittany and Normandy's dairy farming and apples are used to create buttery Breton cookies and the finest *tarte aux pommes*. In the East and Center, Lyon is home to Bernachon, one of France's finest *pâtisseries-confiseries*, while *pain d'épices*, a spicy gingerbread, has been made in Dijon since the fifteenth century. The Southwest is known for its rural Basque cooking, which includes *gâteau basque*, as well as famous *macarons* from Saint Emilion and tarts made with Agen prunes. In the South, with its abundance of fruit, there are candied fruit and *marrons* (chestnuts).

FRUIT CONFITS are a specialty of Provence and were originally a way to store soft fruit through the winter. Lilamand Confiseur is one of the last independent producers of the jewel-like fruits, which must be made with fruits flavorful enough to be tasted through the sugar.

PITHIVIERS

ORIGINATING IN PITHIVIERS IN THE LOIRE VALLEY, THIS PASTRY IS TRADITIONALLY SERVED ON TWELFTH NIGHT, WHEN IT IS KNOWN AS *GALETTE DES ROIS* AND USUALLY CONTAINS A BEAN THAT BRINGS GOOD LUCK TO WHOMEVER FINDS IT IN THEIR SLICE.

FILLING
1/2 cup unsalted butter, at room temperature
1/2 cup superfine sugar
2 large eggs, lightly beaten
2 tablespoons dark rum
finely grated zest of 1 small orange or lemon
3/4 cup ground almonds
2 1/2 tablespoons all-purpose flour

1 batch puff pastry (page 281)
1 egg, lightly beaten
confectioners' sugar

SERVES 6

TO MAKE the filling, beat the butter and sugar together until pale and creamy. Mix in the beaten eggs, little by little, beating well after each addition. Beat in the rum and the orange or lemon zest and then lightly fold in the almonds and flour. Put the filling in the fridge to firm up a little while you roll out the pastry.

CUT the pastry in half and roll cut one half. Cut out an 11-inch circle and place the circle on a large baking sheet lined with waxed paper. Spread the filling over the pastry, leaving a clear border of about 3/4 inch all the way around. Brush a little beaten egg over the clear border to help the two halves stick together.

ROLL OUT the other half of the pastry and cut out a second circle, the same size as the first. Lay this circle on top of the filling and firmly press the edges of the pastry together. Cover and put in the refrigerator for at least 1 hour (several hours or even overnight is fine).

PREHEAT the oven to 425°F. Brush all over the top of the pie with the beaten egg to give it a shiny glaze—be careful not to brush egg on the side of the pie or the layers won't rise properly. Working from the center to the outside edge, score the top of the pithiviers with curved lines in a spiral pattern.

BAKE the pithiviers for 25–30 minutes, or until it has risen and is golden brown. Dust with confectioners' sugar and allow to cool. Cut into slices to serve.

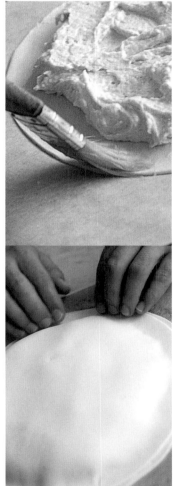

Leave a clear border around the filling, then brush it with egg to help the two halves of the pastry stick together.

Pipe a thick ring of choux pastry over the guide.

PARIS-BREST

THIS LARGE CHOUX PASTRY CAKE WAS NAMED AFTER THE PARIS-BREST BICYCLE RACE. IT WAS INVENTED IN 1891 BY A CANNY PARISIAN BAKER WHO OWNED A SHOP ALONG THE ROUTE AND HAD THE IDEA OF PRODUCING THESE BICYCLE WHEEL-SHAPED CAKES.

1 batch choux pastry (page 282)
1 egg, lightly beaten
1¹/₂ tablespoons sliced almonds
1 batch crème pâtissière
  (page 285)
confectioners' sugar

PRALINE
¹/₃ cup superfine sugar
1 cup sliced almonds

SERVES 6

PREHEAT the oven to 400°F and put the choux pastry in a pastry bag fitted with a wide tip (about ³/₄ inch wide). Draw an 8-inch circle on the back of a piece of waxed paper in a dark pen so that the circle shows through on the other side. Put the paper on a baking sheet, pen side down.

PIPE a ring of pastry over the guide you have drawn. Now pipe another ring of pastry directly inside this one so that you have one thick ring. Pipe another two circles on top of the first two and continue until all the choux pastry has been used. Brush the choux ring with beaten egg and sprinkle with the sliced almonds.

BAKE the choux ring for 20–30 minutes, then reduce the oven to 350°F and bake for another 20–25 minutes. Remove from the baking sheet and place on a wire rack. Immediately slice the ring in half horizontally, making the base twice as deep as the top. Take off the top and scoop out any uncooked pastry from the base. Allow to cool completely.

TO MAKE the praline, grease a sheet of aluminum foil and lay it flat on the work surface. Put the sugar in a small saucepan with ¹/₃ cup water and heat gently until completely dissolved. Bring to a boil and cook until deep golden, then quickly pour in the sliced almonds and pour onto the greased foil. Spread a little and allow to cool. When the praline has hardened, grind it to a fine powder in a food processor or with a mortar and pestle. Mix into the cold crème pâtissière.

SPOON the crème pâtissière into the bottom of the choux pastry ring and cover with the top. Dust with confectioners' sugar to serve.

APPLE TART

1 batch sweet pastry (page 278)
¹/₂ batch crème pâtissière
   (page 285)
4 eating apples
¹/₄ cup apricot preserves

SERVES 8

PREHEAT the oven to 350°F. Roll out the pastry to line a 9-inch round loose-bottomed fluted tart pan. Chill in the refrigerator for 20 minutes.

LINE the pastry shell with a crumpled piece of waxed paper and baking beads (use dried beans or rice if you don't have beads). Blind bake the pastry for 10 minutes, remove the paper and beads and bake for another 3–5 minutes, or until the pastry is just cooked but still very pale.

FILL the pastry with the crème pâtissière. Peel and core the apples, cut them in half and then into thin slices. Arrange over the top of the tart and bake for 25–30 minutes or until the apples are golden and the pastry is cooked. Allow to cool completely, then melt the apricot preserves with 1 tablespoon water, strain to remove any lumps and brush over the apples to make them shine.

APPLE TART

TARTE AU CITRON

1 batch sweet pastry (page 278)

FILLING
4 eggs
2 egg yolks
1 cup superfine sugar
¹/₃ cup heavy cream
1 cup lemon juice
finely grated zest of 3 lemons

SERVES 8

PREHEAT the oven to 375°F. Roll out the pastry to line a 9-inch round loose-bottomed fluted tart pan. Chill in the refrigerator for 20 minutes.

TO MAKE the filling, whisk together the eggs, egg yolks and sugar. Add the cream, whisking all the time, and then the lemon juice and zest.

LINE the pastry shell with a crumpled piece of waxed paper and baking beads (use dried beans or rice if you don't have beads). Blind bake the pastry for 10 minutes, remove the paper and beads and bake for another 3–5 minutes, or until the pastry is just cooked but still very pale. Remove from oven and reduce the temperature to 300°F.

PUT the pan on a baking sheet and carefully pour the filling into the pastry shell. Return to the oven for 35–40 minutes, or until the filling has set. Allow to cool completely before serving.

Whisking the lemon filling for the tarte au citron.

MIXED BERRY TARTLETS

1 batch sweet pastry (page 278)
1 batch frangipane (page 285)
3¹/₄ cup mixed berries
3 tablespoons apricot preserves

MAKES 10

PREHEAT the oven to 350°F. Roll out the pastry about ¹/₈ inch thick and use to line ten 3-inch-wide tartlet pans. Put the frangipane in a pastry bag and pipe into the tartlet pans. Put the pans on a baking sheet and bake for 10–12 minutes, or until golden.

COOL SLIGHTLY on a wire rack, then arrange the berries on top. Melt the preserves with 1 teaspoon water, strain to remove any lumps and brush over the berries to make them shine.

MIXED BERRY TARTLETS

Arrange the pears cut side down in the pastry shell with the stems pointing to the center.

PEAR AND ALMOND TART

1 batch sweet pastry (page 278)
¹/₄ cup superfine sugar
1 vanilla bean
3 pears (ripe but still firm), peeled, halved and cored
3 tablespoons apricot preserves

ALMOND FILLING
²/₃ cup unsalted butter, softened
²/₃ cup superfine sugar
few drops of vanilla extract
2 large eggs, lightly beaten
³/₄ cup ground almonds
finely grated zest of 1 small lemon
3 tablespoons all-purpose flour

SERVES 8

PREHEAT the oven to 375°F. Roll out the pastry to line a 9-inch round loose-bottomed fluted tart pan. Chill in the refrigerator for 20 minutes.

PUT the sugar and vanilla bean in a saucepan. Add the pears and pour in just enough water to cover them, then remove the pears. Bring the water to a simmer and cook for 5 minutes. Add the pears, cover and poach for 5–10 minutes until tender. Drain and allow to cool.

TO MAKE the almond filling, beat the butter, sugar and vanilla extract together until pale and creamy. Beat in the eggs gradually and then fold in the almonds, lemon zest and flour.

LINE the pastry shell with a crumpled piece of waxed paper and baking beads (use dried beans or rice if you don't have beads). Blind bake the pastry for 10 minutes, remove the paper and beads and bake for another 3–5 minutes, or until the pastry is just cooked but still very pale. Reduce the oven to 350°F.

SPREAD three-quarters of the filling in the pastry shell and put the pears on top, cut side down and stem ends in the middle. Fill the gaps with the remaining filling. Bake for 35–40 minutes, or until the filling is golden and firm. Melt the preserves with 1 teaspoon water, strain to remove any lumps and brush over the pears to make them shine.

APPLES AND PEARS IN PASTRY

IN LATE SUMMER AND AUTUMN, WHEN THE ORCHARDS ARE OVERFLOWING WITH FRUIT, THE NORMAN COOK MAKES *BOURDELOTS* OR *DOUILLONS*. THESE PASTRY-WRAPPED APPLES OR PEARS COULD ALSO CONTAIN A DRIZZLE OF CALVADOS.

PASTRY
2/3 cup unsalted butter
1 3/4 cups all-purpose flour
2 tablespoons superfine sugar
1 egg yolk

HAZELNUT FILLING
1/4 cup hazelnuts, finely chopped
1/4 cup unsalted butter, softened
1/3 cup brown sugar
pinch of pumpkin pie spice

2 eating apples
2 pears (ripe but still firm)
juice of 1 lemon
1 egg, lightly beaten

SERVES 4

TO MAKE the pastry, rub the butter into the flour until the mixture resembles fine bread crumbs. Stir in the sugar. Add the egg yolk and 2–3 tablespoons water and stir with a knife to form a dough. Turn out the dough and bring together with your hands. Wrap in plastic wrap and refrigerate for at least 30 minutes. Preheat the broiler.

TO MAKE the hazelnut filling, toast the hazelnuts under the hot broiler for 1–2 minutes or until browned, then cool. Mix the softered butter with the sugar, hazelnuts and pumpkin pie spice. Peel and core the apples and pears, leaving the stems and trimming the bottoms of the pears if they are too big. Roll in the lemon juice and stuff with the hazelnut filling. Reduce the oven to 400°F.

ROLL OUT the pastry to make a 13-inch square, trimming off any uneven edges. Cut into four equal squares and place an apple or pear in the center of each. Brush the edges of the pastry with water and then bring them up so that the corners of each pastry square meet at the top of the fruit. Press the edges together so that the pastry follows the curve of the fruit.

CUT OFF the excess pastry and crimp the edges to seal the fruit packages thoroughly. Use the pastry trimmings to cut out leaves, then stick these onto the fruit by brushing the backs with water.

BRUSH the pastry fruits with the beaten egg to glaze and bake on a lightly greased baking sheet for 35–40 minutes or until the pastry is cooked and browned. Serve with cream.

Bring up the four corners of the pastry square so they meet at the top of the fruit.

Dinner in Saint Rémy.

TARTE TATIN

THIS FAMOUS DESSERT IS NAMED AFTER THE TATIN SISTERS WHO RAN A RESTAURANT NEAR ORLÉANS AT THE BEGINNING OF THE TWENTIETH CENTURY. THEY CERTAINLY POPULARIZED THE DISH, BUT MAY NOT HAVE INVENTED IT THEMSELVES.

3 lb. eating apples
1/4 cup unsalted butter
3/4 cup superfine sugar
1 batch tart pastry (page 278)

CRÈME CHANTILLY
3/4 cup heavy cream
1 teaspoon confectioners' sugar
1/2 teaspon vanilla extract

SERVES 8

PEEL, CORE and cut the apples into quarters. Put the butter and sugar in a deep 10-inch frying pan with a flameproof handle. Heat until the butter and sugar have melted together. Arrange the apples tightly, one by one, in the frying pan, making sure there are no gaps. Remember that you will be turning the tart out with the apples on top, so arrange the apple pieces neatly underneath.

COOK over low heat for 35–40 minutes, or until the apple is soft, the caramel is lightly browned and any excess liquid has evaporated. Baste the apple with a pastry brush every so often, so that the top is caramelized as well. Preheat the oven to 375°F.

ROLL OUT the pastry on a lightly floured surface into a circle slightly larger than the frying pan and about 1/8 inch thick. Lay the pastry over the apple and press down around the edge to enclose it completely. Roughly trim the edge of the pastry and then fold the edge back on itself for a neat finish.

BAKE FOR 25–30 minutes, or until the pastry is golden and cooked. Remove from the oven and allow to rest for 5 minutes before turning out. (If any apple sticks to the pan, just push it back into its place in the tart.)

TO MAKE the crème chantilly, put the cream, confectioners' sugar and vanilla extract in a chilled bowl. Whisk until soft peaks form and then serve with the hot tarte tatin.

Wedge the apples tightly into the pan—they shrink as they cook.

STRAWBERRY MILLEFEUILLE

1 batch puff pastry (page 281)
5 tablespoons sugar
1/2 batch crème pâtissière
   (page 285)
1/2 cup whipping cream
1 3/4 cups strawberries, cut into
   quarters
confectioners' sugar

SERVES 6

PREHEAT the oven to 350°F. Roll out the puff pastry on a lightly floured surface into a rectangle about 1/8 inch thick. Roll the pastry around a rolling pin, then unroll it onto a baking sheet lined with waxed paper. Put in the refrigerator for 15 minutes.

TO MAKE the syrup, put the sugar and 3/4 cup water in a saucepan and boil for 5 minutes, then remove from the heat.

CUT OUT three 12 x 5 inch rectangles from the pastry and place them on a large baking sheet. Prick with a fork, cover with a sheet of waxed paper and place a second baking sheet on top to prevent the pastry from rising unevenly. Bake for 6 minutes, then remove the top baking sheet and waxed paper. Brush the pastry with the syrup and bake for another 6 minutes or until golden on top. Cool on a wire rack.

WHISK the crème pâtissière. Whip the cream and fold into the crème pâtissière. Spread half of this over one pastry rectangle and top with half of the strawberries. Place a second layer of pastry on top and spread with the remaining cream and strawberries. Cover with the last layer of pastry and dust with confectioners' sugar to serve.

Madeleines are baked in small scallop-shaped molds.

MADELEINES

3 eggs
1/3 cup superfine sugar
1 1/4 cups all-purpose flour
1/3 cup unsalted butter, melted
grated zest of 1 lemon and
   1 orange

MAKES 14 (OR 30 SMALL ONES)

PREHEAT the oven to 400°F. Brush a tray of madeleine molds with melted butter and coat with flour, then tap the tray to remove the excess flour.

WHISK the eggs and sugar until the mixture is thick and pale and the whisk leaves a trail when lifted. Gently fold in the flour, then the melted butter and grated lemon and orange zest. Spoon into the molds, leaving a little room for rising. Bake for 12 minutes (small madeleines will only need 7 minutes), or until very lightly golden and elastic to the touch. Remove from the molds and cool on a wire rack.

MADELEINES

GÂTEAU BASQUE

THE BASQUE COUNTRY IS SQUEEZED INTO THE SOUTHWESTERN CORNER OF FRANCE, BORDERED BY THE SEA ON ONE SIDE AND SPAIN ON THE OTHER. JUST ABOUT EVERY BASQUE HOUSEHOLD HAS ITS OWN RECIPE FOR THIS BAKED TART, WHICH IS ALSO KNOWN AS *VÉRITABLE PASTIZA*.

Use the best-quality preserves you can find to spread over the pastry shell. Spoon in the crème pâtissière over the top.

ALMOND PASTRY
13 oz. all-purpose flour
1 teaspoon finely grated lemon zest
1/4 cup ground almonds
2/3 cup superfine sugar
1 egg
1 egg yolk
1/4 teaspoon vanilla extract
2/3 cup unsalted butter, softened

ALMOND CRÈME PÂTISSIÈRE
6 egg yolks
3/4 cup superfine sugar
1/2 cup all-purpose flour
1/3 cup ground almonds
4 cups milk
4 vanilla beans

4 tablespoons thick black cherry or
  plum preserves
1 egg, lightly beaten

SERVES 8

TO MAKE the pastry, mix the flour, lemon zest and almonds together, turn out onto a work surface and make a well in the center. Put the sugar, egg, egg yolk, vanilla extract and butter in the well.

MIX TOGETHER the sugar, eggs and butter, using a pecking action with your fingertips and thumb. Once they are mixed, use the edge of a flexible bladed knife to incorporate the flour, flicking it onto the dough and then chopping through it. Bring the dough together with your hands. Wrap in plastic wrap and put in the refrigerator for at least 30 minutes.

ROLL OUT two-thirds of the pastry to fit a 10-inch tart ring. Trim the edge and chill in the fridge for another 30 minutes. Preheat the oven to 350°F.

TO MAKE the almond crème pâtissière, whisk together the egg yolks and sugar until pale and creamy. Sift in the flour and ground almonds and mix together well. Put the milk in a saucepan. Split the vanilla beans in two, scrape out the seeds and add the beans and seeds to the milk. Bring just to a boil, then strain over the egg yolk mixture, stirring continuously. Pour back into the clean saucepan and bring to a boil, stirring constantly—it will be lumpy at first but will become smooth as you stir. Boil for 2 minutes, then allow to cool.

SPREAD the preserves over the bottom of the pastry shell, then spread with the crème pâtissière. Roll out the remaining pastry to make a top for the pie. Brush the edge of the pastry shell with beaten egg, put the pastry top over it and press together around the side. Trim the edge. Brush the top of the pie with beaten egg and gently score in a criss-cross pattern. Bake for 40 minutes, or until golden brown. Cool for at least 30 minutes before serving, either slightly warm or cold.

RAISIN RUM BABA

THE BABA IS THOUGHT TO HAVE ITS ORIGINS IN POLAND AND WAS INTRODUCED TO FRANCE BY A
PARISIAN PASTRY COOK AFTER A VISIT BY THE POLISH COURT. BABAS CAN BE MADE IN DARIOLE OR
PUDDING MOLDS OR IN A SAVARIN MOLD, AS HERE.

3 teaspoons dried yeast or 2/3 oz.
  fresh yeast
1/3 cup warm milk
1 tablespoon superfine sugar
1 large egg
2 large egg yolks
finely grated zest of 1 small orange
11/3 cups all-purpose flour
1/3 cup raisins
1/4 cup unsalted butter, melted

ORANGE RUM SYRUP
1 cup superfine sugar
2 tablespoons orange juice
4 tablespoons dark rum

SERVES 8

MIX the yeast with half of the warm milk and
1 teaspoon of the sugar. Allow to rest for
10 minutes in a warm place until the yeast
becomes frothy. If the yeast does not bubble and
foam in this time, throw it away and start again.

WHISK together the egg, egg yolks and remaining
sugar and stir in the orange zest. Sift the flour into
a large bowl and make a well in the center. Pour
the yeast mixture and egg mixture into the well
and add the raisins. Gradually stir in the flour,
dribbling in the rest of the warm milk as you do
so. Once the ingredients are thoroughly mixed,
add the melted butter, little by little, mixing well.
Work the dough with your hands for 10 minutes,
raising it high and dropping it into the bowl, until
the dough is very soft. Cover with greased plastic
wrap and allow to rise in a warm place for
11/4 hours or until the dough has doubled in size.

TO MAKE the orange rum syrup, put the sugar in
a saucepan with 11/3 cups water. Bring to a boil,
and boil for 3 minutes. Remove from the heat and
add the orange juice and rum. Set aside.

DEFLATE the dough by punching it with your fist
several times to expel the air, and then lightly
knead it again for a minute. Put it in a buttered
5-cup savarin mold. Cover with greased plastic
wrap and allow to rise in a warm place for
20–30 minutes, or until risen almost to the top
of the pan. Preheat the oven to 375°F.

BAKE the baba for 25–30 minutes, covering the
top with aluminum foil if it is over-browning.
Remove from the oven and, while still in the mold,
prick all over the top of the baba with a skewer.
Drizzle some of the syrup over the top of the baba
and allow it to soak in before drizzling with the
rest. Allow to stand for 15 minutes, before turning
out onto a large serving plate to serve.

Bake the rum baba in the
buttered savarin mold. Keep it in
the mold while you drizzle the
syrup over the top, letting the
syrup soak in completely.

BASICS

Because brioche dough has so much butter in it, you will notice that it is heavier to knead than bread dough.

BRIOCHE

BRIOCHE IS SO BUTTERY THAT YOU CAN SERVE IT UP FOR BREAKFAST WITH NOTHING MORE FANCY THAN SOME GOOD-QUALITY PRESERVES OR CURD. IF YOU HAVE ONE, USE A FLUTED BRIOCHE PAN, IF NOT, AN ORDINARY LOAF PAN WILL BE FINE.

2 teaspoons dried yeast or $1/2$ oz. fresh yeast
$1/4$ cup warm milk
2 tablespoons superfine sugar
$13/4$ cups all-purpose flour
pinch of salt
2 large eggs, lightly beaten
few drops vanilla extract
$1/3$ cup butter, cubed
lightly beaten egg, to glaze

MAKES 1 LOAF

MIX the yeast with the warm milk and 1 teaspoon of the sugar. Allow to stand for 10 minutes in a warm place until the yeast becomes frothy. If the yeast does not bubble and foam in this time, throw it away and start again.

SIFT the flour into a large bowl and sprinkle with the salt and the rest of the sugar. Make a well in the center and add the eggs, vanilla extract and yeast mixture. Use a wooden spoon to mix all the ingredients together, then use your hands to knead the dough for a minute to bring it together. Transfer to a lightly floured work surface and gradually knead in the butter, piece by piece. Knead for 5 minutes, then put the dough in a clean bowl and cover with greased plastic wrap. Allow to rise in a draft-free place for 1–$11/2$ hours or until the dough has doubled in size.

DEFLATE the dough by punching it with your fist several times to expel the air, and then lightly knead it again for a couple of minutes. Shape the dough into a rectangle and place in an 8 x $23/4$ x $31/2$ inch buttered loaf pan. Cover with greased plastic wrap and allow the dough to rise in a draught-free place for 30–35 minutes, or until risen almost to the top of the pan. Preheat the oven to 400°F.

ONCE the brioche has risen, use a pair of scissors to carefully snip into the top of the dough at regular intervals. Snip three times on each side and twice at each end. The cuts should only be about 1 inch deep. This will give the top of the loaf its traditional bubble shape. Brush the top with egg to glaze and bake for 30–35 minutes, or until the top is deeply golden. Turn the hot brioche out of the pan and tap the bottom of the loaf—if it sounds hollow, it is cooked. Put it back in the pan upside-down and return to the oven for 5 minutes to crisp the bottom. Transfer to a wire rack and allow to cool.

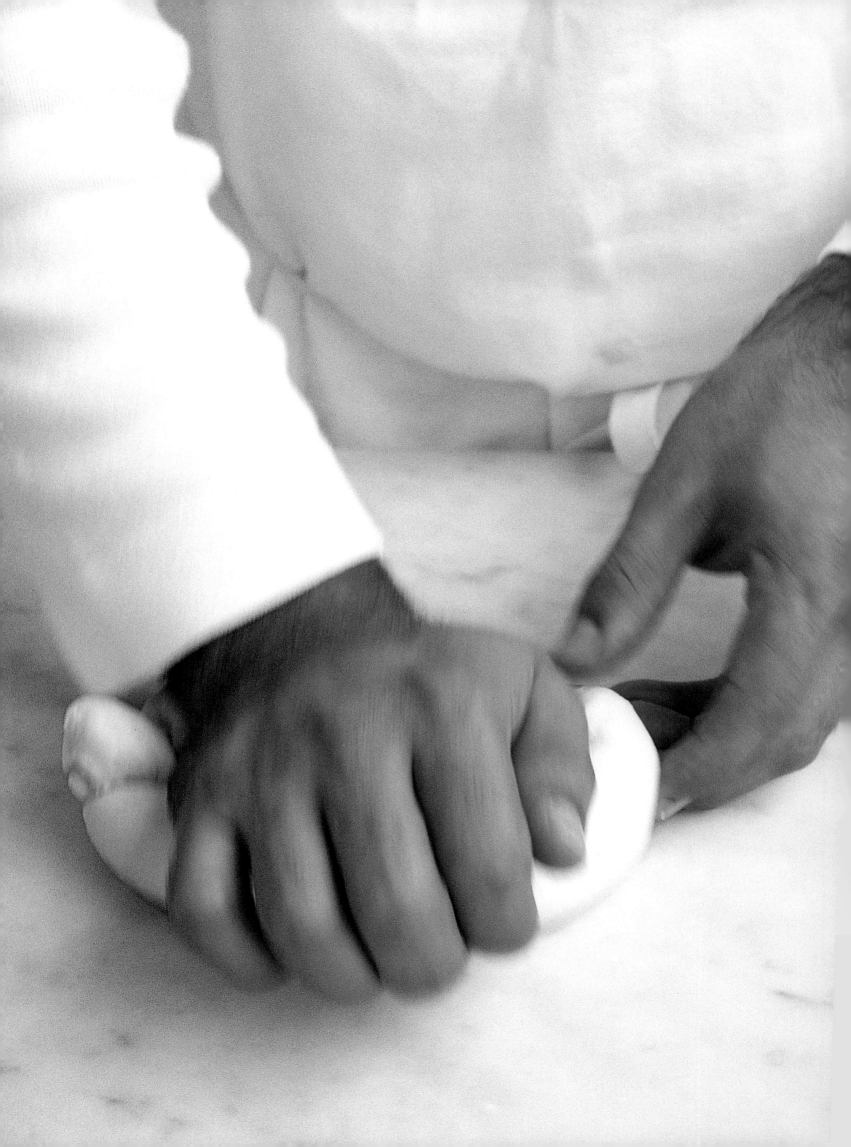

BREAD DOUGH

HAVE LUNCH WITH THICK SLICES OF THIS RUSTIC BREAD WITH UNSALTED BUTTER AND A GOOD CHEESE. THIS IS A BASIC BREAD DOUGH AND IS EASILY FLAVORED—YOU COULD ADD CHOPPED WALNUTS, FRESH HERBS, OLIVES OR CHEESE.

2 teaspoons dried yeast or
   $^1/_2$ oz. fresh yeast
2 cups bread flour
$^1/_2$ teaspoon salt
3 tablespoons olive oil

MAKES 1 LOAF

MIX the yeast with $^1/_2$ cup warm water. Allow to stand for 10 minutes in a warm place until the yeast becomes frothy. If the yeast does not bubble and foam in this time, throw it away and start again.

SIFT the flour into a large bowl and add the salt, olive oil and the yeast mixture. Mix until the dough clumps together and forms a ball.

TURN OUT onto a lightly floured work surface. Knead the dough, adding a little more flour or a few drops of warm water if necessary, until you have a soft dough that is not sticky but is dry to the touch. Knead for 10 minutes, or until smooth, and the impression made by a finger springs back immediately.

RUB the inside of a large bowl with olive oil. Roll the ball of dough around in the bowl to coat it with oil, then cut a shallow cross on the top of the ball with a sharp knife. Leave the dough in the bowl, cover with a kitchen towel or put in a plastic bag and allow to rest in a draft-free place for 1–1$^1/_2$ hours or until the dough has doubled in size (or put it in the refrigerator for 3 hours to rise slowly).

DEFLATE the dough by punching it with your fist several times to expel the air and then knead it again for a couple of minutes. (At this stage the dough can be stored in the refrigerator for 4 hours, or frozen. Bring back to room temperature before continuing.) Allow to rest in a warm place to rise until doubled in size. Place in a pan, on a baking sheet or use as directed in the recipe, then bake at 450°F for 30 minutes. When it is cooked, the base of the bread will sound hollow.

Use flour that is packaged as bread flour. You can also use all-purpose flour or a mixture of all-purpose and whole wheat, but the result won't be as good.

TART PASTRY

1³/4 cups all-purpose flour
pinch of salt
²/3 cup unsalted butter, chilled
    and cubed
1 egg yolk

MAKES 14 OZ.

SIFT the flour and salt into a large bowl, add the butter and rub in with your fingertips until the mixture resembles bread crumbs. Add the egg yolk and a little cold water (about 2–3 teaspoons) and mix with a flexible bladed knife until the dough just starts to come together. Bring the dough together with your hands and shape into a ball. Wrap in plastic wrap and put in the refrigerator to rest for at least 30 minutes. You can also make the dough in a food processor, using the pulse button.

ROLL OUT the pastry into a circle on a lightly floured surface and use to line a tart pan, as directed in the recipe. Trim the edge and pinch around the pastry edge to make an even border raised slightly above the rim of the pan. Slide onto a baking sheet and put in the refrigerator for 10 minutes.

When making the sweet pastry it is easiest to work directly on the work surface.

SWEET PASTRY

2³/4 cups all-purpose flour
small pinch of salt
²/3 cup unsalted butter
³/4 cup confectioners' sugar
2 eggs, beaten

MAKES 1 LB. 6 OZ.

SIFT the flour and salt onto a work surface and make a well in the center. Put the butter into the well and work, using a pecking action with your fingertips and thumb, until it is very soft. Add the sugar to the butter and mix together. Add the eggs to the butter and mix together.

GRADUALLY incorporate the flour, flicking it onto the mixture and then chopping through it until you have a rough dough. Bring together with your hands and then knead a few times to make a smooth dough. Roll into a ball, wrap in plastic wrap and put in the refrigerator for at least 1 hour.

ROLL OUT the pastry into a circle on a lightly floured surface and use to line a tart pan, as directed in the recipe. Trim the edge and pinch around the pastry edge to make an even border raised slightly above the rim of the pan. Slide onto a baking sheet and allow to rest in the refrigerator for 10 minutes.

SWEET PASTRY

PUFF PASTRY

LIGHTNESS IS THE HALLMARK OF GOOD PUFF PASTRY AND THE MANY LAYERS SHOULD RISE WITHOUT STICKING. THE KEY IS TO HAVE THE BUTTER AND PASTRY AT THE SAME CONSISTENCY WHEN YOU ROLL THEM OUT, AND TO KEEP THE ROLLING AND FOLDING AS NEAT AS YOU CAN.

2 cups all-purpose flour
1 teaspoon lemon juice
1 teaspoon salt
2 tablespoons butter, melted
3/4 cup butter, chilled

MAKES 1 LB. 5 OZ.

SIFT the flour into a bowl and make a well in the center. Pour in 1/2 cup water, the lemon juice, salt and melted butter. Draw in the flour with your fingertips, little by little, until you have a rough dough. Turn out onto a work surface and knead with the heel of your hand until the dough is smooth. Shape into a ball and cut a cross on the top. Wrap with plastic wrap and refrigerate for 1–2 hours.

PLACE the chilled butter between two pieces of waxed paper and beat with a rolling pin to make a square 1/2–3/4 inch thick. Keep the butter cool so that it doesn't harden again or melt any further—it needs to be about the same softness as the pastry or it will break up when you roll it.

ON A LIGHTLY floured surface, roll out the dough in four different directions to form a cross large enough to hold the square of butter in its center. Put the butter in the center and fold the four arms of dough over it, one by one, to enclose the butter completely. Position the dough so that it looks like a book with the spine to the left and the open piece of dough to the right. Roll the pastry away from you into a rectangle, keeping the corners as square as you can, then fold the top third down and the bottom third up to make a package of three even layers. Turn the pastry 90 degrees to the right and repeat the rolling, folding and turning, trying to keep the corners neat and square—this will help make the pastry layers even. Wrap in plastic wrap and chill for 30 minutes. (You can mark the pastry with finger indents each time you refrigerate so you remember how many turns you have made.)

REPOSITION the pastry as before, with the hinge to your left, then roll out, fold, turn and chill twice more. Allow to rest for 30 minutes, then make two more turns as before. The pastry is ready to use.

Although it can be time-consuming to make, homemade puff pastry that uses butter will always taste better than commercial pastry, which is often made with vegetable fat.

Sift in the flour and stir until the choux dough comes away from the side of the pan.

CHOUX PASTRY

CHOUX PASTRY

$2/3$ cup unsalted butter
$1^3/4$ cups all-purpose flour, sifted
   twice
7 eggs
1 tablespoon superfine sugar

MAKES 1 LB.

MELT the butter with $1^1/2$ cups water in a saucepan, then bring it to a rolling boil. Remove from the heat and add all the flour at once and a pinch of salt. Return to the heat and beat continuously with a wooden spoon to make a smooth shiny paste that comes away from the side of the pan. Cool for a few minutes.

BEAT IN the eggs one at a time, until shiny and smooth—the mixture should drop off the spoon but not be too runny. Beat in the sugar. Store in a pastry bag in the refrigerator for up to 2 days.

CRÊPES

2 cups all-purpose flour
pinch of salt
1 teaspoon sugar
2 eggs, lightly beaten
$1^2/3$ cups milk
1 tablespoon melted butter
butter or oil, for frying

MAKES 12 SMALL OR
6 LARGE CRÊPES

SIFT the flour, salt and sugar into a bowl and make a well in the center. Mix the eggs and milk together with $1/3$ cup water and pour slowly into the well, whisking all the time to incorporate the flour until you have a smooth batter. Stir in the melted butter. Cover and refrigerate for 20 minutes.

HEAT a crêpe pan or a deep non-stick frying pan and grease with a little butter or oil. Pour in enough batter to coat the bottom of the pan in a thin even layer and pour out any excess. Cook over moderate heat for about a minute, or until the crêpe starts to come away from the side of the pan. Turn the crêpe and cook on the other side for 1 minute or until lightly golden. Stack the crêpes on a plate with pieces of waxed paper between them and cover with aluminum foil while you cook the rest of the batter.

CRÈME PÂTISSIÈRE

6 egg yolks
1/2 cup superfine sugar
1/4 cup cornstarch
1 tablespoon all-purpose flour
2 1/4 cups milk
1 vanilla bean
1 tablespoon butter

MAKES 1 LB.

WHISK together the egg yolks and half the sugar until pale and creamy. Sift in the cornstarch and flour and mix together well.

PUT the milk, remaining sugar and vanilla bean in a saucepan. Bring just to a boil, then strain over the egg yolk mixture, stirring continuously. Pour back into a clean saucepan and bring to a boil, stirring constantly—it will be lumpy at first but will become smooth as you stir. Boil for 2 minutes, then stir in the butter and allow to cool. Transfer to a clean bowl, lay plastic wrap on the surface to prevent a skin from forming and refrigerate for up to 2 days.

CRÈME PÂTISSIÈRE

CRÈME ANGLAISE

1 1/4 cups milk
1 vanilla bean
2 egg yolks
2 tablespoons superfine sugar

MAKES 1 1/4 CUPS

PUT the milk in a saucepan. Split the vanilla bean in two, scrape out the seeds and add the bean and seeds to the milk. (If you don't want the black specks of vanilla seeds, leave the vanilla bean whole.) Bring just to a boil. Whisk the egg yolks and sugar until light and fluffy. Strain the milk over the egg mixture, whisking continuously.

POUR the custard sauce back into the saucepan and cook, stirring, until it is thick enough to coat the back of a wooden spoon. Do not let it boil or the custard sauce will curdle. Strain into a clean bowl, lay plastic wrap on the surface to prevent a skin from forming and refrigerate for up to 2 days.

FRANGIPANE

FRANGIPANE

1 cup unsalted butter, softened
2 cups confectioners' sugar
1 1/3 cups ground almonds
1/3 cup all-purpose flour
5 eggs, lightly beaten

MAKES 1 LB. 10 OZ.

BEAT the butter until very soft. Add the confectioners' sugar, ground almonds and flour and beat well. Add the egg gradually, beating until fully incorporated. Transfer to a clean bowl, cover with plastic wrap and refrigerate for up to 24 hours.

MAYONNAISE

4 egg yolks
1/2 teaspoon white wine vinegar
1 teaspoon lemon juice
2 cups vegetable oil

MAKES 2 CUPS

PUT the egg yolks, vinegar and lemon juice in a bowl or food processor and whisk or mix until light and creamy. Add the oil, drop by drop from the tip of a teaspoon, mixing constantly until the mixture begins to thicken, then add the oil in a very thin stream. (If you're using a processor, pour in the oil in a thin stream with the motor running.) Season well.

MAYONNAISE

VINAIGRETTE

1 garlic clove, crushed
1/2 teaspoon Dijon mustard
2 tablespoons white wine vinegar
6 tablespoons olive oil

MAKES 1/3 CUP

MIX TOGETHER the garlic, mustard and vinegar. Add the oil in a thin stream, whisking continuously to form an emulsion. Season with salt and pepper. Store in a screw-top jar in the refrigerator and shake well before use. You can also add some chopped herbs such as chives or chervil.

BÉCHAMEL SAUCE

1/3 cup butter
1 onion, finely chopped
3/4 cup all-purpose flour
4 cups milk
pinch of nutmeg
bouquet garni

MAKES 3 CUPS

MELT the butter in a saucepan, add the onion and cook, stirring, for 3 minutes. Stir in the flour to make a roux and cook, stirring, for 3 minutes over low heat without allowing the roux to brown.

REMOVE from the heat and add the milk gradually, stirring after each addition until smooth. Return to the heat, add the nutmeg and bouquet garni and cook for 5 minutes. Strain through a fine sieve into a clean pan and lay a buttered piece of waxed paper on the surface to prevent a skin from forming.

VINAIGRETTE

BÉCHAMEL SAUCE

VELOUTÉ SAUCE

1/4 cup butter
2/3 cup all-purpose flour
4 cups hot chicken stock

MAKES 2 CUPS

MELT the butter in a saucepan. Stir in the flour to make a roux and cook, stirring, for 3 minutes over low heat without allowing the roux to brown. Allow to cool to room temperature. Add the hot stock and mix well. Return to the heat and simmer very gently for 10 minutes or until thick. Strain through a fine sieve, cover and refrigerate until needed.

CHÂTEAU MARGAUX is one of Bordeaux's *grands crus classés*, a classification dating back to 1855 when wines from Médoc, Sauternes and one from Graves were classified according to the prices they fetched. The five-tier classification, from *premiers* down to *cinquièmes* (fifth) *crus* (growths), is still used today, with Châteaux Margaux, Haut-Brion, Latour, Lafite-Rothschild and Mouton-Rothschild (elevated to

WINE

FRANCE IS INDISPUTABLY THE CENTER OF THE WINE WORLD, AND GREAT BORDEAUX, BURGUNDIES AND CHAMPAGNES CONTINUE TO SET THE STANDARD TO WHICH OTHERS ASPIRE.

The French were making wines from indigenous vines even before the Romans arrived. Over the centuries, wine-makers have cultivated a staggering number of grape varieties, eventually matching each one up to the right methods of production, the perfect climate and terrain, from the wet North to the cool mountains and the hot Mediterranean. This fact means that today France produces nearly every classic wine in the world.

CLASSIFYING FRENCH WINE

France's *appellation d'origine contrôlée* (AC) is the oldest and most precise wine governing body in the world. The French attach much importance to the notion of *terroir*, that there is a perfect environment in which to grow a wine and that every wine should demonstrate the character of that environment, so the smaller and more pinpointed an *appellation*, the more prestigious it is. Thus, within the broad Bordeaux AC, subregions, such as Médoc, and even individual communities within this, such as Pauillac, may gain their own *appellation*. The AC also defines grape varieties, yields and production methods.

Vin délimité de qualité supérieure (VDQS) classifies less distinguished regions standing between AC and *vins de pays* status. *Vins de pays* (country wines) can be great if they have a strong local character. *Vins de table* should be drinkable.

MINERVOIS red and white wines from Languedoc, France's largest wine-growing area. Good value, the reds are fruity and light with a typical Mediterranean grape blend, including Grenache and Syrah.

CORBIÈRES an *appellation* in Languedoc making good dry white wines and reds — mixing Grenache and Carignan (used in mass-produced wines but here used to give character).

CHÂTEAUNEUF-DU-PAPE great red wines from the papal vineyards of Provence, mixing up to 13 different grape varieties to produce a full-bodied wine that usually needs aging.

GRAVES famed Bordeaux area producing dry Semillon/Sauvignon Blanc whites and rich Cabernet Sauvignon reds. Split in 1987, the outstanding *crus classés* are now in Pessac-Léognan AC.

ALSACE dry white wines from the North. The area produces many varietal (single grape variety) wines that bear the name of the grape, here Pinot Blanc, rather than the region.

MÂCONNAIS a Burgundian district producing decent Gamay and Pinot Noir reds and white Chardonnays, especially the very good Pouilly-Fuissé. In Mâcon, Mâcon-Villages is a superior AC.

MÉDOC Bordeaux's outstanding wine area, producing Cabernet Sauvignon reds. Within Médoc, the greatest areas (Pauillac, Saint Julien and Estèphe and Margaux) have their own *appellations*.

SAUTERNES a Bordeaux region, classified in 1855 and producing the world's most prestigious dessert wines from Semillon, Sauvignon Blanc and Muscadelle grapes.

POUILLY FUMÉ one of the world's great Sauvignon wines, along with neighboring Sancerre. Made in the Loire Valley, it has an elegant gooseberry character and should be drunk young.

NUITS-SAINT-GEORGES situated in the Côte d'Or in the middle of Burgundy, this commune has a number of *premiers crus* producing classic Pinot Noir reds for aging.

BERGERAC east of Bordeaux, this area has the same climate and grapes as its neighbor. Fine reds centering on Cabernet Sauvignon, Franc and Merlot; dry whites based around Sauvignon.

BEAUJOLAIS a Burgundian area producing fruity reds from Gamay grapes to be drunk chilled and young (within weeks for Nouveau). Beaujolais-Villages is a superior *appellation* within Beaujolais.

CHAMPAGNE

THE CELLARS AT TAITTINGER, one of Reim's world-famous champagne houses, date back to the Benedictine monks who first created champagne. Champagne is a mixture of red Pinot Noir and Pinot Meunier and white Chardonnay grapes, carefully picked and pressed to prevent any red skin color leaking into the juice. First a *cuvée* is blended by adding previous years' harvests to the present one, creating a champagne in the house's style (their non-vintage brut; though a vintage may be made in exceptional years). A secondary fermentation is

initiated by adding sugar and yeast (*liqueur de tirage*) before bottling, sealing with a cap and aging slowly in the cold cellars. After a 3-month fermentation, aging continues *sur lie* from one to several years, and a yeasty, less acidic flavor develops. During this time, the upended bottles are turned periodically, called *remuage* (riddling), to slide the sediment into the neck. Finally, *dégorgement* takes place, with the sediment frozen into a plug and ejected when the bottle is opened. The plug is replaced by some sweet wine that determines the sweetness of the champagne.

TYPES OF CHAMPAGNE

VINTAGE this champagne is made only every 3 or 4 years, when an exceptional harvest produces a distinctive, fine wine that is not blended with previous vintages into a house style.

BRUT this is the most common champagne, a dry wine made every year from a mixture of Pinot and Chardonnay grapes, blended with a little wine from previous harvests to create a house style.

ROSÉ usually made from normal white champagne blended with 15% red wine (produced from the same red pinot grapes), rosé is a fruity wine not made in large quantities and good with food.

BLANC DE BLANCS meaning "white of whites" and made just from white Chardonnay grapes, a blanc de blancs has a fine, delicate taste and makes a great apéritif.

this level in 1973) all *premiers crus*. The fact that the classification remains in use reflects the suitability of the *terroir* for growing Cabernet Sauvignon, especially the mild climate and gravelly soil, and also the efforts of the châteaux to maintain standards. At Château Margaux, the land is still worked by hand and a cooper handcrafts the French oak barrels. The best of their elegant wines can be aged for at least 20 years.

READING FRENCH LABELS

CHÂTEAU a Bordeaux wine estate

CLOS on some Burgundies, meaning a walled vineyard

CRU meaning "growth," it refers to wine from a single estate

CRU BOURGEOIS an unofficial level of classification just below Bordeaux's *crus classés*

GRAND CRU CLASSÉ/CRU CLASSÉ a Bordeaux classified in 1855 and usually of a very high quality. Also used in other regions to signify their most prestigious wines

CUVÉE a blended wine from different grapes or vineyards

CUVÉE PRESTIGE a special vintage or blend

MILLÉSIMÉ vintage

MIS EN BOUTEILLE AU CHÂTEAU/DOMAINE estate-bottled, rather than a merchant or cooperative blend

NÉGOCIANT-ÉLEVEUR a wine merchant, often an international firm, who buys grapes to blend and age and finished wines

PROPRIÉTAIRE-RÉCOLTANT growers who make their own wine

WINES can be bought from a *marchand de vin* (wine shop), *négociant* (specialized wine merchant) or *en vrac* (unbottled wine sold by the liter at markets). In wine areas you can also buy directly from the vineyards or from a *cave coopérative* (wine cooperative).

GLOSSARY OF FRENCH FOOD AND COOKING

andouillette A sausage made from pork or veal chitterlings or tripe. Andouillettes are usually broiled and often served with mustard, potatoes or cabbage. Some have an outer layer of lard that melts as they cook.

bain-marie Literally a "water bath" for gentle oven-cooking of delicate terrines and desserts. Usually the dish is placed in a roasting pan, which is half-filled with water.

beurre manié A paste made by mixing together butter and flour. Stirred into sauces at the end of cooking to thicken them.

beurre noisette A simple sauce made by cooking butter until it is brown and "nutty."

bouquet garni A bundle of herbs used to flavor dishes. Made by tying sprigs of parsley, thyme, celery leaves and a bay leaf in either a piece of cheesecloth or portion of leek.

brown stock Stock made from browned beef or veal bones. As beef and veal stock are usually interchangeable, the term "brown stock" is used.

butter Butter is flavored both by the lactic fermentation of cream and the diet of the cows from whose milk it is made. Butter from Normandy and the Alps is high quality and has a sweet flavor. French butter tends not to be heavily salted, with the amount varying between regions—Isigny butter from Normandy is unsalted, while next door in Brittany, butter from Poitou-Charentes is salted. Both butters have AOC status. Use either salted or unsalted butter for savory dishes, but unsalted in sweet recipes.

capers The pickled flowers of the caper bush. They are available preserved in brine, vinegar or salt and should be rinsed well and squeezed dry before use.

cervelas A long, fat pork sausage, often flavored with garlic, pistachios or truffles. It is a boiling sausage (*saucisse à cuire*) and should be poached before browning under the broiler. Ordinary pork sausages flavored with pistachios can be used instead if cervelas are unavailable.

chipolata In France, a chipolata can be as long as an ordinary sausage but is always much thinner. Usually made from pork and pork fat, chipolatas are used as a garnish in French cooking.

clarified butter Made by melting butter so that the fat separates out from the impurities and water. The fat is then either spooned off or the water poured away and the butter allowed to reset. Clarified butter keeps longer than ordinary butter because all the water has been removed and it can be used for cooking at higher temperatures because it has a higher burning point.

confit From the French word for "preserve," confit is usually made from goose or duck meat, cooked in its own fat and then preserved in a jar or pot. It is eaten on its own or added to dishes such as cassoulet for extra flavor.

cornichon The French term for a small gherkin. If you can't find cornichons, use cocktail gherkins instead.

court bouillon A flavored poaching liquid, usually for cooking fish.

couscous Made from very tiny balls of dough, couscous is usually steamed and served like rice with a main meal. Couscous was traditionally made by hand from freshly milled flour and came in different sizes of grain. Now that it is commercially produced, the grains tend to be uniformly quite tiny.

crème de cassis Originating near Dijon in Burgundy, crème de cassis is a black currant liqueur used in desserts and also to flavor the drink kir.

crème fraîche Often used in place of cream in the French kitchen. Lightly fermented, it has a slightly tart taste. Crème fraîche from Isigny has AOC status.

curd cheese A smooth soft cheese made from curds that have not undergone lactic fermentation. Curd cheese is lower in fat than cream cheese but higher in fat than cottage cheese.

Dijon mustard A pale yellow mustard, made from verjuice or white wine and mustard seeds that have been ground to a flour. Originating in Dijon, this style of mustard is now made all over France.

foie gras The enlarged livers of fattened geese or ducks. Regarded as a delicacy, with foie gras from Strasbourg and southwest France both highly regarded.

fromage frais A fresh white cheese with a smooth creamy consistency. There are a number of varieties, many artisan-produced. Fromage blanc is traditionally used in Lyon's *cervelle de canut*. The fat content of fromage frais varies, which may affect its cooking qualities, but generally it makes a good low-fat alternative to cream.

goose fat A soft fat that melts at a low temperature and is used a lot in the cooking of southwest France to give a rich texture to dishes. Duck fat can be substituted, although it needs to be heated to a higher temperature.

Gruyère A pressed hard cheese with a nutty flavor. French Gruyère is available as *Gruyère de Comté*, which can have large holes, and *Gruyère de Beaufort*, which has virtually no holes. Although French Gruyère does have a different flavor than Swiss, the two are interchangeable in recipes.

haricot beans The general French name for beans, though the term is also used just to mean a kind of small, dried bean. Dried haricot beans come in many different varieties, including cannellini, flageolet (white or pale green beans) and navy beans. When slow-cooked in stews such as cassoulet they become tender. They also break down very well when mashed to make a smooth purée.

julienne To cut a vegetable or citrus rind into short, thin "julienne" strips. Vegetables used as a garnish are often julienned for decorative purposes and to ensure quick even cooking.

juniper berries Blackish-purple berries with a resinous flavor. Used in stews and robust game dishes. Use the back of a knife to crush the berries lightly before use to release their flavor.

Madeira A type of fortified wine from the Portuguese island of Madeira. There are a number of different varieties of Madeira, from sweet (Malmsey or Malvasia and Bual), to medium (Verdelho) and dry (Sercial).

Maroilles A square soft cheese with an orange washed-rind and a strong smell but sweet flavor. As an alternative, you could use other washed-rind varieties, such as Livarot, or a cheese with a white-molded rind, such as Camembert.

Mesclun A salad mix containing young lettuce leaves and herbs such as arugula, mâche, dandelion leaves, basil, chervil and endive. Traditionally found all over the south of France.

mussels Grown commercially around the coast of France on *bouchots* (poles) driven into mud flats or in beds in estuaries, mussels can be eaten raw but are usually cooked in dishes such as *moules à la marinière*. French mussels have blue-black shells and vary slightly in size and flavor according to the waters in which they are grown. The mussels grown around Boulogne in northern France are of a very high quality.

olive Grown all over the South the main varieties of French olives include the green pointed Picholines, purple-black Nyons and the small black olives of Nice, used in traditional Niçoise cooking. Fresh green olives are available from the summer and are picked before they start to turn black, while fresh black olives are available from the autumn through winter. Though green and black olives have a different flavor, they can be used interchangeably in recipes unless the final color is a factor.

olive oil Extra-virgin and virgin olive oils are pressed without any heat or chemicals and are best used in simple uncooked dishes and for salads. Pure olive oil can be used for cooking or deep-frying. Olive oil is made in the south of France, and after picking the olives in the autumn, each year's new oil is available in the winter.

orange flower water Produced when the flower of the bitter orange is distilled. Orange flower water is a delicate flavoring used in dessert recipes.

oyster Two main species of oyster are available in France. *Huîtres plates* are European oysters, or natives. They have a flat round shell and are better in the winter months when they are not spawning. The most famous are the *belons* from Brittany. *Huîtres creuses* are the much more common Portuguese (or Pacific) oysters, with deep, bumpy and flaky shells. Some of the best Portuguese oysters are grown in Marennes. *Fines de claires* are oysters grown in water full of algae, giving them a green colour and a distinct, iodine flavor.

poussin A baby chicken weighing about 13 oz–1 lb. Poussin are often butterflied and broiled or stuffed. Usually one poussin is served per person, though slightly bigger ones are adequate for two people.

Puy lentils Tiny green lentils from Puy in central France that are AOC graded. Puy lentils do not need to be presoaked and do not break down when cooked. They have a firm texture and go very well with both meat and fish. Traditionally they are cooked and served with a mustard vinaigrette.

saffron The dried dark orange stigmas of a type of crocus flower, which are used to add aroma and flavor to food. Only a few threads are needed for each recipe as they are very pungent (and expensive).

salt cod Brought to Europe as long ago as the fifteenth century, salt cod's popularity in France is a legacy of the religious need to eat fish on Fridays and feast days. Salt cod is cod that has been gutted, salted and dried, and is different from stockfish (dried cod), which is just dried but not salted. A center-cut fillet of salt cod tends to be meatier than the thinner tail end, and some varieties are drier than others so the soaking time varies.

saucisse à cuire A cooking, or specifically boiling, sausage that is usually larger than an ordinary sausage. *Saucisses à cuire* are poached in liquid, either as part of a dish like *choucroute garnie* or just with red wine.

sweetbreads The pancreas and thymus glands of calves or lambs, sweetbreads are white in color, soft in texture and have an irregular shape. Sweetbreads should be soaked in cold water to remove any blood before they are cooked.

Toulouse sausage A general term for meaty pork broiling sausages, usually sold in a coil.

truffles Considered an expensive delicacy, truffles are a type of fungus and have an earthy smell. The black truffles found in France, specifically around Périgord, are often considered the best black truffles in the world. Truffles are best eaten fresh, but can also be bought preserved in jars, and only need to be used in small amounts to flavor dishes.

vanilla extract Made by using alcohol to extract the vanilla flavor from beans and not to be confused with artificial vanilla essence made with synthetic vanillin. Vanilla extract is very strong and should be used sparingly.

INDEX

BIBLIOGRAPHY

Ayto, John. *The Diner's Dictionary Food and Drink from A to Z*. Oxford University Press, 1993.

Behr, Edward. *The Art of Eating*, no. 48.

Bissell, Frances. *Sainsbury's Book of Food*. Websters International Publishers, 1989.

Christian, Glynn. *Edible France: a Traveler's Guide*. Interlink Books, 1997.

Conran, Caroline and Terence, and Hopkinson, Simon. *The Conran Cookbook*. Conran Octopus, 1997.

Davidson, Alan. *The Oxford Companion to Food*. Oxford University Press, 1999

Dominé, André, and Ditter, Michael. *Culinaria*. Könemann, 1995.

Dominé, André. *Culinaria France*. Könemann, 1999.

Editors of Time-Life Books. *Classic French Cooking*. Time-Life Books Inc, 1978.

Editors of Time-Life Books. *The Cooking of Provincial France*. Time-Life Books Inc 1972.

Editors of Time-Life Books. *The Good Cook: Wine*. Time-Life Books B.V., 1982.

Grigson, Jane. *Charcuterie and French Pork Cookery*. Penguin Books, 1970.

Johnston, Mireille. *Complete French Cookery Course*. BBC Books, 1994.

Masui, Kazuko, and Yamada, Tomoko. *French Cheeses*. Dorling Kindersley, 1996.

Millon, Marc and Kim. *The Food Lover's Companion to France*. Macmillan Travel, 1996.

Sinclair, Charles. *International Dictionary of Food and Cooking*. Peter Collin Publishing Ltd, 1998.

Stobart, Tom. *The Cook's Encyclopaedia*. Grub Street, 1998.

Wells, Patricia. *The Food Lover's Guide to Paris*. Methuen London Ltd, 1984.

THE FOOD OF FRANCE

This edition first published in the United States and Canada in 2001 by Whitecap Books.

First published in 2001 by Murdoch Books® a subsidiary of Mudoch Magazines Australia Pty Ltd.
© Text, design, photography and illustrations Murdoch Books® 2000. All rights reserved.
ISBN 1-55285-189-3

Murdoch Books® Australia
GPO Box 1203, Sydney, NSW 2001
Phone: (02) 8220 2000   Fax: (02) 8220 2558

Publishing Manager: Kay Halsey
Food Editor: Lulu Grimes
Design Concept and Art Direction: Marylouise Brammer
Designer: Susanne Geppert
Editor: Jane Price
U.S. Editor: Kerry MacKenzie
Photographer: Chris L. Jones
Stylist: Mary Harris
Stylist's Assistant: Ben Masters
Additional Photography: Howard Shooter
Additional Recipes: Ruth Armstrong, Michelle Earl, Barbara Lowery, Dimitra Stais, Jody Vassallo, Richard Young, Sophia Young
Map: Russell Bryant

Associate Publisher: Catie Ziller
Production Manager: Liz Fitzgerald
Group General Manager: Mark Smith
Group CEO & Publisher: Anne Wilson

PRINTED IN CHINA by Leefung-Asco Printers Ltd.

Whitecap Books Ltd (Vancouver Office)
351 Lynn Avenue, North Vancouver, BC
Canada V7J 2C4

Whitecap Books (Toronto Office)
47 Coldwater Road, North York, ON
Canada M3B IY8

Graphic Arts Center Publishing
PO Box 10306, Portland, OR
USA 97296-0306

IMPORTANT: Those who might be at risk from the effects of salmonella food poisoning (the elderly, pregnant women, young children and those suffering from immune deficiency diseases) should consult their GP with any concerns about eating raw eggs.

ACKNOWLEDGMENTS

The Publisher wishes to thank the following for their help in making this book possible: Cour des Loges, Lyon; Gérard Ravet, Cour des Loges, Lyon; Danièle Monterrat, Lyon; Michaël Leete, Boulangerie du Pont, Lyon; Jean Perroux, Lyon; Alain Duclot, Lyon; L'Hotel les Ateliers de l'Image, St-Rémy-de-Provence; David and Nitockrees Carpita, Mas de Cornud, St-Rémy-de-Provence; Gerard Driget, St-Rémy-de-Provence; Denis Censi, Fromagerie Du Mistral, St-Rémy-de-Provence; Josette Erard, St-Rémy-de-Provence; Paul Bergese, St-Rémy-de-Provence; Joël Durand, Joël Durand Chocolatier, St-Rémy-de-Provence; Pierre Lilamand, St-Rémy-de-Provence; Van Beeck, Le Petit Duc Patissiers, St-Rémy-de-Provence; Andre Rousson, St-Rémy-de-Provence; Michel Nunes, Aix-en-Provence; Sofitel Marseille Vieux-Port, Marseille; M. Fromion, Marseille; M. et Mme. Delfino, Marseille; M.-J Pichot, Mme. Bizard, Chateau Margaux; Monique Bodin, Christophe Conge, Château Lafite Rothschild; Bristol Hôtel, Périgueux; Gérard Joly, Marchal & Pautet, Périgueux; Jean Paul Armaud, Pondaurat; François Rames, Carves; Angèlique Denoix, St Mayme de Peyrerol; M. Barriere, St Laurent la Vallee; Eric Settbon, St Martin de Riberac; Marc et Marcelle Boureau, Castels; Hotel de l'Université, Paris; Philippe Foulatiere, Hediard, Paris; Marie-Anne Cantin, Paris; Stéphane Nachba, Gérard Mulot, Paris; Corinne Rosa, Paris; Claude et Catherine Ceccaldi, Paris; Vincent Rové, La Sablaise, Paris; Dominique Fenouil, Le Repaire de Bacchus, Paris; M. Jean Luc Poujounan, Poujauran, Paris; Jean Paul Gardil, Paris; Mon Martin Boulangerie, Paris; Sébastien Lay, U.C.L. Isigny-Sainte-Mère, Isigny-Sur-Mer; M. Claude Taittinger, Michèle Barbier, Champagne Taittinger, Reims; Kalinka, Sydney; Camargue, Sydney; Mosaique, Sydney; Brian Allen Antiques, Sydney; McLeod Antiques, Sydney; Peppergreen, Sydney.
Rod Johnson and Kayell Photographic; Nicole Lawless and Kodak; Kylie Goodwin, Qantas; Simon Johnson, Sydney; Sara Schwartz, Tasting Places, London; Mosaique Imports; Corso de Fiori; Will Studd; Max Pesch, Ilve Australia.